CONQUEST
OF THE
ISLE OF ELY

1070 A.D.
THE CAMP OF REFUGE

SAMUEL H. MILLER, F.R.A.S.

KLAUS SCHWANITZ

Publications by Klaus Schwanitz:

SIR JOHN MANDEVILLE	THE TRAVELS - Anno 1322-1356 ISBN-13: 978-1500919290
THE BANISHED	ANNO DOMINI 1519 ISBN-13: 978-1501047633
100 YEAR WAR	CHRONICLES OF THE HUNDRED YEAR WAR

VOL. I.	ISBN-13: 978-1514846056
VOL. II.	ISBN-13: 978-1514846766
VOL. III.	ISBN-13: 978-1514847107
VOL. IV.	ISBN-13: 978-1518782350
VOL. V.	ISBN-13: 978-1519378910
VOL. VI.	ISBN-13: 978-1523290925
VOL. VII.	ISBN-13: 978-1530215683
VOL. VIII.	ISBN-13: 978-1530968350
VOL. IX.	ISBN-13: 978-1533326072
VOL. X.	ISBN-13: 978-1535182973
VOL. XI.	ISBN-13: 978-1536948998
VOL. XII.	ISBN-13: 978-1537798905

SCOTLAND YARD ESCAPED	From London to Australia ISBN 13: 978-1507833759
RAFFLES NEW LIFE	A gentleman thief ISBN 13: 978-1479388851
RAFFLES NEW LIFE	Gentleman Dieb wechselt die Fronten ISBN 13: 978-1463780319
RAFFLES NEW LIFE II.	Scotland Yard entkommen ISBN 13: 978-1478336563
THE GOLF BALL	Or, why I don't want to play golf ISBN-13: 978-1502329189
DER GOLF BALL	Oder, warum ich kein Golf spiele ISBN-13: 978-1502329189
NETTELBECK	Wundersame Lebensgeschichte ISBN 13: 978-1500540883
LICHTENSTEIN	Herzog Ulrich geächtet – Anno 1519 ISBN-13: 978-1502352484

All rights reserved, no part of this publication may be reproduced, distributed, or transmitted in any form, or stored in a data base or retrieval system, without the prior written permission of the copyright holder.
Printed by Createspace.com in the United States of America
First Edition 2016
Copyright © 2016 Klaus Schwanitz

ISBN-13: 978-1539618492
ISBN-10: 1539618498

CONQUEST OF THE ISLE OF ELY

Foreword

Several generations has passed away since "The Camp of Refuge" first issued from the press. Although published anonymously, it shows that its author had a very extensive knowledge of the history and topography of the Fen district.
The book, however, while it embodied much real history, was put forth with no higher pretension than that of a tale, whose characters were historic personages, and whose incidents occurred, in the main, during the Norman Conquest.

Knowing that this interesting book had become very scarce, and thinking that it would prove as acceptable to this, and perhaps to the next, generation as it did to the past—the present publisher determined to offer a new edition to the public; trusting at the same time that its contents will help to foster a loyalty and a love for our English nation.
But with a new edition some few pictures, drawings and maps have been added, not with a view merely to embellish the original work, nor to convert it into a real history, but to assist, in some measure, the youthful reader, or mayhap those, too, who have but limited means of consulting the many sources of information upon which the ground-work of the tale rests.

CONQUEST OF THE ISLE OF ELY

THE CONTENTS.

CHAP.	CONTENT
I.	The Messenger
II.	The Succursal Cell at Spalding
III.	The Great House at Ely
IV.	The Monks of Ely Feast
V.	The Monks of Ely take counsel
VI.	Ivo Taille-Bois and the Ladie Lucia
VII.	Hereward's Return
VIII.	Lord Hereward goes to get his own
IX.	Elfric the ex-novice, and Girolamo of Salerno, prepare to play at devils
X.	The House at Crowland
XI.	The Linden Grove and Ladie Alftrude
XII.	The Marriage and the Ambuscade
XIII.	How Lord Hereward and his Ladie lived at Ey
XIV.	Hereward is made Knight
XV.	The Castle at Cam-Bridge and a Battle
XVI.	The Traitorous Monks of Peterborough
XVII.	Hereward goes to Brunn, and is disturbed there
XVIII.	The Danes and their King's son
XIX.	The Norman Witch
XX.	The Norman Duke tries again
XXI.	The Monks of Ely complain and plot
XXII.	Hereward brings Corn and Wine to Ely
XXIII.	A Chapter and a Great Treason
XXIV.	The Dungeon
XXV.	The Normans in the Camp
XXVI.	A Fire and a Rescue
XXVII.	Hereward still Fights
XXVIII.	The Happy End

CONQUEST OF THE ISLE OF ELY

The Isle of Ely

Cambridge Shire - England

CHAPTER I.

THE MESSENGER

It was long ago; it was in the year of grace one thousand and seventy, or four years after the battle of Hastings, which decided the right of power between the English and Norman nations, and left the old Saxon race exposed to the goading's of the sharp Norman lance, that a novice went on his way from the grand abbey of Crowland to the dependent house or succursal cell of Spalding, in the midst of the Lincolnshire fens.

The young man carried a long staff or pole in his hand, with which he aided himself in leaping across the numerous ditches and rivulets that intersected his path, and in trying the boggy ground before he ventured to set his feet upon it. The upper end of his staff was fashioned like unto the staff of a pilgrim, but the lower end was armed with a heavy iron ferrule, from which projected sundry long steel nails or spikes. It was a fen-pole, such, I wist, as our fenners yet use in Holland, Lindsey, and Kesteven. In a strong and bold hand this staff might be a good war-weapon; and as the young man raised the skirts of his black garment it might have been seen that he had a short broad hunting-knife fastened to his girdle.

He was a fair-haired, blue-eyed, and full-lipped youth, with an open countenance and a ruddy complexion: the face seemed made to express none but joyous feelings, so that the grief and anxiety which now clouded it appeared to be quite out of place. Nor was that cloud always there, for whenever the autumn sun shone out brightly, and some opening in the monotonous forest of willows and alders gave him a pleasant or a varied prospect, or when the bright king-fisher flitted across his path, or the wild duck rose from the fen and flew heaven-ward, or the heron raised itself on its long legs to look at him from the sludge, or the timid cygnet went sailing away in quest of the parent swan, his countenance lighted up like that of a happy thoughtless boy. Ever and anon too some inward emotion made him chuckle or laugh outright. Thus between sadness and gladness the novice went on his way—a rough and miry way proper to give a permanent fit of ill-humor to a less buoyant spirit, for he had quitted the road or causeway which traversed the fens and was pursuing a devious path, which was for the greater part miry in summer, but a complete morass at the present season of the year.

Notwithstanding all his well-practiced agility, and in spite of the good aid of his long staff, he more than once was soused head over ears in a broad water-course. With a good road within view, it may be thought that he had some strong motive for choosing this very bad one; and every time that his path approached to the road, or that the screen of alders and willows failed him, he crouched low under the tall reeds and bulrushes of the fen, and stole along very cautiously, peeping occasionally through the rushes towards the road, and turning his ear every time that the breeze produced a loud or unusual sound. As thus he went on, the day declined fast, and the slanting sun shone on the walls of a tall stone mansion, battlemented and moated—a dwelling-house, but a house proper to stand a siege: and in these years of trouble none could dwell at peace in any house if unprovided with the means of holding out against a blockade, and of repelling siege and assault.

All round this manor-house, to a wide space, the trees had been cut down and the country drained; part of the water being carried off to a neighboring mere, and part being collected and gathered, by means of various cuts, to fill the deep moat round the house.

Here the young man, in fear of being discovered by those who occupied that warlike yet fair-looking dwelling, almost crawled on the ground. Nevertheless he quitted his track to get nearer to the house; and then, cowering among some reeds and bulrushes, he put his open hand above his eyebrows, and gazed sharply at the moat, the drawbridge, the low gateway with its round-headed arch, the battlements, and the black Norman flag that floated over them. The while he gazed, the blast of a trumpet sounded on the walls, and sounded again, and once again; and, after the third blast, a noise as of many horses treading the high road or causeway was heard among the fen reeds. The novice muttered, and almost swore blasphemously, (albeit by the rules of the order he was bound to use no stronger terms than *crede mihi*, or *planè, or certè, or benedicamus Domina;*) but he continued to gaze under his palm until the sounds on the road came nearer and trumpet replied to trumpet.

Then, muttering "This is not a tarrying place for the feet of a true Saxon!" he crawled back to the scarcely perceptible track he had left, and kept on, in a stooping posture but at a rapid pace, until he came to a thick clump of alders, the commencement of a wood which stretched, with scarcely any interruption, to the banks of the river Welland. Here, screened from sight, he struck the warlike end of his staff against the trunk of a tree, and said aloud, "Forty Norman men-at-arms! By Saint Etheldreda and by the good eye-sight that Saint Lucia hath vouch-safed unto me! Forty Norman cut-throats and we in our succursal cell only five friars, two novices, two lay-brothers, and five hinds! And our poor upper buildings all made of wood, old and ready to burn like tow! and not ten bows in the place or five men knowing how to use them! By Saint Ovin and his cross! Were our walls but as strong as those of the monks of Ely, and our war-gear better, and none of us cowards, I would say, 'Up drawbridge! Defy this Norman woodcutter, who felled trees in the forest for his bread until brought by the bastard to cut Saxon throats and fatten upon the lands of our thanes and our churches and monasteries! I would spit at the beard of this Ivo Taille-Bois, and call upon Thurstan my Lord Abbat of Ely, and upon the true Saxon hearts in the Camp of Refuge, for succor!' And the passionate young man struck the trunk of the poor unoffending tree until the bark cracked, and the long thin leaves, loosened by autumn, fell all about him.

He then continued his journey through the low, thick, and monotonous wood, and after sundry more leaps, and not a few sousing's in the water and slips in the mud, he reached the bank of the Welland at a point just opposite to the succursal cell of Spalding. A ferry-boat was moored under the walls of the house. He drew forth a blast horn; but before putting it to his lips to summon the ferryman across, he bethought him that he could not be wetter than he was, that he had got his last fall in a muddy place, and that the readiest way to cleanse himself before coming into the presence of his superior would be to swim across the river instead of waiting to be ferried over. This also suited the impatient mood he was in, and he knew that the serf who managed the boat was always slow in his movements, and at times liable to sudden and unseasonable fits of deafness.

So, throwing his heavy staff before him, like a javelin, and with so much vigor that it reached and stuck deep into the opposite bank, he leaped into the river and swam across after it. Before he came to the Welland the sun had gone down; but it was a clear autumnal evening, and if he was not seen in the twilight by a lay-brother stationed on the top of the house to watch for his return and to keep a look-out along the river, it must have been because the said lay-brother was either drowsy and had gone to sleep, or was hungry and had gone down to see what was toward in the kitchen.

The succursal cell of Spalding was but a narrow and humble place compared with its great mother-house at Crowland: it seemed to stand upon piles driven deep into the marshy ground; the lower part of the building was of stone, brick, and rubble, and very strong; but all the upper part was of wood, even as the wayfaring novice had lamented. A few small round-headed arches, with short thick mullions, showed where was the chapel, and where the hall, which last served as refectory, chapter, and for many other uses. Detached from the chapel was a low thick campanile or bell-tower, constructed like the main building, partly of stone, brick, and rubble, and partly of timber, the upper part having open arches, through which might be seen the squat old bell and the ponderous mallet, which served instead of a clapper.

The Welland almost washed the back of the house, and a deep trench, filled by the water of the river, went round the other sides. Without being hailed or seen by anyone, the young man walked round from the river bank to the front of the house, where the walls were pierced by a low arched gateway and one small grated window a little above the arch. "The brothers are all asleep, and before supper time!" said the novice, "but I must rouse old Hubert." He then blew his horn as loud as he could blow it. After a brief pause a loud but cracked voice cried from within the gates, "Who comes hither, after evening song?" "It is I, Elfric the novice."

"The voice is verily that of child Elfric; but I must see with my eyes as well as hear with mine ears, for the Norman are prowling all about, and these be times when the wolf counterfeited the voice of the lamb."

"Open, Hubert, open," cried the novice, "open, in the name of Saint Chad! For I am wet, tired, and a-hungred, and the evening wind is beginning to blow coldly from the meres. Open thy gate, Hubert, and let fall the bridge; I am so hungry that I could eat the planks! Prithee, is supper ready?"

To this earnest address no answer was returned; but after a minute or two the twilight showed a cowled head behind the grates of the window—a head that seemed nearly all eyes, so intensely did the door-porter look forth across the moat—and then the voice which before had been heard below, was heard above, saying, "The garb and figure be verily those of Elfric, and the water streams from him to the earth. Ho! Elfric the novice — and thou be he—throw back thy hood, and give the sign!"

"Abbat Thurstan and Saint Etheldreda for the East Englanders!" shouted the young man.

Here, another voice was heard from within the building calling out "Hubert, whom challenges? Is it Elfric returning from Crowland?"

"Yea," quote the portarius, "it is Elfric the novice safe back from Crowland, but dripping like a water-rat, and shivering in the wind. Come, help me lower the bridge, and let him in."

The gate was soon opened, and the narrow drawbridge lowered. The youth entered, and then helped to draw up the bridge and make fast the iron-studded door. Within the archway every member of the little community, except those who were preparing the evening repast or spreading the tables in the refectory, and the superior who was prevented by his gout and his dignity from descending to the door-way to meet a novice (be his errand what it might), was standing on tip-toe, and open-mouthed for news; but Elfric was a practiced messenger, and knowing that the bringer of bad news is apt to meet with a cold welcome, and that the important tidings he brought ought to be communicated first to the head of the house, he hurried through the throng, and crossing a cloistered court, and ascending a flight of stairs, he went straight to the cell of Father Adhelm, the sub-prior of Crowland Abbey, who ruled the succursal cell of Spalding.

The monks followed him into the room; but the novices and lay-brothers stopped short at the threshold, taking care to keep the door ajar so that they might hear whatsoever was said within. "I give thee my benison, oh, my child! and may the saints bless thee, for thou art back sooner than I weened. But speak, oh Elfric! Quick! Tell me what glad tidings thou bringest from my Lord Abbat and our faithful brethren at Crowland, and what news of that son of the everlasting fire, our evil neighbor Ivo Taille-Bois?"

After he had reverentially kissed the hand of his superior, Elfric the novice spoke and said, —

"Father, I bring no glad tidings; my news be all bad news! Ivo Taille-Bois is coming against us to complete his iniquities, by finishing our destruction; and the Abbat and our faithful brethren at Crowland are harassed and oppressed themselves, and cannot help us!"

The faces of the monks grew very long; but they all said in one voice, "Elfric, thou dreamest. Elfric, thou speakest of things that cannot be; for hath not my Lord Abbat obtained the king's peace, and security for the lives of all his flock and the peaceful possession of all our houses, succursal cells, churches and chapels, farms and lands whatsoever, together with our mills, fisheries, stews, warrens, and all things appertaining to our great house and order?"

One of the primary duties imposed upon novices was to be silent when the elders spoke. Elfric stood with his hands crossed upon his breast and with his eyes bent upon the floor, until his superior said "Peace, brothers! let there be silence until the youth hath reported what he hath heard and seen." And then turning to Elfric, Father Adhelm added, "Bring you no missive from our good Abbat?"

"Yea," said the novice, "I am the bearer of an epistle from my Lord Abbat to your reverence; and lo! it is here." And he drew forth from under his inner garment a round case made of tin, and presented it most respectfully to the superior.

"I am enduring the pains of the body as well as the agony of the spirit," said the superior, "and my swollen right hand refuses its office; brother Cedric, undo the case."

Cedric took the case, opened it, took out a scroll of parchment, kissed it as if it had been a relic, unrolled it, and handed it to the superior.

"Verily this is a long missive," said the superior, running his eyes over it, "and alack, and woe the while, it commenced with words of ill omen! Brethren my eyes are dim and cannot read by twilight; the body moreover is faint, I having fasted from everything but prayer and meditation since the mid-day refection; and then, as ye can bear witness, I ate no meat, but only picked a stewed pike of the smallest. Therefore, brethren, I opine that we had better read my Lord Abbat's epistle after supper (when will they strike upon that refectory bell?), and only hear beforehand what Elfric hath to say."

The cloister-monks gladly assented, for they were as hungry as their chief, and, not being very quick at reading,

CONQUEST OF THE ISLE OF ELY

were glad that the superior had not called for lights in the cell, and called upon them to read the letter.

"Now speak, Elfric, and to the point; tell the tale shortly, and after the evening meal the lamp shall be trimmed and we will draw our stools round the hearth in the hall, and read the abbat's epistle and deliberate thereupon."

Upon this injunction of Father Adhelm, the youth began to relate with very commendable brevity, that the abbey of Crowland was surrounded and in good part occupied by Norman knights and men-at-arms, who were eating the brotherhood out of house and home, and committing every kind of riot and excess; that the abbat had in vain pleaded the king's peace, and shown the letters of protection granted him by Lanfranc, the new foreign primate of the kingdom; that the Normans had seized upon all the horses and mules and boats of the community; and that the abbat (having received disastrous intelligence from the north and from other parts of England where the Saxon patriots had endeavored to resist the conqueror), had fallen sick, and had scarcely strength to dictate and sign the letter he brought.

"These are evil tidings indeed," said the superior, "but the storm is yet distant, and may blow over without reaching us. It is many a rood from Crowland to Spalding, and there is many a bog between us. Those accursed knights and men-at-arms will not readily risk their horses and their own lives in our fens; and now that Ivo Taille-Bois hath so often emptied our granaries, and hath crippled or carried off all our cattle, we have the protecting shield of poverty.

There is little to be got here but bare walls, and Ivo, having the grant of the neighboring lands from the man they call King William, is not willing that any robber but himself should come hitherward.

His mansion guards the causeway, and none can pass thereon without his *bene placet*. But, oh Elfric! What of the demon-possessed Ivo? Rests he not satisfied with the last spoils he made on our poor house? Abides he not true to his compact that he would come no more, but leave us to enjoy his king's peace and the peace of the Lord? Heeds he not the admonition addressed to him by Lanfranc? Speak, Elfric, and be quick, for methinks I hear the step of the cellarer by the refectory door."

"The strong keep no compact with the weak," responded the novice, "and these lawless marauders care little for William their king, less for their archbishop and nothing for the Lord! While I was hid in Crowland Abbey waiting for my Lord Abbat's letter, I heard from one of the friars who can interpret their speech, that some of these Normans were saying that Ivo Taille-Bois wanted the snug nest at Spalding to put cleaner birds into it: that Ivo had made his preparations to dispossess us. And lo! as I came homeward through the fens, and passed as near as I might to the manor-house which Taille-Bois made his own by forcibly marrying the good Saxon owner of it, I heard the flourish of trumpets, and anon I saw, tramping along the causeway towards the well-garrisoned manor-house, forty Norman men-at-arms!"

"Not so, surely not so, Elfric," said the superior in a quake, "danger cannot be so near us as that!"

"His eyes must have deceived him," cried all the brothers.

"Nay," said the youth, "I saw, as plainly as I now see the faces of this good company, their lances glinting in the setting sun, and their bright steel caps and their grey mail, and...."

"Fen-grass and willows," cried the superior, who seemed determined not to give credit to the evil tidings, "what thou took for spears were bulrushes waving in the breeze, and thy steel-caps and grey mails were but the silvery sides of the willow-leaves turned upwards by the wind! Boy, fasting weakens the sight and makes it dim!"

"Would it were so," quote Elfric; "but so was it not! I heard the trumpet give challenge from the battlements—I heard the other trumpet give response—I heard the tramping of many hoofs along the hard solid causeway; and, creeping nearer to the road, I saw lances and horses and men—and they were even forty!"

"It cannot be," said one of the monks, "for, when he made his last paction with us, Ivo Taille-Bois swore, not only by three Saxon saints but eke by six saints of Normandie, that he would do us and our house no further wrong."

"The senses are deceptions," said another of the brotherhood.

"The foul fiend, who often lurks in these wildernesses and plays fiery pranks in our fens, may have put it into this youth's head to mar our peace with false alarms;" quote another monk.

"Say warning, and not false alarm," rejoined Elfric rather petulantly. "If you will not be warned, you will be surprised in your sleep or at your meals. These forty men-at-arms cannot come hither for other purpose than that of finishing our ruin and driving us hence. As sure as the sun rises they will be here to-morrow morning."

"The boy chafes, and loses respect for his elders," said the monk who had last spoken.

"Let him sup with the cats!" cried the superior.

At this moment a bell was struck below; and at the signal the novices and lay-brothers ran from the door at which they had been listening, and the superior, followed by the monks and at a respectful distance by the reproved and vexed novice, hobbled down stairs to the refectory.

The aspect of that hall, with its blazing wood fire, abundant tapers and torches, and well-spread tables, intimated that the superior's account of the poverty and destitution to which Ivo the Norman had reduced the house was only figurative or comparative. That good father took his place at the head of the table; the monks took their seats according to their degree of antiquity; the novices and the lay-brothers sat below the salt; and poor Elfric, submissive to his penance, sat down cross-legged on the rushes in the middle of the floor, and in the midst of all the cats of the establishment, who, I wist, knew as well as the monks the meaning of the dinner and supper bell, and always trooped into the refectory to share the fragments of the feast.

One of the novices ascended a little pulpit raised high in one of the angles of the hall, and the superior having blessed the good things placed before him, this young novice read from the book of Psalms while the rest of the company ate their meal. After all had been served, even to the meanest of the lay-brothers, Elfric's bread and meat and his stoup of wine were handed to him on the floor—and then was seen what it signified to sup with the cats, for tabbies, greys, blacks, and whites all whisked their tails, and purred and mewed, and scratched round about him, greedy to partake with him, and some of the most daring even dipped their whiskers into his porringer, or scratched the meat from his spoon before it could reach his mouth.

Nevertheless the young man made a hearty meal, and so, in spite of their fears and anxieties, did all the rest of that devout community. As grace was said, and as the reader was descending from the pulpit to do as the others had done, the superior, after swallowing a cup of wine, said rather blithely, "Now trim the good lamp and feed the fire, close the door, and place seats and the reading-desk round the hearth." As the novices and lay-brothers hastened to do these biddings, Father Cedric whispered to the superior, "Would it not be fitting to shut out the young and the un-ordained, and deliberate by ourselves, *maturi fratres*?" "No," replied the superior, "we be all alike concerned; let novices and lay-brothers stay where they are and hear the words of our Lord Abbat. If danger be so nigh, all must prepare to meet it, and some may be wanted to run into Spalding town to call upon all good Christians and true Saxons there to come to the rescue."

Then turning to the youth on the rushes he said, "Elfric the messenger, thou mayest rise and take thy seat in thy proper place: I cannot yet believe all thy news, and thou spokest when thou oughtest not to have spoken; but these are days of tribulation, and mischief may be nearer than we thought it. Yet, blessed be God! That provides food and drink for his creatures, and that makes the bounteous meal and the red wine revives the heart and courage of man, I feel very differently now from what I felt before supper, and can better bear the weight of evil news, and more boldly face the perils that may lie in my path." By words or by looks all the brotherhood re-echoed this last sentiment.

Spalding Abbey

CHAPTER II.

THE SUCCURSAL CELL

The Abbat of Crowland's letter, read aloud and slowly by the cheerful fire, had no note of gladness in it. It began "Woe to the Church! Woe to the servants of God! Woe to all of the Saxon race!" and it ended with, "Woe! Woe! Woe!" It related how all the prelates of English birth were being expelled by foreign priests, some from France and some from Italy; how nearly every Saxon abbat had been deprived, and nearly every religious house seized by men-at-arms and given over to strange shavelings from Normandie, from Anjou, from Picardie, from Maine, from Gascony, and numberless other parts, and how these alien monks, who could not speak the tongue which Englishmen spoke, were occupying every pulpit and confessional, and consigning the people to perdition because they spoke no French, and preferred their old masters and teachers to their new ones, put over them by violence and the sword!

Jealousies and factions continued to rage among the Saxon lords and among those that claimed kindred with the national dynasties; sloth and gluttony, and the dullness of the brain they produce, rendered of no avail the might of the Saxon arm, and the courage of the Saxon heart. Hence a dies iræ, a day of God's wrath. Aldred, the archbishop of York, had died of very grief and anguish of mind: Stigand, the English and the true archbishop of Canterbury, after wandering in the Danelagh and in Scotland, and flying for his life from many places, had gone in helpless condition to the Camp of Refuge in the Isle of Ely: Edgar Etheling, that royal boy, had been deserted by the Danes, who had crossed the seas in many ships to aid him; and he had fled once more in a denuded state to the court of Malcolm Caenmore, the Scottish king. In all the north of England there had been a dismal slaughter: from York to Durham not an inhabited village remained—fire and the sword had made a wilderness there—and from Durham north to Hexham, from the Wear to the Tyne, the remorseless conqueror, Herodes, Herode ferocior, a crueler Herod than the Herod of old, had laid waste the land and slaughtered the people. York Minster had been destroyed by fire, and every church, chapel, and religious house had been either destroyed or plundered by the Normans.

Everywhere the Saxon patriots, after brief glimpses of success, had met with defeat and extermination, save and except only in the Camp of Refuge and the Isle of Ely; and there too misfortune had happened. Edwin and Morcar, the sons of Alfgar, brothers-in-law to King Harold, and the best and the bravest of the Saxon nobles, had quitted the Camp of Refuge, that last asylum of Anglo-Saxon independence, and had both perished. All men of name and fame were perishing. The Saxon commonalty were stupefied with amazement and terror,—*Pavefactus est Populus*. The Normans were making war even upon the dead or upon the tombs of those who had done honor to their country as patriots, warriors, spiritual teachers, and saints. Frithric, the right-hearted Abbat of St. Albans, had been driven from his abbey with all his brethren; and Paul, a young man from Normandie and a reputed son of the intrusive Archbishop Lanfranc, had been thrust in his place.

And this Paul, as his first act in office, had demolished the tombs of all his predecessors, whom he called rude and idiotic men, because they were of the English race!

And next, this Paul had sent over into Normandie for all his poor relations and friends—men ignorant of letters and of depraved morals—and he was dividing among this foul rapacious crew the woods and the farms, all the possessions and all the offices of the church and abbey of St. Albans. Crowland was threatened with the same fate, and he, the abbat, was sick and brokenhearted, and could oppose the Normans only with prayers—with prayers to which, on account of the sins of the nation, the blessed Virgin and the saints were deaf. The brethren in the succursal cell at Spalding must look to themselves, for he, the abbat, could give them no succor; and he knew of a certainty that Ivo Taille-Bois had promised the cell to some of his kith and kin in foreign parts.

The reading of this sad letter was interrupted by many ejaculations and expressions of anger and horror, grief and astonishment; and when it was over, the spirits of the community were so depressed that the superior thought himself absolutely compelled to call upon the cellarer and bid him fill the stoups again, to the end that there might be another short Biberes. When the monks had drunk in silence, and had crossed themselves after the draught, they began to ask each other what was to be done?

For they no longer doubted that Elfric had seen the forty men-at-arms in the neighborhood, or that Ivo Taille-Bois would be thundering at their gate in the morning. Some proposed sending a messenger into Spalding town, which was scarcely more than two good bow-shots distant from the cell, lighting the beacon on the tower, and sounding all the blast-horns on the house-top to summon the whole neighborhood to their aid; but the superior bade them reflect that this would attract the notice of Ivo Taille-Bois, and be considered as an hostile defiance; that the neighborhood was very thinly peopled by inexpert and timid serfs, and that most of the good men of Spalding town who possessed arms and the art of wielding them had already taken their departure for the Camp of Refuge. At last the superior said, "We cannot attempt a resistance, for by means of a few lighted arrows the children of Satan would set fire to our upper works, and so burn our house over our heads. We must submit to the will of Heaven, and endeavour to turn aside the wrath of our arch-persecutor. Lucia, the wife of Ivo Taille-Bois, was a high-born Saxon maiden when he seized upon her (after slaying her friends), and made her his wife in order to have the show of a title to the estates. As a maiden Lucia was ever good and Saxon-hearted, especially devout to our patron saint, and a passing good friend and benefactress to this our humble cell. She was fair among the daughters of men, fairest in a land where the strangers themselves vouchsafe to say that beauty and comeliness abound; she may have gotten some sway over the fierce mind of her husband, and at her supplications Ivo may be made to forego his wicked purposes. Let us send a missive to the fair Lucia."

Here Brother Cedric reminded Father Adhelm that a letter would be of little use, inasmuch as the fair Lucia could not read, and had nobody about her in the manor-house that could help her in this particular. "Well then," said the superior, "let us send that trusty and nimble messenger Elfric to the manor-house, and let him do his best to get access to the lady and acquaint her with our woes and fears. What sayest thou, good Elfric?"

Albeit the novice thought that he had been but badly rewarded for his last service, he crossed his arms on his breast, bowed his head, and said, "Obedience is my duty. I will adventure to the manor-house, I will try to see the Lady Lucia, I will go into the jaws of the monster, if it pleaseth your reverence to command me so to do. But, if these walls were all of stone and brick, I would rather stay and fight behind them: for I trow that the fair Lucia hath no more power over Ivo Taille-Bois than the lamb hath over the wolf, or the sparrow over the sparrow-hawk."

"But," said the superior, "unless Heaven vouchsafe a miracle, we have no other hope or chance than this. Good Elfric, go to thy cell and refresh thyself with sleep, for thou hast been a wayfarer through long and miry roads, and needest rest. We too are weary men, for we have read a very long letter and deliberated long on weighty trying business, and the hour is growing very late. Let us then all to bed, and at earliest morning dawn, after complines, thou wilt gird up thy loins and take thy staff in thine hand, and I will tell thee how to bespeak the Lady Lucia, an thou canst get to her presence. I will take counsel of my pillow, and call upon the saints to inspire me with a moving message that I shall send."

Elfric humbly saluted the superior and all his elders by name, wished them a holy night, and withdrew from the refectory and hall to seek the rest which he really needed: but before entering his cell he went to the house-top to look out at the broad moon, and the wood, and the river, and the open country, intersected by deep cuts and ditches, which lay in front of the succursal cell. The night had become frosty, and the moon and the stars were shining their brightest in a transparent atmosphere. As the novice looked up the course of the Welland he thought he distinguished something afar off floating on the stream. He looked again, and felt certain that a large boat was descending the river towards the house.

He remained silent and almost breathless until the vessel came so near that he was enabled to see that the boat was filled with men-at-arms, all clad in mail, who held their lances in their hands, and whose shields were fastened to the sides of the boat, glittering in the moonlight.

"I count forty and one lances and forty and one shields," said the youth to himself, "but these good friars will tell me that I have seen bulrushes and willow-leaves." He closed his eyes for a time and then rubbed them and looked out again. There was the boat, and there were the lances and the shields and the men-at-arms, only nearer and more distinct, for the current of the river was rapid, and some noiseless oars or paddles were at work to increase the speed without giving the alarm. "I see what is in the wind," thought Elfric; "the Normans would surprise us and expel us by night, without rousing the good people of Spalding town."

He ran down the spiral staircase; but, short as was the time that he had been on the housetop, every light had been extinguished in the hall during the interval, every cell-door had been closed; and a chorus of loud snores that echoed along the corridor told him that, maugre their troubles and alarms, all the monks, novices, and lay-brothers were already fast asleep. "I will do what I can do," said the youth, "for if I wake the superior he will do nothing. If the men of Spalding town cannot rescue us, they shall at least be witnesses to the wrongs put upon us. Nay, Gurth the smith, and Wybert the wheelwright, and Nat the weaver, and Leolf the woodsman, be brave-hearted knaves, and have the trick of archery. From the yon side of those ditches and trenches, which these heavy-armed Normans cannot pass, perchance a hole or two may be driven into their chain jerkins!"

Taking the largest horn in the house he again ascended to the roof, and turning towards the little town he blew with all his strength and skill, and kept blowing until he was answered by three or four horns in the town.

By this time the boat was almost under the walls of the monastery, and an arrow from it came whistling close over the youth's head. "There are neither battlements nor parapets here," said he, "and it is now time to rouse the brethren." In a moment he was in the corridor rapping at the doors of the several cells, wherein the monks slept on, not hearing the blowing of the horns; but before half the inmates were roused from their deep slumber the Normans had landed from the boat, and had come round to the front of the house shouting, "Taille-Bois! Taille-Bois! Notre Dame to our aid! and Taille-Bois to his own! Get up, ye Saxon churls that be ever sleeping or eating, and make way for better men!"

The superior forgot his gout and ran to the hall. They all ran to the hall, friars, novices, lay-brothers, and hinds, and lights were brought in and hurried deliberations commenced, in which every one took part. Although there was overmuch sloth, there was little cowardice among these recluses. If there had been any chance of making good the defense of the house, well I ween the major part of them would have voted for resistance; but chance there was none, and therefore, with the exception of Elfric, whose courage, at this time of his life, bordered on rashness, they all finally agreed with the superior that the wisest things to do would be to bid Hubert the portarius throw open the gate and lower the bridge; to assemble the whole community in the chapel, light up all tapers on the high altar and shrines, and chant the *Libera Nos Domine*—Good Lord deliver us!

"It is not psalmody that will save us from expulsion," thought Elfric.

Now Hubert the porter was too old and too much disturbed in spirit to do all that he had to do without help; and Father Cedric bade the sturdy novice go and assist him.

"May I die the death of a dog—may I be hanged on a Norman gibbet," said Elfric to himself, "if I help to open the gates to these midnight robbers!" And instead of following Hubert down to the gate, he went again (*sine Abbatis licentiâ*, without license or knowledge of his superior) to the house-top, to see whether any of the folk of Spalding town had ventured to come nigh. As he got to the corner of the roof from which he had blown the horn, he heard loud and angry voices below, and curses and threats in English and in Norman French. And he saw about a score of Spalding-men in their sheepskin jackets and with bows and knives in their hands, menacing and reviling the mail-clad men-at-arms. The Saxons soon got themselves well covered from the foe by a broad deep ditch, and by a bank; but some of the Normans had brought their bows with them, and a shaft let fly at the right moment when one of the Saxons was exposing his head and shoulders above the bank, took effect, and was instantly followed by a wild scream or yell—"Wybert is down! Wybert is slain!"

"Then this to avenge him, for Wybert was a good man and true;" and Elfric, who had brought a bow with him from the corridor, drew the string to his ear and let fly an arrow which killed the Norman that had killed Wybert the wright. It was the men-at-arms who now yelled; and, even as their comrade was in the act of falling, a dozen more arrows came whistling among them from behind the bank and made them skip.

Ivo Taille-Bois lifted up his voice and shouted, "Saxon churls, ye mean to befriend your fainéant monks; but if ye draw another bow I will set fire to the cell and grill them all!"

This was a terrible threat, and the poor men of Spalding knew too well that Ivo could easily do that which he threatened. The noise had reached the chapel, where the superior was robing himself, and Father Cedric came to the house-top to conjure the Saxons to retire and leave the servants of the saints to the protection of the saints. At the top of the spiral staircase he found the novice with the bow in his hand; and he said unto him, "What dost thou here, *et sine licentiâ*"?

"I am killing Normans," said Elfric; "but Wybert the wright is slain, and the men of Spalding are losing heart."

"Mad boy, get thee down, or we shall all be burned alive. Go help Hubert unbar the gate and drop the bridge."

"That will I never, though I break my monastic vow of obedience," said the youth.

"But hark! The chain rattles!—the bridge is down—the hinge creaks—by heaven! The gate is open—Ivo Taille-Bois and his devils are in the house! Then is this no place for me!"

And before the monk could check him, or say another word to him, the novice rushed to the opposite side and leaped from the roof into the deep moat. Forgetting his mission—which was to conjure the Saxons in the name of Father Adhelm the superior of the house not to try the arms of the flesh,—old Cedric followed to the spot whence the bold youth had taken his spring, but before he got there Elfric had swum the moat and was making fast for the Welland, in the apparent intention of getting into the fens beyond the river, where Norman pursuit after him could be of no avail.

The monk then went towards the front of the building and addressed the Saxons who still lingered behind the ditch and the bank, bemoaning the fate of Wybert, and not knowing what to do. Raising his voice so that they might hear him, Cedric beseeched them to go back to their homes in the town; and he was talking words of peace unto them when he was struck from behind by a heavy Norman sword which cleft his cowl and his skull in twain:

and he fell over the edge of the wall into the moat. Some of the men-at-arms had seen Elfric bending his bow on the house-top, and the Norman who had been slain had pointed, while dying, in that direction. After gaining access they had slain old Hubert and the lay-brother who had assisted him in lowering the drawbridge; and then, while the rest rushed towards the chapel, two of the men-at-arms found their way to the roof, and there seeing Cedric they dispatched him as the fatal archer and as the daring monk who had blown the horn to call out the men of Spalding. As Father Cedric fell into the moat, and the Normans were seen in possession of the cell, the men of Spalding withdrew, and carried with them the body of Wybert. But if they withdrew to their homes, it was but for a brief season and in order to carry off their moveable goods and their families; for they all knew that Ivo Taille-Bois would visit the town with fire and sword. Some fled across the Welland and the fens to go in search of the Camp of Refuge, and others took their way towards the wild and lonesome shores of the Wash.

But how fared the brotherhood in the chapel below? As Ivo Taille-Bois at the head of his men-at-arms burst into the holy place—made holy by the relics of more than one Saxon saint, and by the tomb and imperishable body of a Saxon who had died a saint and martyr at the hand of the Danish Pagans in the old time, before the name of Normans was ever heard of—the superior and friars, dressed in their stoles, as if for high mass, and the novices and the lay-brothers, were all chanting the Libera Nos; and they seemed not to be intimidated or disturbed by the flashing of swords and lances, or by the sinful imprecations of the invaders; for still they stood where they were, in the midst of tapers and flambards, as motionless as the stone effigies of the saints in the niches of the chapel; and their eyes moved not from the books of prayer, and their hands trembled not, and still they chanted in the glorious strain of the Gregorian chant (which Time had not mended), *Libera Nos Domine!* "Good Lord deliver us!" and when they had finished the supplication, they struck up in a more cheerful note, *Deus Noster Refugium*, God is our Refuge.

Fierce and unrighteous man as he was, Ivo Taille-Bois stood for a season on the threshold of the chapel with his mailed elbow leaning on the font that held the holy water; and, as the monks chanted, some of his men-at-arms crossed themselves and looked as if they were conscious of doing unholy things which ought not to be done. But when the superior glanced at him a look of defiance, and the choir began to sing *Quid Gloriaris?* "Why boasteth thou thyself, thou tyrant, that thou canst do mischief?" Ivo bit his lips, raised up his voice—raised it higher than the voices of the chanting monks, and said, "Sir Priest, or prior, come forth and account to the servant of thy lawful King William of Normandie for thy unlawful doings, for thy gluttonies, backslidings, and rebellions, for thy uncleanliness of life and thy disloyalty of heart!" But Father Adhelm moved not, and still the monks sang on and they came to the verses—"Thou hast loved to speak all words that may do hurt; oh! Thou false tongue—therefore shall God destroy thee forever: He shall take thee and pluck thee out of thy dwelling."

"False monk, I will first pluck thee out of thine," cried Ivo, who knew enough church Latin to know what the Latin meant that the monks were chanting; and he strode across the chapel towards the superior, and some of his men-at-arms strode hastily after him, making the stone floor of the chapel ring with the heavy tread of their iron-bound shoon; and some of the men-at-arms stood fast by the chapel door, playing with the fingers of their gloves of mail and looking in one another's eyes or down to the ground, as if they liked not the work that Ivo had in hand. The monks, the novices, the lay-brothers, all gathered closely round their superior and linked their arms together so as to prevent Ivo from reaching him; and the superior, taking his crucifix of gold from his girdle, and raising it high above his head and above the heads of those who girded him in, and addressing the Norman chief as an evil spirit, or as Sathanas the father of all evil spirits, he bade him avaunt! Ivo had drawn his sword, but at sight of the cross he hesitated to strike, and even retired a few steps in arrears.

The monks renewed their chant; nor stopped, nor were interrupted by any of the Normans until they had finished this Psalm. But when it was done Ivo Taille-Bois roared out, "Friars, this is psalmody enough! Men-at-arms, your trumpets! Sound the charge." And three Normans put each a trumpet to his lips and sounded the charge; which brought all the men-at-arms careering against the monks and the novices and the lay-brothers; so that the living fence was broken and some of the brethren were knocked down and trampled underfoot, and a path was opened for Ivo, who first took the golden crucifix from the uplifted hand of Father Adhelm and put it round his own neck, and then took the good father by the throat and bade him come forth from the chapel into the hall, where worldly business might be done without offering insult or violence to the high altar.

"I will first pour out the curses of the church on thy sacrilegious head," said the superior, throwing off the Norman count, and with so much strength that Ivo reeled and would have fallen to the ground among the prostrate monks, if he had not first fallen against some of his men-at-arms. Father Adhelm broke away from another Norman who clutched him, but in so doing he left nearly all his upper garment in the soldier's hand, and he was rent and ragged and without his crucifix when he reached the steps of the altar and began his malediction.

"Stop the shaveling's tongue, but shed no blood here," cried Ivo; "seize him, seize them all, and bring them into the refectory!"—and so saying the chief rushed out of the chapel into the hall. It was an unequal match—thirty-nine men-at-arms against a few monks and boys and waiting men; yet before the superior could be dragged from the high altar, and conveyed with all his community into the hall, several of the Normans were made to measure their length on the chapel floor (they could not wrestle like our true Saxons), and some of them were so squeezed within their mail sleeves and gorgets by the grip of Saxon hands, that they bore away the marks and smarts that lasted them many a day. It was for this that one of them cut the weazen of the sturdy old cook as soon as he got him outside the chapel door, and that another of them cut off the ears of the equally stout cellarer.

At last they were all conveyed, bound with their cords or girdles, into the hall. The Taille-Bois, with his naked sword in his hand, and with a man-at-arms on either side of him, sat at the top of the hall in the superior's chair of state; and the superior and the rest of the brotherhood were brought before him like criminals.

"Brother to the devil," said Ivo, "what was meant by thy collecting of armed men—rebel and traitor serfs that shall rue the deed!—thy sounding of horns on the house-top; thy fighting monks that have killed one of my best men-at-arms; thy long delay in opening thy doors to those who knocked at them in the name of King William; thy outrages in the chapel, and all thy other iniquities which I have so often pardoned at the prayer of the Lady Lucia? Speak, friar, and tell me why I should not hang thee over thine own gateway as a terror and an example to all the other Saxon monks in this country, who are all in their hearts enemies and traitors to the good king that God and victory have put over this land!"

Had it not been that Father Adhelm was out of breath, from his wrestling in the Chapel, I wist he never would have allowed Ivo Taille-Bois to speak so long without interruption. But by the time the Norman paused, the superior had partly recovered his breath; and he did not keep the Norman waiting for his answer.

"Son of the fire everlasting," cried Adhelm, "it is for me to ask what meanest thou by thy transgressions, past and present? Why hast thou from thy first coming among us never ceased from troubling me and these other servants of the saints, the brothers of this poor cell? Why hast thou seized upon and emptied our granaries and our cellars (more the possessions of the saints and of the poor than our possessions)? Why hast thou carried off the best of our cattle? Why hast thou and thy people lamed our horses and our oxen, and killed our sheep and poultry? Why hast thou caused to be assailed on the roads, and beaten with staves and swords, the lay-brothers and servants of this house? Why didst thou come at the dead of night like a chief of robbers with thy men-at-arms and cut-throats to break in upon us and to wound and slay the servants of the Lord, who have gotten thy king's peace, and letters of protection from the Archbishop Lanfranc? Oh, Ivo Taille-Bois! tell me why thou shouldst not be overtaken by the vengeance of man's law in this world, and by eternal perdition in the next?"

Ivo was not naturally a man of many words; and thinking it best to cut the discussion short, he grinned a grim grin, and said in a calm and business-like tone of voice, "Saxon! We did not conquer thy country to leave Saxons possessed of its best fruits. This house and these wide domains are much too good for thee and thine: I want them, and long have wanted them, to bestow upon others. Wot ye not that I have beyond the sea one brother and three cousins that have shaved their crowns and taken to thy calling — that in Normandie, Anjou, and Maine there are many of my kindred and friends who wear hoods and look to me for provision and establishment in this land of ignorance and heresy, where none of your home-dwelling Saxon monks know how to make the tonsure in the right shape?"

"Woe to the land, and woe to the good Christian people of it!" said the superior and several of his monks; "it is then to be with us as with the brotherhood of the great and holy abbey of St. Albans! We are to be driven forth empty-handed and brokenhearted, and our places are to be supplied by rapacious foreigners who speak not and understand not the tongue of the English people! Ah woe! was it for this that Saxon saints and martyrs died and bequeathed their bones to our keeping and their miracles to our superintendence; that Saxon kings and queens descended from their thrones to live among us, and die among us, and enrich us, so that we might give a beauty to holiness, a pomp and glory to the worship of heaven, and ample alms, and still more ample employment to the poor? Was it for this the great and good men of our race, our thanes and our earls, bequeathed lands and money to us? Was it to fatten herds of alien monks, who follow in the bloody track of conquest and devastation, and come among us with swords and staves, and clad in mail even like your men-at-arms, that we and our predecessors in this cell have labored without intermission to drain these bogs and fens, to make roads for the foot of man through this miry wilderness, to cut broad channels to carry off the waste waters to the great deep, to turn quagmires into bounteous corn fields, and meres into green pastures?"

While the Saxon monks thus delivered themselves, Ivo and his Normans (or such of them as could understand what was said) often interrupted them, and spoke in this wise—"King William hath the sanction of his holiness the Pope for all that he hath done or doth. Lanfranc loveth not Saxon priests and monks, and Saxon priests and monks love not the king nor any of the Normans, but are ever privately preaching and prating about Harold and Edgar Etheling, and putting evil designs into the heads of the people. The Saxon saints are no saints: who ever heard their names beyond sea? Their half-pagan kings and nobles have heaped wealth here and elsewhere that generous Norman knights and better bred Norman monks might have the enjoyment of it. The nest is too good for these foul birds: we have better birds to put into it. Let us then turn these English out of doors."

The last evil deed was speedily done, and superior, monks, novices, lay-brothers, were all thrust out of the gateway, and driven across the bridge. If the well-directed arrow of Elfric had slain one man-at-arms and the folk of Spalding town had slightly wounded two or three others, the Normans had killed Father Cedric, Hubert the porter, and the man that assisted him, had killed the cook, and cut off the ears of the cellarer. The conquerors therefore sought to shed no more blood, and the Taille-Bois was satisfied when he saw the brotherhood dispossessed and turned out upon the wide world with nothing they could call their own, except the sandals on their feet, and the torn clothes on their backs, and two or three church books.

When a little beyond the moat they all shook the dust from their feet against the sons of the everlasting fire; and the superior, leisurely and in a low tone of voice, finished the malediction which he had begun in the chapel against

Ivo Taille-Bois. This being over, Father Adhelm counted his little flock and said, "But oh, my children, where is the good Cedric?"

"Cedric was killed on the house-top, and lies dead in the moat," said one of the lay-brothers who had learned his fate when the rest of the community was ignorant of it.

"Peace to his soul, and woe to him that slew him!" said the superior; "but where is Elfric? I see not the brave boy Elfric."

"I saw Elfric outside the walls of our house and running for the Welland, just as the Normans were admitted," said the lay-brother who had before spoken, "and it must have been he that sent the arrow through the brain of the man-at-arms that lies there on the green sward."

"He will send his arrows through the brains of many more of them," said the superior. "My children, I feel the spirit of prophecy speaking within me, and I tell ye all that Elfric, our whilom novice, will live to do or cause to be done more mischief to the oppressors of his country than all the chiefs that have taken up arms against them. He hath a head to plan, and a heart to dare, and a strong hand to execute. I know the course he will take. He will return to the Isle of Ely, the place of his birth, in the midst of the many waters, and throw himself into the Camp of Refuge, where the Saxon motto is 'Death or Independence.'"

Before moving to the near bank of the Welland, or to the spot to which the Normans had sent down the ferry-boat, Father Adhelm again counted his little flock, and said, "Cedric lies dead in the moat, Hubert and Bracho lie cold under the archway, Elfric the novice is fled to be a thorn in the sides of these Normans, but, oh tell me! Where is good Oswald the cook?"

"After they had dragged your reverence into the hall, a man-at-arms cut his throat, even as Oswald used to cut the throats of swine; and he lies dead by the chapel-door."

"*Misericordia!* (O mercy on us!) Go where we will, we shall never find so good a cook again!"

Although it seemed but doubtful where or when they should find material for another meal the afflicted community repeated the superior's alacks and *Misericordia's!* mourning the loss of old Oswald as a man and as a Saxon, but still more as the best of cooks.

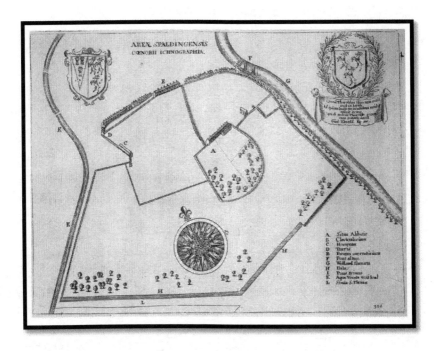

Precinct of the Priory of Spalding

CHAPTER III.

THE GREAT HOUSE AT ELY

Islands made by the sea, and yet more islands, inland, by rivers, lakes, and meres, have in many places ceased to be islands in everything save only in name. The changes are brought about by time and the fluctuations of nature, or by the industry and perseverance of man.

We, the monks of Ely that now live (*Henrico Secundo, regnante*), have witnessed sundry great changes in the Fen Country, and more changes be now contemplated; in sort that in some future age, men may find it hard to conceive, from that which they see in their day, the manner of country the Fen country was when the Normans first came among us. Then, I wist, the Isle of Ely was to all intents an inland island, being surrounded on every side by lakes, meres and broad rivers, which became still broader in the season of rain, there being few artificial embankments to confine them, and few or no droves or cuts to carry off the increase of water towards the Wash and the sea. The isle had its name from Helig or Elig, a British name for the Willow, which grew in great abundance in every part of it, and which formed in many parts low but almost impenetrable forests, with marshes and quagmires under them, or within them. Within the compass of the waters, which marked the limits of the country, and isolated it from the neighboring countries—which also from south to north, for the length of well-nigh one hundred miles, and from east to west, for the breath of well-nigh forty miles, were a succession of inland islands, formed like Ely itself—there were numerous meres, marshes, rivers, and brooks. The whole isle was almost a dead flat, with here and there an inconsiderable eminence standing up from it. These heights were often surrounded by water; and when the autumnal or the spring rains swelled the meres and streams, and covered the flats, they formed so many detached islets.

Though surrounded and isolated, they were never covered by water; therefore it was upon these heights and knolls that men in all times had built their towns, and their churches and temples. Communications were kept up by means of boats, carricks, and skerries, and of flat-bottomed boats which could float in shallow water; and, save in the beds of the rivers, and in some of the meres, the waters were but shallow even in the season of rains. But if it was a miry, it was not altogether a hungry land. When the waters subsided, the greenest and richest pasture sprung up in many parts of the plain, and gave sustenance to innumerable herds. The alluvial soil was almost everywhere rich and productive; and the patches which had been drained and secured, rewarded the industry and ingenuity of the inhabitants with abundant crops.

The Roman conquerors, with amazing difficulty, had driven one of their military roads through the heart of the country; but this noble causeway was an undeviating straight line, without any branches or cross roads springing from it; and it was so flanked in nearly its whole extent by meres, pools, rivers, rivulets, swamps, and willow forests, that a movement to the one side or the other was almost impracticable, unless the Romans, or those who succeeded the conquerors in the use of the causeway, embarked in boats and travelled like the natives of the country. In all times it had been a land of refuge against invaders. In the days of Rome the ancient

CONQUEST OF THE ISLE OF ELY

Britons rallied here, and made a good stand after all the rest of England had been subdued. Again, when Rome was falling fast to ruin, and the legions of the empire had left the Britons to take care of themselves, that people assembled here in great numbers to resist the fierce Saxon invaders.

Again, when the Saxons were assailed by the Danes and Norwegians, and the whole host of Scandinavian rovers and pirates, the indwellers of the Isle of Ely, after enjoying a long exemption from the havoc of war and invasion, defied the bloody Dane, and maintained a long contest with him; and now, as at earlier periods, and as at a later date, the isle of Ely became a place of refuge to many of the people of the upland country, and of other and more open parts of England, where it had not been found possible to resist the Danish battle-axes.

The traditions of the ancient Britons had passed away with that unhappy and extinct race; but the whole fenny country was full of Saxon traditions, and stories of the days of trouble when war raged over the isle and the fierce Danes found their way up the rivers, which opened upon the sea, into the very heart of the country. The saints and martyrs of the district were chiefly brave Saxons who had fought the Danes in many battles, and who had fallen at last under the swords of the unconverted heathen.

The miracles that were wrought in the land of many waters were for the most part wrought at the tombs of these Saxon warriors. The legends of patriotism were blended with the legends and rites of religion. Every church had its patriot saint and martyr; in every religious house the monks related the prowess, and chanted daily requiems, and said frequent masses to the soul of some great Saxon warrior who had fallen in battle; or to some fair Saxon maid or matron, who had preferred torture and death to a union with a pagan; or to some Saxon queen or princess, who, long before the coming of the Danes, and at the first preaching of the Gospel among the Saxons by Saint Augustine and his blessed followers, had renounced a throne and all the grandeurs and pleasures of the world, and all her riches, (*relictis fortunis omnibus!*) to devote herself to the service of heaven, to found a monastery, and to be herself the first lady abbess of the monastery she founded.

The foremost and most conspicuous of all the heights in this fen country was crowned by the abbey and conventual house of Ely, around which a large town, entirely governed by the Lord Abbat, (or, in the Lord Abbat's name, by the Cellarius of the abbey), had grown. The first conventual church was founded in the time of the Heptarchy, about the year of our Lord six hundred and seventy, by Saint Etheldreda, a queen, wife, virgin, and saint. Etheldreda was wife to King Egfrid, the greatest of the Saxon kings, and daughter of Anna, king of the East Angles, whose dominions included the isle of Ely, and extended over the whole of Suffolk and Norfolk.

This the first abbey church was built by Saint Wilfrid, bishop of York, who, with his sainted companion, Benedict, bishop of Northumberland, had travelled in far countries to learn their arts, and had brought from Rome into England painted glass, and glaziers, and masons, and all manner of artificers. When the Church was finished, a monastery was built and attached to it by the same royal devotee. Neither the love of her husband nor any other consideration could make Etheldreda forego her fixed purpose of immuring herself in the cloisters. Many of her attached servants of both sexes, whom she had converted, followed her to Ely, and were provided with separate and appropriate lodgings. Etheldreda was the first abbess of Ely; and after many years spent in the exercise of devotion, in fasting, penitence, and prayer, she died with so strong an odor of sanctity that it could not be mistaken; and she was canonized forthwith by the pope at Rome. Some of her servants were beatified: one, the best and oldest of them all, Ovin, who was said to descend from the ancient Britons, and who had been minister to her husband the king, or to herself as queen, was canonized soon after his death. Huna, her chaplain, after assisting at her interment, retired to a small island in the Fens near Ely, where he spent the rest of his days as an anchorite, and died with the reputation of a saint.

Many sick resorted to Huna's grave and recovered health. Her sister Sexburga was the second abbess of Ely, and second only to herself in sanctity. She too was canonized; and so also were her successors the abbesses Ermenilda and Withburga. The bodies of all the four lay in the choir of the church. The house had had many good penmen, and yet, it was said that they had failed to record all the miracles that had been wrought at these tombs. But the holiness of the place had not always secured it. In or about the year the unbelieving Danes, by ascending the Ouse, got unto Ely, slew all the monks and nuns, and plundered and destroyed the abbey.

And after this, Saxon kings, no better than heathens, annexed all the lands and revenues of the house to the crown, to spend among courtiers and warriors the substance which Saint Ermenilda and the other benefactors of the abbey had destined to the support of peace-preaching monks, and to the sustenance of the poor. And thus fared it with the abbey of Ely, until the reign of the great and bountiful King Edgar, who in course of his reign founded or restored no fewer than fifty monasteries. In the year this ever-to-be-revered king (*Rex Venerandus*) granted the whole of the island of Ely, with all its appurtenances, privileges, and immunities, to

CONQUEST OF THE ISLE OF ELY

Ethelwald, bishop of Winchester, who rebuilt the church and the monastery, and provided them well with monks of the Benedictine order. The charter of Edgar, as was recorded by that king's scribe in the preamble to it, was granted "not privately and in a corner, but in the most public manner, and under the canopy of heaven." The charter was confirmed by other kings, and subsequently by the pope. The great and converted Danish King Canute, who loved to glide along the waters of the river and listen to the monks of Ely singing in their choir, and who often visited the Lord Abbat, and feasted with him at the seasons of the great festivals of the church, confirmed the charter; and the cartularies of the house contained likewise the confirmation of King Edward the Confessor, now a saint and king in heaven, *(in cœlo sanctus et rex.)*

Theoretical and fabulous are the tales of those who say that the Saxons had no majestic architecture; that their churches and abbeys and monasteries were built almost entirely of wood, without arches or columns, without aisles or cloisters; and that there was no grandeur or beauty in the edifices of England until after the Norman Conquest.

The abbey built at Ely in the tenth century by the Saxon bishop Ethelwald was a stately stone edifice, vast in its dimensions, and richly ornamented in its details. Round-headed arches rested upon rows of massive columns; the roof of the church and the roof of the great hall of the abbey were arched and towering; and, high above all, a tower and steeple shot into the air, to serve as a landmark throughout the flat fenny country, and a guide to such as might lose themselves among the meres and the labyrinths of the willow forests. If the monks of Ely were lords of all the country and of all the people dwelling in it, those people and all honest wayfarers ever found the hospitable gates of the abbey open to receive them; and all comers were feasted, according to their several degrees, by the Lord Abbat, the prior, the cellarer, the hospitaller, the pietancer, or some other officer of the house. Twenty knights, with their twenty squires to carry arms and shield, *(arma ac scuta),* did service to the Lord Abbat as his military retainers; and in his great stables room was left for many more horses. The house had had many noble, hospitable, Saxon-hearted heads, but never one more munificent and magnificent than the Abbat Thurstan.

He had been appointed to the dignity in the peaceful days of Edward the Confessor; but King Harold, on ascending the throne, had shown him many favors, and had given him the means of being still more generous. This last of our Saxon kings had begun his reign with great popularity, being accessible, affable, and courteous to all men, and displaying a great regard for piety and justice. In the Confessor's time, under the title of earl, he had ruled as a sovereign in Norfolk and Suffolk and part of Cambridge, and he was a native of East Anglia. He had been open-handed and open-hearted. From all these reasons the people of this part of England were singularly devoted to his cause, and so thoroughly devoted to his person that they would not for a very long time believe that he had perished in the battle of Hastings; their hope and belief being that he had only been wounded, and would soon re-appear among them to lead them against the Norman.

When Duke William had been crowned in Westminster Abbey, and when his constantly reinforced and increasing armies had spread over the country, many of the great Saxon heads of religious houses, even like the Abbat of Crowland, had sent in their submission, and had obtained the king's peace, in the vain hope that thus they would be allowed to retain their places and dignities, and preserve their brethren from persecution, and the foundations over which they presided from the hands of foreign spoilers and intruders. Not so Thurstan, my Lord Abbat of Ely. He would not forget the many obligations he owed, and the friendship and fealty he had sworn to the generous, lion-hearted Harold; and while the lands of other prelates and abbots lay open everywhere to the fierce Norman cavalry, and their hinds and serfs, their armed retainers and tenants, and all the people dwelling near them, were without heart or hope, and impressed with the belief that the Normans were invincible, Thurstan, from the window of the hall, or from the top of the abbey tower, looked across a wide expanse of country which nature had made defensible; and he knew that he was backed by a stout-hearted and devoted people, who would choke up the rivers with the dead bodies of the Normans, and with their own corpses, ere they would allow the invaders to reach the abbey of Ely and the shrine of Saint Etheldreda.

Hence Thurstan had been emboldened to give shelter to such English lords, and such persecuted Saxons of whatsoever degree, as fled from the oppression of the conquerors to the Isle of Ely. Thanes dispossessed of their lands, bishops deprived of their mitres, abbots driven from their monasteries to make room for foreigners, all flocked hither; and whether they brought much money or rich jewels with them, or whether they brought nothing at all, they all met with a hospitable reception: so large and English was the heart of Abbat Thurstan. When it was seen that William was breaking all the old and free Saxon institutions, and the mild and equitable laws of Edward the Confessor, which he had most solemnly sworn to preserve and maintain; that the promptest submission to the conqueror ensured no lasting safety to life or property; and that the Normans, one and all, laity and clergy, knights and bishops, were proclaiming that all men of Saxon blood ought to be disseized of their property, and ought to be reduced to servitude and bondage, and were acting as if this system could soon be established, more and more fugitives came flying into the fen country. The town of Ely was roomy, but it was crowded; vast were the monastery, and hospitium, and dependencies, but they were crowded also: and far and near, on the dry hillocks, and in the green plains fenced from the waters, were seen huts and rude tents, and the blue smoke of many fires rising above the grey willows and alders.

It were long to tell how many chiefs and nobles of fame, and how many churchmen of the highest dignity, assembled at dinner-time, and at supper-time, in my Lord Abbat's great hall, where each had his seat according to his rank, and where the arms of every great chief were hung behind him on the wall, and where the banner of every chief and noble floated over his head, pendant from the groined roof. All the bravest and most faithful of the Saxon warriors who had survived the carnage of Hastings, and of the many battles which had been fought since that of Hastings, were here; and in the bodies of these men, scarred with the wounds inflicted by the Norman lances, flowed the most ancient and noble blood of England.

They had been thanes and earls, and owners of vast estates, but now they nearly all depended for their bread on the Lord Abbat of Ely. Stigand, the dispossessed Saxon Primate of all England, was here; Egelwin, the dispossessed Saxon Bishop of Durham, was here; Alexander, Bishop of Lincoln, was here; and on one side of Alexander sat the good Bishop of Lindisfarne, while on the other side of him the pious Bishop of Winchester ate the bread of dependence and sorrow. Among the chiefs of great religious houses were Eghelnoth the Abbat of Glastonbury, and Frithric the most steadfast and most Saxon-hearted of all Lord Abbats.

A very hard man, an unlettered, newly-emancipated serf, from one of the hungriest parts of Normandie or Maine, had taken possession of the great house at Glastonbury, and had caused the bodies of his predecessors, the abbots of English race, to be disinterred; and, gathering their bones together, he had cast them in one heap without the gates, as if, instead of being the bones of holy and beatified monks, they had been the bones of sheep, or oxen, or of some unclean animals.

Frithric of Saint Albans, who had been spiritual and temporal lord of one of the fairest parts of England, of nearly all the woodland and meadow-land and corn-fields that lay between Saint Albans and Barnet on the one side, and between Luton and Saint Albans on the other side—Frithric, who had maintained one score and ten loaf-eaters or serving men in his glorious abbey, had wandered alone and unattended through the wilds and the fens, begging his way and concealing himself from Norman pursuit in the huts of the poorest men; and he had brought nothing with him to Ely save two holy books which had comforted him on his long wayfaring, and which he carried under his arm.

Every great house was wanted by the conquerors for their un-ecclesiastical kindred; but Saint Albans was one of the greatest of them all, and Frithric had done that which the Normans and their duke would never forgive. When, months after that great assize of God's judgment in battle, the battle of Hastings, (and after that the traitorous Saxon Witan, assembled in London, had sent a submissive deputation to William the Bastard at Berkhamstead to swear allegiance to him, and to put hostages into his hand,) the Normans were slaying the people, and plundering and burning the towns and villages, upon drawing nigh unto Saint Albans, they found their passage stopped by a multitude of great trees which had been felled and laid across the road, and behind which—if there had not been traitors in London and false Saxons everywhere—there would have been posted expert archers, and valorous knights and hardy yeomen, and nathless every monk, novice, lay-brother, and hind of the abbey, in such sort that the invaders and their war-horses would never have gotten over those barricades of forest trees, nor have ever ascended the hill where the great saint and martyr Albanus suffered his martyrdom in the days of the Dioclesian persecution, and where Offa the true Saxon king of Mercia erected the first church and the first great monastery for one hundred monks, that they might keep alive the memory of the just, and pray over his tomb seven times a-day.

Wrathful was Duke William; for, albeit none stood behind those ramparts of timber to smite him and his host, he could not win forward, nor enter the town, nor approach the abbey, until his men-at-arms and the followers of his camp should with long toil clear the road, and remove one after the other those stout barriers of forest trees. Red was he in the face as a burning coal when he summoned to his presence Frithric the Lord Abbat, and demanded whose work it was, and why these oaken barriers were raised in the jurisdiction of the monastery.

Abbat Frithric, whose heart was stouter than his own oaks, looked, as became the free descendant of Saxon thanes and Danish princes, right into the eyes of the conqueror, and said unto him in a loud voice, "I have done the duty appertaining to my birth and calling; and if others of my rank and profession had performed the like, as they well could and ought, it had not been in thy power to penetrate into the land thus far!" We have said his voice was loud when he spoke to the conqueror: it was so loud that the hills re-echoed it, and that men heard it that were hid in the woods to watch what the Normans would do, and avoid their fury; and when the echoes of that true Saxon voice died away, the thick growing oaks seemed to speak, for there came voices from the woods on either side the road, shouting, "Hail! all hail! Lord Frithric, our true Lord Abbat! If every Saxon lord had been true as he, Harold would now be king!"

Quoth Duke William, in an angered voice, "Is the spirituality of England of such power? If I may live and enjoy that which I have gotten, I will make their power less; and especially I mind to begin with thee, proud Abbat of Saint Albans!"

And how behaved Abbat Frithric when his domains were seized, and ill-shaven foreign monks thrust into his house, and savage foreign soldiers?—when, after that the conqueror had sworn upon all the relics of the church of Saint Albans, and by the Holy Gospels, to respect the abbey and all churches, and to preserve inviolate the good and ancient laws which had been established by the pious kings of England, and more especially by King Edward the Confessor, he allowed his Normans to kill the Saxon people without bot or compensation, plundered every church in the land, oppressed and despoiled all the abbeys, ploughed with ploughshares of red hot iron over the faces of all Saxons, and yet demanded from Frithric and his compeers a new oath of allegiance, and fuller securities for his obedience—what then did the Lord Abbat of Saint Albans?

He assembled all his monks and novices in the hall of the chapter, and taking a tender farewell of them, he said, "My brothers, my children, the time is come when, according to Scripture, I must flee from city to city before the face of our persecutors—*Fugiendum est a facie persequentium a civitate in civitatem.*" And rather than be forsworn, or desert the good cause, or witness without the power of remedying them the sufferings and humiliations and forcible expulsions of his monks, he went forth and became a wanderer as aforesaid, until he crossed the land of willows and many waters, and came unto Ely, a lone man, with nought but his missal and his breviary under his arm.

Now the Abbat Frithric was old when these years of trouble began; and constant grief and toil, and the discomforts of his long journey on foot from the dry sunny hill of Saint Albans to the fens and morasses of Ely, had given many a rude shake to the hour-glass of his life. Since his arrival at Ely he had wasted away daily: every time that he appeared in the hall or refectory he seemed more and more haggard and worn: most men saw that he was dying, but none saw it so clearly as himself. When the young and hopeful would say to him, "Lord Frithric, these evil days will pass away, the Saxons will get their own again, and thou wilt get back as a true Saxon to thine own abbey," he would reply, "Young men, England will be England again, but not in my day; my next move is to the grave: Saint Albans is a heavenly place, but it is still upon earth, and, save the one hope that my country may revive, and that the laws and manners and the tongue of the Saxons may not utterly perish, my hopes are all in heaven!"

Some of the best and wisest of those who had sought for refuge in the Isle of Ely feared that when this bright guiding light should be put out, and other old patriots, like the Abbat Frithric, should take their departure, the spirit which animated this Saxon league would depart also, or gradually cool and decline.

CHAPTER IV.

THE MONKS OF ELY FEAST

It was on a wet evening in Autumn, as the rain was descending in torrents upon swamps that seemed to have collected all the rains that had been falling since the departure of summer, and just as the monks of Ely were singing the Ave Maria (*Dulce, cantaverunt Monachi in Ely!*) that Elfric, the whilom novice of Spalding, surrounded by some of the Lord Abbat's people, and many of the town folk, who were all laughing and twitching at his cloak, arrived at the gate of the hospitium.

Our Lord Abbat Frithric had brought with him two holy books. Elfric, our novice, had brought with him two grim Norman heads, for he had not been idle on the road, but had surprised and killed on the borders of the fen country, first one man-at-arms, and then another; and the good folk of Ely were twitching at his mantle in order that they might see again the trophies which he carried under his broad sleeve. At his first coming to the well-guarded ford across the Ouse, the youth had made himself known.

Was he not the youngest son of Goodman Hugh, who dwelt aforetime by Saint Ovin's Cross, hard by the village of Haddenham, and only a few bow-shot from the good town of Ely. And when the Saxons had seen the two savage Norman heads, and had looked in the youth's face, the elders declared that he was the very effigies of the Goodman Hugh; and some of the younkers said that, albeit his crown was shorn, and his eye not so merry as it was, they recalled his face well, and eke the days when Elfric the son of Goodman Hugh played at bowls with them in the bowling-alley of Ely, and bobbed for eels with them in the river, and went out with them to snare wild water-fowl in the fens. Judge, therefore, if he met not with an hospitable reception from town and gown, from the good folk of Ely, and from all the monks!

So soon as Elfric had refreshed himself in the hospitium, he was called to the presence of Abbat Thurstan, and in truth to the presence of all the abbat's noble and reverend guests, for Thurstan was seated in his great hall, where the servitors were preparing for the supper. Elfric would have taken his trophies with him, but the loaf-man who brought the message doubted whether the abbat would relish the sight of dead men's heads close afore suppertime, and told him that his prowess was already known; and so Elfric proceeded without his trophies to the great hall, where he was welcomed by the noble company like another David that had slain two Goliaths.

When he had told the story of Ivo Taille-Bois' long persecution and night attack, and his own flight and journey, and had answered numerous questions put to him by the grave assembly, Abbat Thurstan asked him whether he knew what had happened at Spalding since his departure, and what had become of Father Adhelm and his monks, and what fate had befallen the good Abbat of Crowland.

"After my flight from the succursal cell," said the youth, "I dwelt for a short season at Crowland, hidden in the township, or in Deeping-fen, whither also came unto the abbey Father Adhelm and the rest of that brotherhood of Spalding; and there we learned how Ivo Taille-Bois had sent over to his own country to tell his kinsmen that he had to offer them a good house, convenient for a prior and five friars, ready built, ready furnished and well provided with lands and tenements; and how these heretical and unsound Norman monks were hastening to cross the Channel and take possession of the succursal cell at Spalding. My Lord Abbat of Crowland, having what they call the king's peace, and holding the letters of protection granted by Lanfranc".... "They will protect no man of Saxon blood, and the priest or monk that accepts them deserves excommunication," said Frithric, the Abbat of Saint Albans.

"Amen!" said Elfric; "but our Abbat of Crowland, relying upon these hollow and rotten reeds, laid his complaints before the king's council at that time assembled near unto Peterborough, and sought redress and restitution. But the Normans sitting in council not only refused redress and absolved Taille-Bois, but also praised him for what he had done in the way of extortion, pillage, sacrilege, and murder; and"....

"My once wise brother thy Abbat of Crowland ought to have known all this beforehand," said the Abbat of Saint Albans; "for do not these foreigners all support and cover one another, and form a close league, bearing one upon another, even as on the body of the old dragon scale is laid over scale?"

"*Sic est*, my Lord Abbat," said the youth, bowing reverentially to the dignitary of the church and the best of Saxon patriots, "so is it my lord! And dragons and devils are these Normans all! Scarcely had the decision of the king's council reached our house at Crowland, ere it was surrounded by armed men, and burst open at the dead of night, as our poor cell at Spalding had been, and Father Adhelm and all those who had lived under his rule at Spalding, were driven out as disturbers of the king's peace! I should have come hither sooner, but those to whom my obedience was due begged me to tarry awhile. Now I am only the forerunner of Father Adhelm and his brethren, and of my Lord Abbat of Crowland himself; for the abbat can no longer bear the wrongs that are put upon him, and can see no hope upon earth, and no resting-place in broad England, except in the Camp of Refuge."

"Another abbat an outcast and a wanderer! This spacious house will be all too full of Saxon abbots and bishops: but I shall make room for this new comer," said Frithric of Saint Albans to Egelwin, Bishop of Durham.

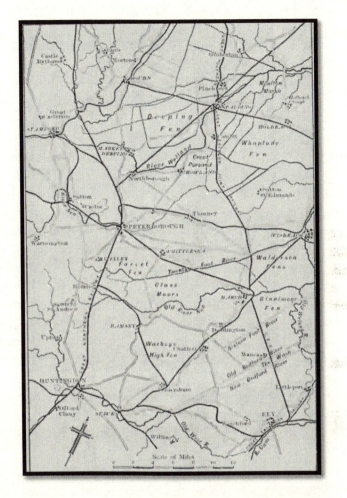

District of Peterborough

Divers of the monks of Ely, and specialiter the chamberlain, who kept the accounts of the house, and the cellarer, who knew the daily drain made on the wine butts, looked blank at this announcement of more guests; but the

CONQUEST OF THE ISLE OF ELY

bounteous and big-hearted Abbat of Ely said, "Our brother of Crowland, and Father Adhelm of Spalding, shall be welcome here—yea, and all they may bring with them; but tell me, oh youth, are they near at hand, or afar off in the wilderness?"

"The feet of age travel not as fast as the feet of youth," said Elfric, "age thinks, youth runs. I wot I was at Ramsey mere before they got to the Isle of Thorney, and crossed the Ouse before they came to the Nene, but as, by the blessing of the saints," and the youth might have said, in consequence of exercise and low living, "Father Adhelm's podagral hath left him, they can hardly fail of being here on the day of Saint Edmund, our blessed king and martyr, and that saint's day is the next day after to-morrow."

"It shall be a feast-day," said Thurstan; "for albeit Saint Edmund be not so great a saint as our own saint, Etheldreda, the founder of this house, and the monks of Saint Edmund-Bury (the loons have submitted to the Norman!) have more to do with his worship than we have, King Edmund is yet a great saint—a true Saxon saint, whose worship is old in the land; and it hath been the custom of this house to exercise hospitality on his festival. Therefore will we hold that day as we have been wont to hold it; and our brothers from Crowland and Spalding, who must be faring but badly in the fens, shall be welcomed with a feast."

So bounteous and open-handed was the true Saxon Abbat of Ely. But the chamberlain set his worldly head to calculate the expense, and the cellarer muttered to himself, "By Saint Withburga and her holy well, our cellars will soon be dry!"

On Saint Edmund's eve, after evening service in the choir and after saying his prayers apart in the chapel of Saint Marie, Frithric, the Abbat of Saint Albans departed this life. His last words were, that England would be England still; and all those who heard the words and had English hearts, believed that he was inspired, and that the spirit of prophecy spoke in his dying voice. The Abbat of Crowland was so near, that he heard the passing-bell, as its sad sounds floated over the fens, telling all the faithful that might be there of their duty to put up a prayer for the dead. On Saint Edmund's day the way-farers from Crowland arrived, and that abbat took possession of the cell, and of the seat in the refectory which had been occupied by Frithric. Fitting place was also found for Father Adhelm, who had grown so thin upon the journey that even Elfric scarcely knew him again. The feast in the hall was as magnificent as any that had been given there to King Canute, or even to any that had been given in the happy days of King Edward the Confessor; and the appetites of the company assembled were worthy of the best times. Fish, flesh, and fowl, and pasties of venison—nothing was wanting. The patrimony of Saint Etheldreda, the lands and waters appertaining unto the abbey, and administered by the bountiful abbat, furnished the best portions of the feast.

Were there in the world such eels and eel-pouts as were taken in the Ouse and Cam close under the walls of the abbey? Three thousand eels, by ancient compact, do the monks of Ramsey pay every Lent unto the monks of Peterborough, for leave to quarry stone in a quarry appertaining to Peterborough Abbey; but the house of Ely might have paid ten times three thousand eels, and not have missed them, so plenty were there, and eke so good! The fame of these eels was known in far countries; be sure they were not wanting on this Saint Edmund's day. The streams, too, abounded with pike, large and fit for roasting, with puddings in their bellies; and the meres and stagnating waters swarmed with tench and carp, proper for stewing. Ten expert hinds attended to these fresh-water fisheries, and kept the abbat's stews and the stews of the house constantly filled with fish. It is said by an ancient historian that here in the fenny country is such vast store of fish as astonishes strangers; for which the inhabitants laugh at them: nor is there less plenty of water-fowl; and for a single halfpenny five men may have enough of either, not only to stay their stomachs, but for a full meal! Judge, then, if my Lord Abbat was well provided. It was allowed on all sides that, for the Lenten season, and for all those fast-days of the Church when meat was not to be eaten, no community in the land was so well furnished as the monks of Ely; and that their fish-fasts were feasts. While the brethren of other houses grew thin in Quadragesima, the monks of Ely grew fat.

Other communities might do well in roast meats and baked meats; but for a fish dinner—for a banquet in Lent—there was not in the land anything to compare with the dinners at Ely! Nor was there lack of the fish that swim the salt sea, or of the shell-fish that are taken on the sea-coast, or of the finny tribes that come up the river to spawn; the fishermen of Lynn were very devout to Saint Etheldreda, and made a good penny by supplying the monks; they ascended the Ouse with the best of their sea-fish in their boats, and with every fish that was in season, or that they knew how to take. And so, at this late November festival there were skates and plaice, sturgeon and porpoises, oysters and cockles spread upon my Lord Abbat's table.

Of the sheep and beeves we speak not; all men know the richness of the pasture that springs up from the annually inundated meadows, and the bounty of the nibbling crop that grows on the upland slopes with the wild thyme and the other savory herbs that turn mutton into venison. Of the wild boars of the forest and fen only the hure or head was served up in this Aula Magna, the inferior parts being kept below for the use of the lay-brothers and hinds, or to be distributed by the hospitaller to the humbler degrees of pilgrims and strangers, or to be doled out to the poor of the town of Ely—for wot ye, when the Lord Abbat Thurstan feasted in Ely none fasted there: no!

Not the poorest palmer that ever put cockle-shell in his cap or took the pilgrim's staff in his hand to visit the blessed shrine of Saint Etheldreda! Of the wild buck, though less abundant in this fenny country than the boar, nought was served up for my Lord Abbat and his own particular guests except the tender succulent haunch; the lay-brothers and the loaf-eaters of the house, and the poor pilgrims and the poor of the town, got all the rest. The fat fowls of Norfolk, the capons of Caen in Normandie, and the pavoni or peacocks that first came from Italy a present from the *Legatus à latere* of his holiness the Pope, were kept and fattened in my Lord Abbat's farm-yard; and well did his coquinarius know how to cook them!

To the wild-fowl there was no end, and Elfric, our bold novice, the son of Goodman Hugh, who dwelt by Saint Ovin's Cross, hard by the village of Haddenham, and who had been a fen-fowler from his youth, could have told you how facile it was to ensnare the crane and the heron, the wild duck and teal, and the eccentric and most savory snipe. Well, we ween, before men cut down the covering woods, and drained the marshes, and brought too many people into the fens and too many great ships up the rivers, the whole land of Saint Etheldreda was like one great larder; and my Lord Abbat had only to say, "Go forth and take for me so many fowl, or fish, or boars," and it was done. It is an antique and venerable proverb, that which sayeth good eating demands good drinking. The country of the fens was not productive of apple-trees, and the ale and beer that were drunk in the house, and the mead and idromel likewise, were brought from Norfolk and other neighboring countries; but the abbat, and the officials, and the cloister monks drank better wine than apple-wine, better drink than mead or than pigment, for they drank of the juice of the generous vine, which Noah planted on the first dry hill-side he found. The monks of Glastonbury and Waltham, and of many other houses of the first reputation, cultivated the grape on their own soil, where it seldom would ripen, and drank English grape-wine much too sour and poor.

Not so our lordly monks of Ely! They sent the shipmen of Lynn to the Elbe, and to the Rhine, and to the Mosel, to bring them more generous drink; and they sent them to the south even so far as Gascony and Espaing for the ruby wine expressed from the grapes which grow in the sunniest clime. In the good times four keels, two from the German Ocean and two from the Gulf of Biscaye, steered every year through the sand-banks of the Wash to Lynn, and from Lynn up the Ouse even unto Ely, where the tons were landed and deposited in the cellars of the abbey, under the charge of the sub-cellarer, a lay-brother from foreign parts, who had been a vintner in his youth. And in this wise it came to be a passant saying with men who would describe anything that was super-excellent—

"It is as good as the wine of the monks of Ely!" Maugre the cellarer's calculation of quantities, the best wine my Lord Abbat had in hand was liberally circulated at the feast in silver cups and in gold-mounted horns. Thus were the drinks equal to the viands, as well in quantity as in quality; and if great was the skill of the vintner, great also was the skill of the cook. In other houses of religion, and in houses, too, of no mean fame, the monks had often to lament that their coquinarius fed them over long on the same sort of dishes; but it was not so with our monks of

Ely, who possessed a cook that had the art of giving variety to the selfsame viands, and who also possessed lands, woods, and waters that furnished the most varied materials for the cook to try his skill upon. As Father Adhelm finished his last slice of porpoise, curiously condimented with Eastern spices, as fragrant to the nose as they were savory to the palate, he lifted up his eyes towards the painted ceiling, and said, "I did not hope, after the death of Oswald our cook at Spalding, to eat of so perfect a dish on this side the grave!"

Flowers there were none to strew upon the floor; but the floor of the hall was thickly strewed with sweet-smelling hay, and with the rushes that grow in the fens; and the feet of the loaf-men of the abbat and of the other servitors that waited on the lordly company made no noise as they hurried to and fro with the dishes and the wine-cups and drinking-horns. While dinner lasted, nought was heard but the voice of the abbat's chaplain, who read the Psalms in a corner of the hall, the rattle of trenchers and knives, and, timeously, such ejaculations as these! "How good this fish! How good this flesh! How good this fowl! How fine this pasty! How rich this wine!" But when the tables were cleared, and grace after meat had been said, and my Lord Abbat's cupbearer had filled the cup of every guest with bright old Rhenish, Thurstan stood up at the head of the table, and said,

"Now drink we round to the health of England's true king, and this house's best friend, the Saxon-hearted Harold, be he where he will! And may he soon come back again! Cups off at a draught, while we drink Health to King Harold!"

"We drink his health, and he is dead—we wish him back, and he is lying in his coffin in the church of the abbey of Waltham, safe in the keeping of the monks of Waltham! The wine is good, but the toast is foolish." Thus spoke the envious prior to the small-hearted cellarer. But the rest of the goodly company drank the wassail with joy and exultation, and seemingly without any doubt that Harold was living and would return. In their minds it was the foul invention of the enemy—to divide and discourage the English people—which made King Harold die at Hastings. Who had seen him fall? Who had counted and examined that noble throng of warriors that retreated towards the sea-coast when the battle was lost by foul treachery, and that found boats and ships, and sailed away for some foreign land? Was not Harold in that throng, wounded, but with no deadly wound? Was it not known throughout the land that the Normans, when they counted the slain, not being able to find the body of Harold, sent some of our Saxon slaves and traitors to seek for it—to seek but not to find it? Was it not a moldering and a mutilated corpse that the Normans caused to be conveyed to Waltham, and to be there entombed, at the east end of the choir, as the body of King Harold? And did not the monks of Waltham close up the grave with brick-work, and inscribe the slab, *Hic jacet Harold infelix*, without ever seeing who or what was in the coffin? So reasoned all of this good company, who loved the liberties of England, and who had need of the sustaining hope that the brave Harold was alive, and would come back again.

Other wassails followed fast one upon the other. They were all to the health's of those who had stood out manfully against the invader, or had preferred exile in the fens, and poverty in the Camp of Refuge to submission to the conqueror. "Not less than a brimming cup can we drink to the last arrived of our guests, our brother the Lord Abbat of Crowland, and our brother the prior of Spalding," said Thurstan, filling his own silver cup with his own hand until the Rhenish ran over upon the thirsty rushes at his feet.

"Might I be allowed," said Father Adhelm at a later part of the feast, "might my Lord Abbat vouchsafe me leave to call a wassail for an humble and unconsecrated member of the Saxon church—who is nevertheless a child of Saint Etheldreda, and a vassal of my Lord Abbat, being native to this place—I would just drink one quarter of a cup, or it might be one half, to Elfric the Novice, for he travelled for our poor succursal cell when we were in the greatest perils; he carried my missives and my messages through fire and water; he forewarned us of our last danger and extremity; and, albeit he had not our order for the deed, and is thereby liable to a penance for disobedience—he slew with his arrow Ivo Taille-Bois' man-at-arms that had savagely slain good Wybert our wheel-wright."

"Aye," said Thurstan, "and he came hither across the fens as merry as David dancing before the ark; and he brought with him the heads of two Norman thieves who, with their fellows, had been murdering our serfs, and trying to find an opening that should lead them to the Camp of Refuge! Father Adhelm, I would have named thy youth in time; but as thou hast named him, let us drink his name and health even now! And let the draught be one half cup at least;—'Elfric the novice of Spalding!'"

"This is unbecoming our dignity and the dignity of our house: next we shall waste our wine in drinking wassail to our loaf-eaters and swineherds," muttered the cellarer to the prior.

But while the cellarer muttered and looked askance, his heart not being Saxon or put in the right place, the noblest English lords that were there, and the highest dignitaries of the church, the archbishop and the bishops, the Lord Abbats, and the priors of houses, that were so high that even the priors were styled Lords, Domini, and wore mitres, stood on their feet, and with their wine-cups raised high in their hands, shouted as in one voice, "Elfric the novice;" and all the obedientiarii or officials of the abbey of Ely that were of rank enough to be bidden to my Lord Abbat's table, stood up in like manner and shouted, "Elfric the novice!" and, when the loud cheering was over, off went the wine, and down to the ringing board the empty silver cups and the golden-bound horns. He who had looked into those cups and horns might have smiled at Father Adhelm's halves and quarters: they were nearly all filled to the brim: yet when they had quitted the lip and were put down upon the table, there was scarcely a heel-tap to be found except in the cup of the cellarer and in that of the envious prior of Ely. So strong were the heads and stomachs of our Saxon ancestors before the Normans came among us and brought with them all manner of people from the south with all manner of effeminacies.

Judge ye if Elfric was a proud man that day! At was sail-time the wide doors of the Aula Magna were thrown wide open; and harpers, and meni-singers, and men that played upon the trumpet, the horn, the flute, the pipe and tabor, the cymbal and the drum, or that touched the strings of the viola, assembled outside, making good music with instrument and voice; and all that dwelt within the precincts of the abbey, or that were lodged for the nonce in the guest-house, came, and they chose, to the threshold of the hall, and saw and heard what was doing and saying inside and what outside.

Now Elfric was there, with palmers and novices trooping all around him, and repeating (albeit dry-mouthed and without cups or horns to flourish) the wassail of the lords and prelates, "Elfric the novice!" If at that moment my Lord Abbat Thurstan or Father Adhelm had bidden the youth go and drive the Normans from the strong stone keep of their doubly-moated and trebly-walled castle by Cam-Bridge, Elfric would have gone and have tried to do it. He no longer trod upon base earth; his head struck the stars, as the poets say.

The abbat's feast, which began at one hour before noon, did not end until the hour of Ave Maria; nay, even then it was not finished, but only suspended for a short season by the evening service in the choir; for, after one hour of the night, the refectoriarius, or controller of the refectory, re-appeared in the hall with waxen torches and bright lanterns, and his servitors spread the table for supper.

As Abbat Thurstan returned to the refectory, leading by the hand his guest the Abbat of Crowland, that dispossessed prelate said to his host, "Tonight for finishing the feast; to-morrow morning for counsel."

"Aye," responded Thurstan, "to-morrow we will hold a chapter,—our business can brook no further delay—our scouts and intelligencers bring us bad news,—King Harold comes not, nor sends—the Camp of Refuge needs a head—our warriors want a leader of fame and experience, and one that will be true to the Saxon cause, and fearless. Woe the while! where so many Saxons of fame have proved traitors, and have touched the mailed hand of the son of the harlot of Falaise in friendship and submission, and have accepted as the gift of the butcher of Hastings the lands and honours which they held from their ancestors and the best of Saxon kings—where, I say, may we look for such a Saxon patriot and liberator? Oh, Harold! my lord and king, why tarriest thou? Holy Etheldreda, bring him back to thy shrine, and to the Camp of Refuge, which will cease to be a refuge for thy servants if Harold cometh not soon! But, courage my Lord of Crowland! The Philistines are not upon us; our rivers and ditches and marshes and meres are not yet drained, and no Saxon in these parts will prove so accursed a traitor as to give the Normans the clue to our labyrinths. The saint hath provided another joyous meal for us. Let us be grateful and gay to-night; let us sup well and strongly, that we may be invigorated and made fit to take strong and wise counsel in the morning."

And heartily did the monks of Ely and their guests renew and finish their feast, and hopefully and boldly did they speak of wars and victories over the Normans, until the drowsiness of much wine overcame them, and the sub-chamberlain of the house began to extinguish the lights, and collect together the torches and the lanterns, while the cellarer collected all the spoons, taking care to carry the Lord Abbat's spoon in his right hand, and the spoons of the monks in his left hand, according to the statutes of the Order. It was the last time that the feast of Saint Edmund the Martyr was kept in the true Saxon manner in the great house at Ely. The next year, and the year following that, the monks had little wine and but little ale to drink; and after the long years of trouble although the cellars were getting filled again, the true old Saxon brotherhood was broken up and mixed, a foreigner was seated in the place of Abbat Thurstan, and monks with miss-shaven tonsures and miss-shaped hoods and gowns filled all the superior offices of the abbey, purloining and sending beyond sea what my Lord Thurstan had spent in a generous hospitality, among true-born and generous-hearted Englishmen.

But in this nether world even the gifts of saints and the chartered donation of many kings are to be kept only by the brave and the united: conquest recognizes no right except as a mockery: the conquered must not expect to be allowed to call their life and limbs their own, or the air they breathe their own, or their wives and children their own, or their souls their own: they have no property but in the grave, no right but to die at the hour appointed for them. Therefore let men perish in battle rather than outlive subjugation, and look for mercy from conquerors!

And, therefore, let all the nations of the earth be warned by the fate of the Anglo Saxons to be always one-hearted for their country.

This patriotic and eloquent appeal may be very appropriately reiterated at the present day. The sentiment which it inculcates is as essential now as it was when the Saxons were defending the "Camp of Refuge."

Is it not consolidation rather than extension which is needed for the well-being of our country? Will not the future greatness of our nation hinge upon the development of the highest principles of humanity—the unity, loyalty and virtue of its peoples?

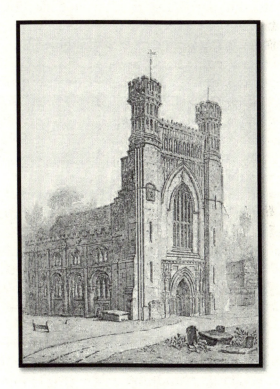

Thorney Abbey

CHAPTER V.

THE MONKS OF ELY TAKE COUNSEL

At as early an hour as the church services and devotional exercises would allow, Thurstan opened a chapter in the chapter-house, which stood on the north side, hard by the chief gate of the church. As his lordship entered, he said—the words that were appointed to be said on such occasions—"May the souls of all the deceased brethren of this house, and the souls of all true believers, rest in peace!" And the convent replied, "Amen!" Then the Lord Abbat spoke again, and said, "Benedicite," and the convent bowed their heads. And next he said, "Oh Lord! In thy name!" and then, "Let us speak of the order." And hereupon all present crossed themselves, and bent their heads on their breasts, and the business of the chapter commenced.

Only the prior, the sub-prior, the cellarer or bursar, the sacrist, and sub-sacrist, the chamberlain or treasurer, and the other chief officials or obedientiarii, and the other cloistered monks, maturi fratres, whose novitiate had been long passed, and whose monastic vows had been all completed, had the right of being present in chapter, and of deliberating and voting upon the business of the house and order. All that passed in chapter was, in a manner, *sub sigillo confessionis*, and not to be disclosed by any deliberating member to the rest of the convent, or to any of them, and much less was it to be revealed to any layman, or to any man beyond the precincts of the abbey. In these consultations, on the day next after the festival of Saint Edmund's, the monks of Ely sat long with closed doors.

When they came forth of the chapter-house it was noticed that the face of the Lord Abbat was very red, and that the faces of the prior and cellarer were very pale. A lay-brother, who had been working on the top of the chapter-house out-side, repairing some chinks in the roof, whispered to his familiars that he had heard very high words passing below, and that he had distinctly heard my Lord Abbat say, "Since the day of my election and investiture no brother of this house has been loaded with chains, and thrown into the underground dungeon; but, by the shrine of Saint Etheldreda, were I to find one traitor among us, I would bind him and chain him, and leave him to rot! And were there two of our brotherhood unfaithful to the good cause, and to King Harold, and plotting to betray the last hopes of England and this goodly house, and its tombs and shrines and blessed relics, to the Norman, I would do what hath been done aforetime in this abbey—I would bury them alive, or build them up in the niches left in our deep foundation walls!"

Now the gossips of the house, making much out of little, went about the cloisters whispering to one another that some sudden danger was at hand, and that my Lord Abbat suspected the prior and the cellarer of some secret correspondence with the Norman knights that garrisoned Duke William's castle near unto Cam-Bridge.
"If it be so," said Elfric, the novice from Spalding, "I would advise every true Saxon monk, novice, and lay-brother, to keep their eyes upon the cellarer and the prior!"
"That shall be done," said an old lay-brother.
"Aye, we will all watch their outgoings and their comings in," said several of the gossips; "for the prior is a hard-dealing, peremptory man, and cunning and crafty at the same time, never looking one in the face; and ever since

last pasque the cellarer hath shown an evil habit of stinting us underlings and loaf-eaters in our meat and drink."

"He hath ever been given too little to drink himself to be a true Saxon," said another; "we will watch him well!"

And they all said that they would watch the cellarer and eke the prior; that they would forever love, honor, and obey Thurstan their good and bountiful Lord Abbat; and that they would all die with swords or spears in their hands rather than see the Normans enter the Camp of Refuge. So one-hearted was the community at this time.

Shortly after finishing the chapter in the usual manner, and coming out with his chaplains, singing *Verba Mea*, Lord Thurstan went into his own hall, and there assembled all the high and noble guests of the house, whether laics, or priests, or monks, and all the obedientiarii and cloistered brothers of the abbey, except the prior and the cellarer, who had gone to their several cells with faces yet paler than they were when they came forth from the chapter-house.

In my Lord Abbat's hall no business was discussed that appertained exclusively to the house or order: the deliberations all turned upon the general interests of the country, or upon the means of prolonging the struggle for national independence. Thurstan, after reminding the assembly that the Saxon heroes of the Camp of Refuge had foiled the Normans in two attempts they had made to penetrate into the Isle of Ely—the one in the summer of the present year, and the other in the summer of the preceding year, one thousand and sixty-nine—and that it was four good years since the battle of Hastings, which William the Norman had bruited on the continent as a victory which had given him possession of all England, frankly made it known to all present that he had certain intelligence that the Normans were making vast preparations at Cam-Bridge, at Bury, at Stamford, at Huntingdon, and even at Brunn, in order to invade the whole fenny country, and to press upon the Isle of Ely and the Camp of Refuge from many opposite quarters. My Lord Abbat further made it known that the duke had called to this service all his bravest and most expert captains, and a body of troops that had been trained to war in Brittanie and in other parts wherein there were fens and rivers and meres, and thick-growing forests of willow and alder, even as in the country of East Anglia. He also told them how Duke William had sworn by the splendor of God's face that another year should not pass without seeing the Abbey of Ely in flames, the Camp of Refuge broken into and scattered, the rule of the Normans established over the whole land, and the refractory Saxons exterminated.

"Now," said my Lord Abbat, "it behaves us to devise how we shall withstand this storm, and to select some fitting and experienced captain that shall have authority over all the fighting men of our league, and that shall be able to measure swords with these vaunted leaders from foreign parts. Our brave Saxon chiefs in the camp, or in this house, and now present among us, are weary of their jealousies of one another, and have wisely agreed to obey, one and all, one single leader of experience and fame and good fortune, if such a leader can anywhere be found, having a true Saxon heart within him, and being one that hath never submitted to or negotiated with the invader. Let us then cast about and try and find such a chief. Let everyone speak his mind freely, and then we can compare and choose."

Some named one chief, and some another: many brave and expert men were named successively and with much applause, and with many expressions of hope and confidence; but when Father Adhelm, the expelled prior of the succursal cell at Spalding, stood up in his turn, and with the briefest preamble named Hereward the son of Leofric, the late Lord of Brunn, Hereward the truest of Saxons, the other chiefs seemed to be all forgotten, even by those who had severally proposed them, and the assembly listened in silence, or with a silence interrupted only by shouts of triumph, while this good prior and whilom neighbor of Hereward related the chief events of that warrior's life, and pointed out the hereditary and the personal claims he had to the consideration of his countrymen.

Ever since the earliest days in which the Saxons gained a footing on the land, the Lords of Brunn, the ancestors of Hereward, had been famed for their valor in the field, famed for their prudence in the Witan and in all other councils, had been famed above all their neighbors for their hospitality! And when the Saxons embraced the Gospel as preached by Saint Augustine and his disciples, who had been so devout as the Lords of Brunn? Who so bountiful to the shrines of saints and religious houses? who so ready to fight unto death in defense of the church? Notable it was, and known unto all that dwelt in the land of fens, that the house of Crowland, and the house of Ely, and the shrine of Saint Etheldreda, had been served in the hour of need by many of Hereward's forefathers.

When the unconverted, heathenish Danes were ravaging the country, and burning all the monasteries, and tethering their horses in the chapels of royal palaces, one Lord of Brunn fought in the ranks by the side of Friar Tolli, from sunrise to sunset, for the defense of the Abbey of Crowland, nor ceased fighting until three of the Danish sea-kings had been slain, and the monks had had time to remove their relics, and their books, and their sacred vases, into the impenetrable marshes of that vicinity. Another Lord of Brunn, who at the call of the monks had marched across the fens with all his people, and with all of his family that could wield a sword, had perished close under the walls of Ely Abbey, after defeating the Pagans, and driving them back towards their ships. The blood of each of these Lords of Brunn ran in the veins of Hereward, and his deeds had proved him worthy of the blood.

In his youth—in the days of Edward the Confessor—when the cunning Normans were beginning to beset the court of the childless king, and to act as if the inheritance was already their own, and the people of England already their slaves, it chanced that our Hereward, who had been on a pilgrimage to Canterbury, came back to the sea by Dover, and found Count Eustace of Boulogne, and his French men-at-arms engaged in a fierce quarrel with the men of Dover, and galloping through the streets with their naked swords in their hands, striking men and women, and crushing divers children under their horses' hoofs. Hereward, though but a stripling, drew his blade, rallied the dull townsfolk, who before had no leader, (and so were fighting loosely and without order, and without any science of war,) and renewing the battle at a vantage, he slew with his own hand a French knight; and then the men of Dover slew nineteen of the strangers, wounded many more, and drove Count Eustace and the rest out of the town to fly in dismay back to king Edward.

Later, when Harold, as earl of the eastern counties, and chief of king Edward's armies, marched into Wales to curb the insolent rage of King Griffith, Hereward attended him, and fought with him among the mountains and glens, and lakes and morasses of Wales, until that country was reduced by many victories, and Harold took shipping to return to King Edward with the head of Griffith stuck upon the rostrum or beak of his galley. Later still, when Hereward was of manly age, and King Edward the

Confessor was dead, having bequeathed his crown to Harold, and Harold as our true king raised his banner of war to march against his own unnatural brother Earl Tostig, who had brought the King of Norway and a great army of Norwegians into the country of York to deprive him of his throne or dismember his kingdom, Hereward marched with him with many of his father's stout men of Brunn, and fought under Harold's eye in the great battle at Stamford Bridge—that battle which ceased not until Earl Tostig and the king of Norway were both slain, and the river was choked up with the Norwegian dead. From Stamford Bridge the march of bold Harold was to Hastings, for the Normans had landed while he had been vanquishing the Norwegians.

On that long and rapid march, when hundreds of tried soldiers lagged behind, Hereward kept pace with his royal master; and when the battle was arrayed he was seen riding by Harold's side; and when the battle joined, his battle-axe was seen close by the battle-axes of Harold and the king's two loyal and brave brothers, Gurth and Leofwin, dealing terrible blows, and cutting the steel caps and the coats of mail of the Normans like chaff. Saxons, remember that he fought at Hastings through nine long hours, and did not yield until ye saw that ye were betrayed! Separated from his king in the fury of the last melée, Hereward attempted to rally the East Angles and the men of Kent; and failing in that, and hearing a mighty rumor that Harold the king was slain, he galloped to the port of Winchelsea with a few of his father's trusty people, and there embarked for foreign parts, vowing that he would never bow his head to the conqueror.

The father of Hereward, being old and infirm, and infected by the unmanly fears which made so many Saxons throw aside the sword before the conquest of England was well begun, had made haste to tender his allegiance to the son of the harlot, had obtained his peace, and had been allowed to retain his lordship of Brunn, after paying sundry fines for his son's patriotism. But latterly the old Lord of Brunn had been gathered to his fathers, and a Norman chief had seized his manor-house and all his lands, and was now keeping them as his patrimony. Such, being told briefly, was the story which Father Adhelm told to my Lord Abbat of Ely and his guests and officials; and when he had done, he asked, where could a better chief be found for the Camp of Refuge than Hereward the true Saxon, and legitimate Lord of Brunn? And, hereupon, there was a clapping of hands and shouting of voices in all that noble and devout assembly—a shouting so loud that it echoed through all the abbey, and was heard as far off as Saint Ovin's Cross; and the indwellers of the town of Ely, albeit they knew not what it meant, took up the cry, and shouted, "Hereward to the Camp of Refuge! Hereward for England!"

"Bethinks me," said the cautelous Abbat of Crowland, when the noise had ceased, "that perchance Hereward will not come to us at our summons. He must know how false our country has proved to herself, and how great the progress the conqueror hath made in it: his lands and all his inheritance are gone, a price is set upon his head in England, and his valor and experience in war, and his other good qualities, have made for him a prosperous and honorable home in a foreign land. While yet in my poor house at Crowland, a shipman from the Wash, who trades to the opposite coast, told me that he had lately seen at Ypres my Lord Hereward, living in great affluence and fame; and the mariner further told me that Hereward had said to him that he would never went back to a land of cowards and traitors; that he had carved himself out new estates in the fattest lands of the Netherlands, and that

England had nothing to give him except dishonor or a grave."

These representations damped the hopes of some of the company; but as Hereward's mind could not be known without a trial, it was determined to send some trusty messenger across the seas, who might gain access to the presence of the chief, and at the same time purchase and bring back with him a supply of arms and warlike harness, with other things much needed in the Camp of Refuge. The difficulties of this embassage struck all that were present: "And who," said the Lord Abbat, "shall be this trusty and expert messenger?"

"Were it not for the greenness of his years and the lowliness of his condition," said the Prior of Spalding, "I would even venture to recommend for the mission my bold-hearted, clear-headed, and nimble-footed novice, Elfric."

"Brother, thou hast said it," responded Thurstan; "thy novice shall go! Let the youth be summoned hither."

The novice was soon kneeling at my Lord Abbat's feet, and was soon made acquainted as well with the difficult task he was expected to perform, as with the uncomfortable doubts which had been propounded by the Abbat of Crowland. When asked by his own immediate superior, Father Adhelm, whether he would undertake the task, he answered, "Marry and that I will right gladly. When I first went to Spalding, I knew well Hereward, the son of the Lord of Brunn, and some of those that were nearest to him. If England is to be saved, he is the man that will save it. I would go to the world's end to find him and bring him hither. I love my country, and I love travelling better than my meat and drink. I have often prayed to Saint Ovin that he would vouchsafe me the grace of going into foreign parts! Moreover, my prime duty is obedience to my superiors. Let me depart instantly, and I will the sooner bring you back Lord Hereward!"

"Thou art very confident," said the Abbat of Crowland: "how knowest thou that Hereward will come with thee?"

"My lord and master," said the novice, "I ween I can take over with me a word of command, or a prayer more potential than a command, and one which Hereward could not withstand even if he were king of all the Netherlands' country, and sure death stood upon the English beach to seize him on return!"

"What does this young man mean?" said the Abbat of Crowland.

Elfric blushed, stammered, and could not go on.

"What dost thou mean?" said his Prior of Spalding.

Elfric stammered more than before, which angered his superior, and brought down some harsh words upon his head.

"Nay," said the good old Bishop of Lindisfarne, "chide not the young man, but give him to collect his thought and frame his speech. He may know more of Lord Hereward than anyone here knoweth. But... but I hope that this novice of a goodly house doth not think of employing any witchcraft or unlawful spell! *De maleficio libera nos*! From witchcraft and sacrilege, and all the arts of the devil, good Lord deliver us!"

The bishop crossed himself; they all crossed themselves; and Elfric not only crossed himself, but likewise said "*Libera nos!*" and "Amen!" But when he had so done and so said, his merry eye twinkled, and there was as much of a smile about his mouth as the reverence due to the company allowed of in a novice.

"If there be magic," said he, "it is all white magic; if there be a spell, it is not an unholy spell." And as Elfric said these words he looked into the good-natured, right hearty and right English face of my Lord Abbat Thurstan.

"Speak on, boy," said the abbat; "speak out, my brave boy, and fear nought!"

Being thus heartened, Elfric said: "Then, to speak with reverence before this noble and reverend company, I wot well there were, when I was first at Spalding, and when my Lord Hereward was at Brunn, certain love-passages...."

"Certain what?" said the expelled Abbat of Cockermouth, who was somewhat deaf.

"Love-passages," said Elfric, looking very archly, and with a laugh in his eyes, if not on his lips; "certain love-passages between the son of the Lord of Brunn and the noble maiden Alftrude, the young daughter and heiress to the lord of the neighboring town, that old Saxon lord, Albert of Ey."

"Truth, the two houses stood not very far apart," said the Abbat of Crowland; "but Albert of Ey was no friend to the old Lord of Brunn."

"Most true, my lord; but Albert died before his neighbor, and left his wide estates to his fair daughter Alftrude, having first given her in ward to this Lanfranc, who is by some called Archbishop of Canterbury, and whose will and power few can gainsay. Moreover, the Ladie Alftrude is cousin to the Ladie Lucia, whom Ivo Taille-Bois hath made his wife; and as that arch-enemy of our house extends his protection to his wife's cousin, not wishing that her lands should be seized by any hungry Norman other than a relation of his own, the heiress of Ey hath been allowed to live in the old manor-house, and to enjoy such proportion of her father's wealth as Lanfranc chooseth to allow her. Many Norman knights have sought her hand, as the best means of obtaining her land, but the Saxon maiden had ever said nay! And Lanfranc, who hath done violence to the very church for his own interest, and Ivo Taille-Bois, who got his own Saxon wife by violence, have hitherto had power enough to prevent any great wrong or violence being done to Ladie Alftrude, the heiress of Ey. Now the Ladie Alftrude remembers the times that are past, and sighs and weeps for the return of Hereward, vowing that she will wed none but him, and that——"

"Thou seemeth well informed in these matters," said one of the monks; "but prithee, how didst thou obtain thine information?"

Elfric stammered a little, and blushed a good deal as he said, "The young Ladie Alftrude hath long had for her handmaiden one Mildred of Hadenham, a daughter of my late father's friend, a maiden well behaved and well favored, and pious withal; and when I was sent to the manor-house of Ey upon the business of our own house at Spalding, and when I met Mildred at the church, or wake, or fair, we were ever wont to talk about my Lord Hereward and my Ladie Alftrude, as well as of other matters."

"Father Adhelm," said my Lord Abbat of Crowland in a whisper, "surely thou hast allowed too much liberty to thy convent."

"My lord," replied the Prior of Spalding, "It is but a novice that speaks; Elfric is not a cloister monk."

"No, and never will be," said the Abbat of Crowland, in another whisper.

"I now see thy spell," said Thurstan, addressing Elfric, who was standing silent, and still blushed; "I now see the witchcraft that thou wouldest use. And dost thou believe that the Ladie Alftrude so loves Hereward that she will jeopardize her estates for him, and call home and marry him, though an outlaw? And dost thou believe that Lord Hereward so loveth the Ladie Alftrude as to quit his new-found fortunes for her, and to come at her bidding into England?"

"I believe in loving hearts," replied Elfric; "I believe in all that Mildred ever told me about Ladie Alftrude; and I can guess better than your shipman and trader of the Wash what it was that made Lord Hereward talk so high about his greatness in foreign parts, and vilipend his own country, and made declarations that he would never return to a land of cowardice, and treachery, and falsehood. The exile hath heard that the Ladie Lucia hath become the wife of Ivo-Taille-Bois, probably without hearing the violence and the craft which brought about that unholy marriage; and probably without knowing how much the Ladie Lucia grieves, and how very a prisoner she is in her own manor-house, and in the midst of her own lands and serfs. My Lord Hereward may also have heard some unlucky rumors about a marriage between the Lady Alftrude and some brother or cousin of Taille-Bois, which idle gossips said was to take place with the sanction of Lanfranc; and judge ye, my lords and holy fathers, whether this would not be enough to drive Hereward mad! But a little wit and skill, and a little good luck, and all these cross and crooked things may be made straight. If I can win to see the Ladie Alftrude, and get from her some love-token and some comfortable messages to the exiled Lord of Brunn, and if I can declare and vow, of mine own knowledge, that the heart of the fair Saxon is aye the same, write me down a traitor or a driveller, my lords, and I bring not Hereward back with me."

"Of a surety he will do it," said Abbat Thurstan, rubbing his hands joyously.

"I understand not much of this love logic, but I think he will do it," said the Abbat of Crowland.

"He will do anything," said the Prior of Spalding; "but once let loose on this wild flight, we shall never again get the young hawk back to hand."

The rest of the business was soon arranged, and precisely and in every part as the novice himself suggested. No one thought of exacting oaths of fidelity from Elfric. His faith, his discretion, and his valor had been well tried already, and his honest countenance gave a better assurance than oaths and bonds. As Saxon monks were the least acceptable of all visitors to the Normans, and as the dress of monk or palmer no longer gave protection to any man of English birth, and as the late novice of Spalding might chance to be but too well known in Ivo Taille-Bois' vicinity, Elfric disguised himself as one of the poorest of the wandering minstrels—half musician, half beggar and idiot; and in this guise and garb, he, on the second day after the feast of Saint Edmund, set out alone to find his way across the fens, through the posts and watches of the Normans, and so on to the manor-house and the jealously guarded bower of the Ladie Alftrude.

He was to return to Ely, if good fortune attended him, within seven days; and then he would be ready to proceed to the country of the Netherlanders, to seek for Lord Hereward, and to purchase the warlike harness that was wanted. As soon as he had taken his departure from the abbey, a quick boat was sent down the Ouse with orders to the steadiest and oftenest-tried shipman of Lynn to get his good bark in readiness for a sea-voyage, and to bring it up to Ely, in order to take on board an important passenger bound on an embassage for my Lord Abbat.

Although the love of the Lady Alftrude might perchance bring back Lord Hereward, it was not likely that it should buy from the trading men of Ypres, or Ghent, or Bruges, the bows and the cross-bows, the swords and the lance heads, the coats of mail, and the other gear that were so much wanted; and therefore Abbat Thurstan, after collecting what little he could from his guests and in the

Camp of Refuge, and after taking his own signet-ring from his finger, and his own prelatic cross of gold and chain of gold from his neck, called upon the chamberlain and the cellarer and the sacrist for all the coin that had been put by the pilgrims into the shrine-box. This time the livid-faced cellarer was silent and obedient; but the chamberlain, demurring to the order of my Lord Abbat, said, "Surely these contributions of the faithful were at all times devoted to the repairing and beautifying of our church!"

"Thou sayeth it," quoth my Lord Abbat; "but if we get not weapons and harness wherewith to withstand the invaders, we shall soon have no church left us to repair or beautify. By the holy face and incorruptible body of Saint Etheldreda, I will strip her very shrine of the gold plates which adorn it, and of the silver lamps which burn before it, and melt the gold and the silver, and barter the ingots for arms, rather than see the last refuge of my countrymen broken in upon, and the accursed Normans in my house of Ely!"

"But doth not this savor of sacrilege?" said the sacrist.

"Not so much as of patriotism and of real devotion to our saint and foundress. Saint Etheldreda, a true Saxon and East Anglian saint, will approve of the deed, if it should become necessary to strip her shrine. Her honor and sanctity depend not on lamps of silver and plates of gold, however rich and rare: the faithful flocked to her tomb, and said their orisons over it when it was but a plain stone block, with no shrine near it; and well I ween more miracles were wrought there, in the simple old times, than we see wrought now. Should the Normans get into our church, they will strip the shrine, and we do not; and they will rifle the tombs of Saint Sexburga, Saint Ermenilda, and Saint Withburga and cast forth the bodies of our saints upon the dung-heap!

Oh, sacrist! Know ye not how these excommunicated foreigners are everywhere treating the saints of Saxon birth, and are everywhere setting up strange saints, whose names were never before heard by Englishmen, and cannot be pronounced by them! The reason of all this is clear: our Saxon hagiology is filled with the names of those that were patriots as well as saints, and we cannot honor them in one capacity without thinking of them in the other."

"This is most true," said the chamberlain; "and the Normans are likewise setting up new shrines to the Blessed Virgin, and bringing in Notre Dames, and our Ladie of Walsingham, and other Ladies that were never heard of before; and they are enforcing pilgrimages in wholly new directions! If these things endure, alack and woe the while for our house of Ely and for the monks of Saint Edmund's-Bury, and for all Saxon houses! Our shrine boxes will be empty; we shall be neglected and forgotten in the land, even if the Normans do not dispossess us."

Minstrels

CHAPTER VI.

IVO TAILLE-BOIS AND THE LADIE LUCIA

Within the moated and battlemented manor-house near to the banks of the Welland, which Elfric had stopped to gaze upon as he was travelling from Crowland to Spalding, there was held a feast on the fourth day after the feast of Saint Edmund, for the said fourth day from the great Saxon festival was the feast-day of some saint of Normandie or of Anjou, and the Ladie Lucia, maugre her sorrow and affliction, had given birth to a male child a moon ago, and the child was to be baptized on this day with much rejoicing. Ivo Taille-Bois and his Norman retainers were glad, inasmuch as the birth of a son by a Saxon wife went to secure them in their possession of the estates; and the Ladie Lucia was glad of heart, as a mother cannot but rejoice at the birth of her first-born; and her Saxon servants, and all the old retainers of her father's house, and all the Saxon serfs, were glad, because their future lord would be more than one half Saxon, being native to the country, a child of the good Ladie Lucia, the daughter of their last Saxon lord.

So merry were all; that grievances seemed to be forgotten: the Normans ceased to oppress and insult; the Saxons ceased, for the time being, to complain. The feast was very bountiful, for the Ladie Lucia had been allowed the ordering of it; and the company was very numerous and much mixed, for many Saxons of name had been bidden to the feast, and pledges had been given on both sides that there should be a truce to all hostilities and animosities; that there should be what the Normans called the Truce of God until the son of Ivo Taille-Bois and Lucia, the presumptive heir to all the lands of the old lord, should be christened, and his christening celebrated in a proper manner. No less a man than the prelate Lanfranc had interfered in making this salutary arrangement. And for the first time since the death of her father, Lanfranc's fair ward, the Ladie Alftrude, had come forth from her own manor-house to attend at the earnest invitation of her cousin the Ladie Lucia. The Saxon heiress had come attended by sundry armed men and by two aged English priests who stood high in the consideration and favor of the potent Lanfranc.

When, landing from her boat (the country was now nearly everywhere under water), she walked up to the gate of the house, and entering, drew aside her wimple and showed her sweet young face and bright blue eyes, there rose a murmur of admiration from all that were assembled there: the Saxons vowed in good old English that the Ladie Alftrude was the fairest and noblest maiden in all England; and the Normans swore in Norman-French and with many a Vive Dieu that they had never beheld anything equal to her either on the other side of the seas or on this! Nay, some of the Norman knights, and more than one whose beard was growing grey while he was yet in poverty or wholly unprovided with any English estate, forgot the broad lands that Alftrude inherited, to think only of her beautiful face.

Yet when Alftrude kissed her fair cousin and her cousin's child, and sat down by the side of the Lady Lucia at the top of the hall, it was hard to say which was the more lovely, the young matron, or the scarcely younger maiden.

"Benedicite," said a young monk of Evreux who had come over for promotion in some English abbey, "but the daughters of this land be fair to look upon!"

"They be," said a starch man in mail, "and they will conquer the conquerors of England, and soon cause the name and distinction of Norman to be swallowed up and forgotten in the country."

"Had I come hither before taking my vows at Evreux, the devil might have been a monk for me, but I would have been none of it!"

Peaceably, ay, and merrily, passed off the day. The fair Ladie Alftrude stood at the font, and was one of the sponsors for her cousin's first-born. The banquet succeeded to the baptism, and dancing and music in the hall followed on the banquet. The old times seemed to be coming back again, those peaceful days of good King Edward, *Cœli deliciæ*, when every free-born Englishman enjoyed his own, and every noble thane or earl held hospitality to be one of his primary duties.

But Ivo Taille-Bois, though he boasted of being cousin to Duke William, was a greedy low-born churl, and therefore he needs must mar the happiness of his young wife (who ever since the birth of her son had been striving to forget how she had been made his wife), by talking of his unprovided brother, who had arrived in England, and was now tarrying about the Conqueror's court in the hope of obtaining from Lanfranc the hand of his rich Saxon ward. The Ladie Lucia, knowing full well how her cousin's heart lay toward Hereward, tried often to change the strain, but her Norman lord, forgetful even of courtesy to his guests, would still keep vexing her ear with his brother's suit, and instead of continuing to be thankful to his saints for his own good fortune in getting so vast an heritage, and so fair a wife, and then so promising a child, he spoke as though he should feel himself a beggar until all the domains of the Ladie Alftrude were in the hands of his family. An anger that would not be concealed flashed in his eye whenever he saw any well-fared knight or gallant youth discoursing with Alftrude, and whether it were a Norman or a Saxon his wrath seemed equal. Desperate thoughts and dark designs flitted through his mind. At one time he thought that now that he had got the young heiress into his house he would forcibly keep her where she was until his brother should arrive and press his own suit in the ungodly manner of the first Norman conquerors; but he cowered under the dread of Lanfranc and a Norman sentence of excommunication, and he saw that the thing was not to be done without great peril and much bloodshed under his own roof, for the Saxon guests were numerous far above the Normans, and though, mayhap, several of his Norman guests would not have scrupled about the deed if it had been for their own profit, they could not be expected to concur in it, or even to allow it, when it was only for the profit of him and his brother.

Vanity, thy name was Norman! There was young Guiscard of Avranches, there was tall Etienne of Rouen (and verily a tall and well-proportioned young man was he, and one that could talk glibly both in English and in French), there was Baldwin of the Mount, a most nimble dancer, and with a fine gilded cloak over his shoulders and not a crown in his purse (even like all the rest of them); there was old Mainfroy of La Perche, who had followed Robert Guiscard into Italy and Grecia, and had lost an eye and half of a nose in those wars before Ladie Alftrude was born; and there was old Drogo from Chinon, who looked as though he had added to his own nose that half of a nose Mainfroy had lost (so hugeous and misshapen was Drogo's nose!); and not one of these gay knights but thought that the Lady Alftrude having once seen and heard him must prefer him to all the world. In their own conceit they were, one and all of them, already Lords of Ey and husbands of Alftrude. Judge ye then whether Ivo

Taille-Bois could have safely ventured to stay his fair guest against her will, or shut up his wife's cousin in close bower for his as yet unknown and unseen brother!

But there was now in the hall a merrier eye, and one more roguish withal, than ever shone under the brows of a Norman. The drawbridge being down, and the gate of the house wide open, that all who list might enter and partake according to his degree of some of the good things that were provided, a young Saxon glee-man or minstrel came over the bridge unchallenged, and only paused under the low archway of the gate. His dress was tattered and torn, and not free from the mud and slime of the fens, but sweet and clear was his voice, and merry and right old English his song; and so all the Saxons that heard him gave him welcome, and bade him enter the hall and sing a lay in honor of the Ladie Lucia and of her first-born son, who would be good lord to all Saxon folk as his grandfather had been before him. But before going into the hall, where the feast was just over, and all the tables cleared, the glee-man went aside into the buttery to renew his strength with a good meal, and refresh his voice with a cup of good wine.

When he entered the hall the old Saxon seneschal cried, "A glee-man! Another glee-man come to sing an English song!" The Norman minstrels looked scornfully at him and his tattered cloak; and the Saxon minstrels asked of one another who he might be; for none of them knew him, albeit the minstrels, like the beggars and other happy vagabonds of old England, were united in league and brotherhood, in sort that every minstrel of East Anglia was thought to know every other minstrel or glee-man of that country. But when the new and unknown comer had played his preludium on his Saxon lyre of four strings, and had sung his downright Saxon song with a voice that was clear as a bell, and at times loud as a trumpet, the

English part of the company, from the highest degree to the lowest, shouted and clapped their hands; and all the English minstrels vowed that he was worthy of their guild; while even the Norman glee-men confessed that, although the words were barbarous and not to be understood by civil men, the air was good, and the voice of the best.

Whether the words were ancient as the music, or whether they were made in part or wholly for the occasion by the singer, they went deep into the hearts both of the Ladie Alftrude and the Ladie Lucia; and while the young matron of the house put a little ring into a cup, and bade her little Saxon page fill the cup with the best wine, and hand it to the Saxon minstrel, the maiden Alftrude went straight to the spot where that minstrel was standing, and asked him to sing his song again. And when the glee-man had knelt on his knee to the mistress of the house, and had drained her cup of wine until not so much as the ghost of a drop was left in it, and when he had sung his song over again, and more deftly and joyously than he had sung it before, the Lady Alftrude still kept near him, and, discoursing with him, took three or more turns across the lower part of the hall. Saxon lords and Saxon dames and maidens of high degree were ever courteous to the poor and lowly, and ever honored those who had skill in minstrelsy.

At first the Ladie Alftrude smiled and laughed as if at some witty conceit let fall by the minstrel; but then those who watched her well, and were near enough to see, saw a cloud on her brow and a blush on her cheek, and then paleness, and a short gasping as if for breath. But all this passed away, and the maiden continued to discourse calmly with the minstrel, and whenever the minstrel raised his voice it was only to give utterance to some pleasant gibe.

Ivo Taille-Bois, albeit he had seen him often under another hood, might not know him, and all the English glee-men might continue to wonder who he was; but we know full well that the minstrel was none other than Elfric the novice. He had found his way unscathed to Ey, and not finding the Ladie Alftrude there, he had followed her to the manor-house of her fair cousin, well pleased that such a celebration and feast would make easy his entrance into the house. A maiden of Alftrude's degree could not travel and visit without a featy handmaiden attendant upon her. Rough men that bend bows and wield swords and spears, and make themselves horny fists, are not fit to dress a ladie's hair or tie her sandals; and well we ween it becomes not priests with shaven crowns to be lacing a maiden's bodice; and so, besides the armed men and the two churchmen, the Ladie Alftrude had brought with her Mildred of Hadenham, that maiden well-behaved and well-favored and pious withal, whom Elfric was wont to entertain with talk about my Lord Hereward, as well as of other matters.

Now Mildred of Hadenham was there at the lower end of the hall, seated among other handmaidens; and as soon as Elfric entered, or, at the latest, as soon as he finished the first verse of his song, she knew who the minstrel was as well as we do. While the Ladie Alftrude was before their eyes, few of the noble company cared to look that way or upon any other than her; but if a sharp eye had watched it would have seen that Mildred several times blushed a much deeper red than her mistress, and that the young glee-man's eyes were rather frequently seeking her out.

And at last, when the Ladie Alftrude returned to her cousin at the head of the hall, and the floor of the hall was cleared for an exhibition of dancers, the glee-man, after some gyrations, found his way to the side of Mildred of Hadenham, and kept whispering to her, and making her blush even redder than before, all the other handmaidens wondering the while, and much envying Mildred, for, albeit his cloak was tattered and his hose soiled, the young minstrel, besides having the sweetest voice, was surpassingly well-favored in form and face, and had the happiest-looking eye that ever was seen.

The Ladie Alftrude talked long in a corner with her cousin the Ladie Lucia, and then there was a calling and consulting with Mildred of Hadenham, as though her mistress's head-gear needed some rearrangement. And after this the two cousins and the waiting-woman quitted the hall, and went into an upper and inner chamber, and tarried there for a short while, or for about the time it takes to say a score of Aves. Then they come back to the hall, and the Ladie Lucia and the Ladie Alftrude sit down together where the company is most thronged. But where is the curiously delicate little ring that was glittering on Ladie Alftrude's finger?... Ha! Ha! We wot well that Elfric hath got it, and other love-tokens besides, that he may carry them beyond seas, and bring back Hereward to his ladie-love and to England that cannot do without him. But where is that merriest of glee-men?...

Many in the hall were asking the question, for they wanted to hear him again. But Elfric was gone, and none seemed to know how or when he went. Mayhap, maid Mildred knew something about it, for when the English part of the company began to call for the glee-man with the tattered cloak, that he might sing another merry song, she turned her face to the wall and wept.

Well, I ween, had our simple dull Saxons outwitted the nimble-witted Normans! Well had the minstrel and the ladies and the waiting-maid played their several parts! Could Ivo Taille-Bois but have known his errand, or have guessed at the mischief that he was brewing for him, either Elfric would never have entered those walls, or he would never have left them alive.

Ivo de Taillebois and his fighters

CHAPTER VII.

HEREWARD'S RETURN

There may be between Thamesis and the Tyne worse seas and more perilous rocks; but when the north-east wind blows right into that gulf, and the waves of the German Ocean are driven on by the storms of winter, the practiced mariner will tell ye that the navigation of the Wash, the Boston Deeps, and the Lynn Deeps, is a fearful thing to those who know the shoals and coasts, and a leap into the jaws of death to those that know them not. Besides the shallows near shore, there be sandbanks and treacherous shoals in the middle of the bay, and these were often shifting their places or changing their shapes.

Moreover, so many rivers and broad streams and inundations, that looked like regular rivers in the wet seasons of the year, poured their waters into the Wash, that it required all the skill of the mariner and pilot to find a way into the proper bed of any one particular river, as the Ouse, the Nene, or the Welland. Here are many quick-sands, fatal to barks, when concealed under the water; and even in summer-tide, when the waters are dried, the shepherds and their flocks, are often taught by a woeful experience that these quick-sands have a wonderful force in sucking in and holding fast whatsoever cometh upon them. In this sort the perils of shipmen are not over even when they reach the shore, and are advancing to tread upon what seemeth like terra firma. The Wash and its sand-banks and the quick-sands had made more East-Anglian widows and orphans than were made by any other calamity besides, save always the fierce Norman conquest.

It was under one of the fiercest and loudest tempests that ever blew from the sky of winter, and upon one of the roughest seas that ever rolled into the Wash, that five barks, which seemed all to be deeply laden and crowded with men, drove past the shoal called the Dreadful, and made for that other shoal called the Inner Dousing. The sun, which had not been visible the whole day, now showed itself like a ball of fire as it sank in the west behind the flats and fens of Lincolnshire; and when the sun was down the fury of the tempest seemed to increase.

When they had neared the Inner Dousing, four of the barks took in all their sail and lay-to as best they could in the trough of the sea; but the fifth bark stood gallantly in for the Wash, with nearly all her sails up. Swift as it bounded over the waves, it was dark night before the foremost bark reached the little cape where stands the chapel of our Ladie.

Here the bark showed three lights at her mast-head and then three lights over her prow, and then three over her stern. Quickly as might be, these lights from on board the fifth and foremost bark were answered by three times three of lights on the belfry of Our Ladie's chapel; and had it not been for the roaring of the winds and the loud dashing of the sea on the resounding shore, those on land by Our Ladie's chapel might have heard a three times three of hearty cheers from those on shipboard, and those on the ship might have heard every cheer given back with interest and increase by the crowd of true Saxons that stood by the chapel.

The bark next showed at her masthead a broad blue light, such as had never been seen before in these parts; and presently from the lee side of the Inner Dousing four other bright blue lights gleamed across the black sky; and having in this wise answered signal, the four barks followed in the track of the fifth and came up with it off

Our Ladie's chapel. Still keeping a little in advance, like the pilot and admiral of the little fleet, the bark that had first reached the coast glided into Lynn Deeps; and as it advanced towards the mouth of the Ouse, signal-lights or piloting lights rose at every homestead and hamlet, from Kitcham to Stone's-end, from Stone's-end to Castle Rising, and from Castle Rising to the good town of Lynn. And besides these stationary lights, there were other torches running along the shore close above the line of sea foam.

And much was all this friendly care needed, the deeps being narrow and winding and the shoals and sand-banks showing themselves on every side, and the wind still blowing a hurricane, and the masts of the barks bending and cracking even under the little sail that they now carried. On this eastern side of the Wash few could have slept, or have tarried in their homes this night; for when—near upon midnight, and as the monks of Lynn were preparing to say matins in the chapel of Saint Nicholas—the five barks swirled safely into the deep and easy bed of the Ouse, and came up to the prior's wharf, and let go their anchors, and threw their stoutest cordage ashore, to the end that the mariners there might make them fast, and so give a double security against wind and tide, the wharf and all the river bank was covered with men, women, and children, and the houses in the town behind the river bank were nearly all lighted up, as if it had been Midsummer's eve, instead of being the penultimate night of the Novena of Christmas.

It was not difficult to make out that the foremost of the barks and one other belonged to Lynn, inasmuch as the Lynn folk leaped on board of them as soon as they were made fast at the wharf, calling upon their town fellows, their brothers or sons, and hugging them more Saxonico when they found them out on the crowded decks. The other barks were of foreign structure, and the mariners seemed to be all foreigners; but the many passengers in each of them were all Englishmen and landsmen besides; for they had all been very sea-sick, and were now very impatient to get their feet upon dry land.

The first that landed from the foremost bark was a tall, robust, and handsome man, dressed as Saxon noblemen and warriors were wont to dress before the incoming of the ill fashions of Normandie.

He carried in his right hand a long straight and broad sword, the blade of which was curiously sheathed, and the hilt of which formed a cross. When he had crossed the plankings of the wharf, and reached the solid ground, he knelt on one knee and kissed the cross of his sword; and then throwing himself prone upon the earth, and casting wide his arms as though he would embrace it and hug it, he kissed the insensate soil, and thanked his God and every saint in the Saxon calendar for that he had been restored to the land which gave him birth, and which held the dust and bones of his fathers.

Some who had seen him in former days on the Spalding side of the Wash, and some who had been apprised of his coming, began instantly to shout, "It is he!—it is Lord Hereward of Brunn! It is Hereward the Saxon! It is the Lord of Brunn, come to get back his own and to help us to drive out the Normans."

The shouts were taken up on every side, mariners and landsmen, foreigners and home-born fens men, and women and children, crying, "It is Hereward the Saxon! Long live the young Lord of Brunn, who will never shut his hall-door in the face of a poor Englishman, nor turn his back on a Frenchman!" Some hemmed him in, and kissed his hands, and the sheath of his long straight sword, and the skirts of his mantle, and the very sandals on his feet; while others held their glaring torches close over his head, that they might see him and show him to their mates. It was one Nan of Lynn, and a well-famed and well-spoken woman, that said, as she looked upon the Lord Hereward, "We Englishwomen of the fens will beat the men-at-arms from Normandie, can we be but led by such a captain as this; with that steel cap on his head, and that scarlet cloak over his shoulders, he looks every inch as stalwart and as handsome a warrior as the archangel Michael, whose portraiture we see in our church!"

The person nearest in attendance on Lord Hereward was that lucky wight Elfric, who had been to seek him in foreign parts; but it was Elfric no longer attired either as a tattered minstrel or as a shaveling novice, but as something betwixt a blithesome page and an armed retainer. He too had more than one tear of joy in his eye as he trod upon the shore; but this tender emotion soon gave way to a hearty if not boisterous mirth, and so he kept shouting, "Make way for Hereward the Lord of Brunn!" and kept squeezing the hands of all the men and women and children he knew in Lynn, as they walked towards the convent where Hereward was to rest until daylight.

Next to Elfric, the man that seemed most entirely devoted to the service and to the person of Hereward was a slight, slim man of middle stature and very dark complexion; his hair was long, and would have been blacker than the plumage of the raven save that time had touched it here and there with grey; his nose was arched like the beak of a goshawk; and his eye, that looked out from under a very black and bushy but very lofty eyebrow, was blacker and keener than the eye of any hawk or other fowl of prey. Some who had seen now and then a wandering Israelite, thought that this stranger looked marvelously like a Jew; but this was a marvelous mistake. None could think him either young or handsome; yet was there something about his person and in his face that none could help looking at, and then remembering for aye. Among the stout Saxons were some that could have taken the dark, slim stranger between their finger and thumb, and have squeezed the life out of him with as much ease as boys crack nuts; but there was a quickness and sharpness in the stranger's eye that seemed to say he could outwit them all if he chose. On the way to the convent Hereward several times addressed him in some foreign tongue, and seemed by his looks to be taking advice of him.

As the convent was but a dependency of my Lord Abbat Thurstan, and a succursal cell to Ely, ye may judge whether the Lord of Brunn and those who came with him met with hospitality! Saxons and strangers (and all landed from the barks as soon as might be, and hastened to the convent) found suppers and beds, or suppers and clean sweet rushes to lie upon, either with the sub-prior or in the guest-house. In the morning, as soon as it was light, Hereward, Elfric, and the dark stranger, and a score of armed men, re-embarked in the good ship that had brought them to Lynn, and proceeded up the river Ouse, leaving the other four barks at their moorings under the prior's wharf.

These four craft were to keep a good look-out, and in case of any armed ships coming into the Wash they were to run, through the most intricate passage, for Spalding; but if no enemy should appear (and of this there was scarcely a chance, as the weather continued stormy, and the Normans were bad seamen, and very badly provided with shipping), they were all to wait at Lynn until Lord Hereward should come back from Ely to lead them to Spalding, and, farther still, to his own house at Brunn.

Broad and free was the river Ouse, and up as high as the junction of the Stoke Lord Hereward's bark was favored by the tide as well as by the wind. Above the Stoke the tide failed; but the wind blew steadily on, and many boats, with lusty rowers in them, came down from Ely and Chettisham and Littleport, and took the bark in tow, for the signal-lights and fires which had guided the fleet into Lynn had been carried across the fens and to the Abbey of Ely, and had told my Lord Abbat that the Lord Hereward was come.

No bark had ever made such voyage before, nor have many made it since; but a good while before the sun went down our Lynn mariners made their craft fast to my Lord Abbat's pier, and Hereward and his bold and trusty followers landed in the midst of a throng ten times greater and ten times more jubilant than that which had welcomed them at Lynn. Before quitting the ship Elfric put on his monastic habit. This he did not do without a sigh; and he carried with him under his novice's gown the gay dress he had worn while in foreign parts and on shipboard. Maybe he expected that services might be required from him in which such an attire would be useful; or perhaps he hoped that his superior of Spalding and the Abbat of Crowland would, in considering the services he had rendered already, determine in their wisdom that the dress and calling of a monk were not those which suited him best.

Although not bound by any irrevocable vow, Elfric was bound by the ties of gratitude to Father Adhelm, who had taken him into the succursal cell at Spalding when a very young and helpless orphan; and Elfric would never have been the man he proved himself if he had been forgetful of duties and obligations.

At the outer gate of the convent Lord Hereward was met and embraced and welcomed by the high-hearted abbat of the house, by the Archbishop Stigand, the Abbat of Crowland, and by all the prelates and high churchmen; and next by all the cloistered monks of Ely; and next by the lay lords and the Saxon warriors of all parts: and all this right reverend and right noble company shouted, "Welcome to our chief and our deliverer! Honor and welcome to the young Lord of Brunn!"

As Thurstan led the Saxon hero by the hand towards his own Aula Magna, he said, "But for the solemn season, which brooks not much noise," (the town folk, and the hinds that had come in from the fens, and the novices and lay-brothers, were continuing to shout and make noise enough to wake the dead that were sleeping in the cloisters), "we would have received you, my lord, with a great clattering of bells and show of flags and banners! Nevertheless thou comest at a most suitable moment and on the very verge of the most joyous of all seasons; 'tis the vigil of the Nativity. On this Christmas eve, like all well-regulated religious houses and all good Christians, we fast upon a banquet of eels and fish. At midnight we have the midnight mass, chanted in our best manner; and to-morrow we feast indeed, and give up all our souls to joy. To-morrow, then, our bells shall be struck upon so that the Norman knights and men-at-arms shall hear them in Cam-Bridge Castle, and shall tremble while they hear! And our Saxon flags, and the banners of our saints, yea, the great banner of Saint Etheldreda itself, shall be hung out on our walls! And when the other duties of the day are over, we will sing a *Te Deum laudamus* for thy coming. My Lord Hereward, I have not known such joy, or half so much hope, since the day on which our good Edward (*Rex venerandus*) put this ring upon my finger and confirmed my election as abbat of this house! My hope then was that I should be enabled to be a good ruler of this ancient brotherhood, and good lord to all the Saxon folk that dwell on the land of Saint Etheldreda. Now my higher hope is that thou wilt be enabled, oh Hereward, to free all England from this cruel bondage!"

The young Saxon noble, being wholly a man of action, and gifted with much modesty, made but a very short reply to this and to other very long speeches; he simply said that he had come back to get back his own, and to help his good countrymen to get back their own; that the Norman yoke was all too grievous to be borne; that it was very strange and very sorrowful that brave King Harold came not back to his faithful people of East-Anglia; and that, until King Harold should come, he, Hereward, would do his best for his friends and for himself.

Though all were eager to be informed of the strength which the Lord of Brunn brought with him, and of the plans he proposed to pursue, Thurstan thought it churlish to question any man fasting. Hereward, however, declared that he had fared well on board the bark, and could well wait till supper-time. And so, having closed the doors of the abbat's great hall, the lords and prelates proceeded to deliberate with the dispossessed Lord of Brunn.

The sum of Hereward's replies to many questions and cross-questions (he having no genius for narration) was simply this:—Elfric had found him out in Flanders, and had delivered to him letters, and messages, and tokens which had determined him to quit his adoptive country and return to England. Many English exiles who had been living in the Netherlands had made up their minds to come over with him. Such money as they could command among them all, or borrow at interest from the traders of Flanders, who seriously felt the loss of their trade with England, had been applied to the purchase of warlike harness, and to the hiring and equipping of three foreign barks.

The master of a bark from Lynn that chanced to be in those parts had offered his bark and the services of himself and crew for nothing, or for what his liege lord the Abbat of Ely might at any time choose to give him. The gold and silver which my Lord Abbat had sent with Elfric had been properly and profitably employed; and, besides spear-heads, and swords, and bows, and jackets of mail, the Lynn bark now lying at my Lord Abbat's pier, and the other Lynn bark left behind at that town, had brought such a quantity of Rhenish and Mosel wine as would suffice for the consumption of the whole house until next Christmas.

Counting the men that had come in all the barks, there were more than one hundred and ten true-hearted Saxons, well-armed and equipped, and well-practiced in the use of arms, as well in the Saxon fashion as in the fashions used abroad; and every one of these men was proper to become a centurion, or the trainer and leader of a hundred of our fen-men. It was Lord Hereward's notion that our great house at Ely and the Camp of Refuge would be best relieved or screened from any chance of attack, by the Saxons making at once a quick and sharp attack all along the Norman lines or posts to the north and north-west of the Isle of Ely, or from Spalding to Brunn, and Crowland, and Peterborough.

Some thought that his lordship preferred beginning in this direction because his own estates and the lady of his love were there: we will not say that these considerations had no weight with him, but we opine that his plan was a good one, and that no great commander, such as Hereward was, would have begun the war upon the invaders in any other manner, time or place. Twenty of the armed men he had brought with him from their wearisome exile—or more than twenty if my Lord Abbat thought fit—he would leave at Ely; with the rest, who had been left with the ships at Lynn, he would go to the Welland river, and make a beginning.

"But thou canst not go yet awhile," said Abbat Thurstan, thinking of the Christmas festivals and of the Rhenish wines; "thou canst not quit us, my son, until after the feast of the Epiphany! 'Tis but twelve days from to-morrow, and the Normans are not likely to be a-stirring during those twelve days."

"True, my Lord Abbat," said Hereward, "the Normans will be feasting and rejoicing; but it is on that very account that I must go forthwith in order to take them unprepared and attack their bands separately, while they are feasting. An ye, holy brothers, give me your prayers, and the saints grant me the success I expect, I shall have recovered for ye the house at Spalding and the abbey of Crowland, and for myself mine humble house at Brunn, before these twelve days be over."

"Then," said the abbat, "thou mayest be back and keep the feast of the Epiphany with us."

Hereward thought of keeping the feast in another place and with a different company, but the eager hospitality of Thurstan was not to be resisted, and so he promised that he would return, if he could do so without detriment to the business he had on hand. But when he spoke of setting forth on the morrow after high mass, not only the Lord Abbat, but every one that heard him, raised his voice against him, and Hereward yielded to the argument that it would be wicked to begin war on Christmas Day, or to do any manner of thing on that day except praying and feasting. Something did Hereward say in praise of Elfric, and of the ability, and courage, and quickness of invention he had displayed while on his mission in foreign parts, and on shipboard.

"Albeit," said he, "I would not rob my good friends the Abbat of Crowland and the Prior of Spalding of so promising a novice, I needs must think that he would make a much better soldier than monk; nor can I help saying that I would rather have Elfric for my messenger and aid in the field than any Saxon youth I know, whether of low degree or high."

"My good brother of Crowland and I have been thinking of these things," said Abbat Thurstan; "and these are surely days when the saints of England require the services of men with steel caps on their heads as much as they require the services of men with shaven crowns. Not but that some of us that wear cowls have not wielded arms and done good battle in our day for the defense of our shrines and houses."

At this moment the eels and fish of the Christmas-eve supper were already, and the best cask of Rhenish which the bark had brought up to my Lord Abbat's pier was broached.

Hereward – the Wake

CHAPTER VIII.

LORD HEREWARD GOES TO GET HIS OWN

In no time had there been at the house of Ely so great and glorious a festival of the Nativity as that holden in the year of Grace one thousand and seventy, the day after the return of the Saxon commander Hereward, Lord of Brunn. Learned brothers of the house have written upon it, and even to this day the monks of Ely talk about it. On the day next after the feast, several hours before sunrise, the mariners in the unloaded bark were getting all ready to drop down the Ouse to the good town of Lynn, and Lord Hereward was communing with the Abbat Thurstan, the Abbat of Crowland, and the Prior of Spalding, in my Lord Abbat's bedchamber.

The rest of the prelates and lay lords were sleeping soundly in their several apartments, having taken their leave of Hereward in a full carouse the night before. Many things had been settled touching correspondence or communication, and a general co-operation and union of all the Saxons in the Camp of Refuge and all that dwelt in the fen country, whether in the isle of Ely, or in the isle of Thorney, or in Lindsey, or in Holland, or in other parts. Fresh assurances were given that the chiefs and fighting men would all acknowledge Hereward as their supreme commander, undertaking nothing but at his bidding, and looking to none but him for their orders and instructions. Abbat Thurstan agreed to keep the score of men that had been brought up to Ely in the bark, but he demurred about receiving and entertaining, as the commander of these men, the dark stranger with the hooked nose and sharp eye. Hereward said that the stranger was a man remarkably skilled in the science of war, and in the art of defending places. Thurstan asked whether he were sure that he was not a spy of the Normans, or one that would sell himself to the Normans for gold?

Then the Lord of Brunn told what he knew, or that which he had been told, concerning the dark stranger. He was from Italy, from a region not very far removed from Rome and the patrimony of Saint Peter; from the name of his town he was hight Girolamo of Salerno. His country has been all invaded, and devastated, and conquered by Norman tribes, from the same evil hive which had sent these depredators into merry England to make it a land of woe. Robert Guiscard, one of twelve brothers that were all conquerors and spoilers, had driven Girolamo from his home and had seized upon his houses and lands, and had abused the tombs of his ancestors, even as the followers of William the Bastard were now doing foul things with the graves of our forefathers.

After enduring wounds, and bonds, and chains, Girolamo of Salerno had fled from his native land forever, leaving all that was his in the hands of the Normans, and had gone over into Sicily to seek a new home and settlement among strangers. But the Normans, who thought they had never robbed enough so long as there were more countries before them which they could rob and conquer, crossed the sea into Sicily under Roger Guiscard, the brother of Robert, and made prey of all that fair island seven years before the son of the harlot of Falaise crossed the Channel and came into England.

Now Girolamo of Salerno had vowed upon the relics of all the saints that were in the mother-church of Salerno, that he would never live under the Norman tyranny; and sundry of the Norman chiefs that went over with Roger Guiscard to Palermo had vowed upon the crosses of their swords that they would hang him as a dangerous man if they could but catch him. So Girolamo shook the dust of Sicily and Mongibel from his feet, and, crossing the seas again, went into Grecia. But go where he would, those incarnate devils the Normans would be after him! He had not long lived in Grecia ere Robert Guiscard came over from Otrantum and Brundisium, to spoil the land and occupy it; therefore Girolamo fled again, cursing the Norman lance.

He had wandered long and far in the countries of the Orient: he had visited the land of Egypt, he had been in Palestine, in Jerusalem, in Bethlehem; he had stood and prayed on the spot where our Lord was born, and on the spot where He was crucified; but, wearying of his sojourn among Saracens, he had come back to the Christian west to see if he could find some home where the hated Normans could not penetrate, or where dwelt some brave Christian people that were hopeful of fighting against those oppressors.

He was roaming over the earth in quest of enemies to the Normans when Hereward met him, two years ago, in Flanders, and took his hand in his as a sworn foe to all men of that race. Was, then, Girolamo of Salerno a likely man to be a spy or fautor to the Normans in England? Thurstan acknowledged that he was not. "But," said he, "some men are so prone to suspicion that they suspect everybody and everything that is near to them; and some men, nay, even some monks and brothers of this very house, are so envious of my state and such foes to my peace of mind, that whenever they see me more happy and fuller of hope than common, they vamp me up some story or conjure some spectrum to disquiet me and sadden me! Now, what said our prior and cellarer no later than last night? They said, in the hearing of many of this house, inexpert novices as well as cloister-monks, that the dark stranger must be either an unbelieving Jew or a necromancer; that when, at grand mass, the host was elevated in the church, he shot glances of fire at it from his sharp eyes; and that when the service was over they found him standing behind the high altar muttering what sounded very like an incantation, in a tongue very like unto the Latin."

Hereward smiled and said, "Assuredly he was but saying a prayer in his own tongue. My Lord Abbat, this Girolamo of Salerno, hath lived constantly with me for the term of two years, and I will warrant him as true a believer as any man in broad England. He is a man of many sorrows, and no doubt of many sins; but as for his faith!—why he is a living and walking history of all the saints and martyrs of the church, and of every miraculous image of Our Ladie that was ever found upon earth. His troubles and his crosses, and his being unable to speak our tongue, or to comprehend what is said around him, may make him look moody and wild, and very strange: and I am told that in the country of his birth most men have coal-black hair and dark flashing eyes; but that in Salerno there be no Israelites allowed, and no necromancers or warlocks or witches whatsoever; albeit, the walnut-tree of Beneventum, where the witches are said to hold their Sabbath, be not very many leagues distant. In truth, my good Lord Abbat, it was but to serve you and to serve your friends and retainers, that I proposed he should stay for a season where he is; for I have seen such good proofs of his skill in the stratagems of war, and have been promised by him so much aid and assistance in the enterprises I am going to commence, that I would fain have him with me.

I only thought that if he stayed a while here in quiet, he might learn to speak our tongue; and that if during my absence the Normans should make any attempt from the side of Cam-Bridge upon this blessed shrine of Saint Etheldreda, he might, by his surpassing skill and knowledge of arms, be of use to your lordship and the good brothers."

"These are good motives," said Thurstan, "and do honor to thee, my son. It is not in my wont to bid any stranger away from the house.... But—but this stranger doth look so very strange and wild, that I would rather he were away. Even our sub-sacrist, who hath not the same nature as the prior and cellarer, saith that all our flaxen-headed novices in the convent are afraid of that thin dark man, and that they say whenever the stranger's large black eye catches theirs they cannot withdraw their eyes until he turns away from them. I think, my Lord Hereward, the stranger may learn our tongue in thy camp. I believe that the Normans will not try on this side now that the waters are all out, and our rivers and ditches so deep; and if they do we can give a good account of them—and I really do think that thou wilt more need than we this knowing man's services:—what say ye, my brother of Crowland?"

The Abbat of Crowland was wholly of the opinion of the Abbat of Ely, and so likewise was the Prior of Spalding. It was therefore agreed that Girolamo of Salerno should accompany the young Lord of Brunn.

"But" said Hereward, "in proposing to leave you this strange man from Italy, I thought of taking from you, for yet another while, that Saxon wight Elfric, seeing that he knoweth all this fen country better than any man in my train; and that, while I am going round by the river and the Wash, I would fain dispatch, by way of the fens, a skilled and trustful messenger in the direction of Ey...."

"To salute the Ladie Alftrude, and to tell her that thou art come," said the Abbat of Crowland.

"Even so," quoth Hereward; "and to tell her moreover to look well to her manor-house, and to let her people know that I am come and that they ought to come and join me at the proper time."

"It is clear," said the Prior of Spalding, "that none can do this mission and it be not Elfric, who knoweth the goings and comings about the house at Ey...."

"Aye, and the maid-servant that dwelled within the gates," quoth the Abbat of Crowland.

The Prior of Spalding laughed, and eke my Lord Abbat of Ely; and when he had done his laugh, Thurstan said "This is well said, and well minded; and as we seem to be all agreed that, upon various considerations, it would be better to unfrock the young man at once, let us call up Elfric, and release him from his slight obligations, and give him to Lord Hereward to do with him what he list. What say ye my brothers?"

The two dignified monks said "yea;" and Elfric being summoned was told that henceforth he was Lord Hereward's man, and that he might doff his cucullis, and let his brown locks grow on his tonsure as fast as they could grow.

The monk that sleeps in his horse-hair camise, and that has nothing to put on when he rises but his hose and his cloak, is not long a-dressing; yet in less time than ever monk attired himself, Elfric put on the soldier garb that he had worn while abroad. And then, having received from Hereward a signet-ring and other tokens, and a long message for the Ladie Alftrude, together with instructions how he was to proceed after he had seen her; and having bidden a dutiful farewell and given his thanks to the Prior of Spalding and to the two abbots, and having gotten the blessing of all three, Elfric girded a good sword to his loins, took his fen-staff in his hand, and went down to the water-gate to get a light skerry, for the country was now like one great lake, and the journey to Ey must be mostly made by boat.

CONQUEST OF THE ISLE OF ELY

It was now nigh upon day-dawn. The Lord Abbat and a few others accompanied the Lord of Brunn to the pier, and saw him on board; then the mariners let go their last mooring, and the bark began to glide down the river.

Before the light of this winter day ended, Hereward was well up the Welland, and the whole of his flotilla was anchored in that river not far from Spalding, behind a thick wood of willows and alders, which sufficed even in the leafless season to screen the barks from the view of the Norman monks in the succursal cell.

As soon as it was dark, Hereward the liberator took one score and ten armed men into the lightest of the barks, and silently and cautiously ascended the river until he came close to the walls of the convent. The caution was scarcely needed, for the Normans, albeit they were ever reproaching the Saxons with gluttony and drunkenness, were feasting and drinking at an immoderate rate, and had taken no care to set a watch. Brightly the light of a great wood fire and of many torches shone through the windows of the hall as Hereward landed with his brave men and surrounded the house, while the mariners were taken good care of the ferry-boat.

"If these men were in their own house," said Hereward, "it is not I that would disturb their mirth on such a night; but as they are in the house of other men, we must even pull them forth by the ears. So! Where be the ladders?"

A strong ladder brought from the bark was laid across the moat, and ten armed men passed one by one over this ladder to the opposite side of the moat. The well-armed men were led by the brother of Wybert the wright, and by another of the men who had fled from Spalding town on that wicked night when Ivo Taille-Bois broke into the house. Now these two men of Spalding well knew the strong parts and the weak parts of the cell—as well they might, for they had often helped to repair the woodwork and the roof of the building. Having drawn the strong ladder after them to the narrow ledge of masonry on which they had landed, they raised it against the wall, and while some steadied it, first one armed man and then another climbed up by the ladder to the top of the stone and brick part of the walls. Then the brother of Wybert climbing still higher, by clutching the beams and the rough timber got to the house-top, and presently told those below in a whisper that all was right, that the door at the head of the spiral staircase was unfastened and wide open.

In a very short time ten armed men and the two hinds from Spalding town were safe on the roof; and the brother of Wybert said, "Now Saxons!" and as he heard the signal, Lord Hereward said, "Now Saxons, your horns!" And three stout Saxons, well skilled in the art of noise-making, put each his horn to his mouth and sounded a challenge, as loud as they could blow. Startled and wrathful, but not much alarmed, was the intrusive prior from Angers when he heard this noise, and bade his Angevin sacrist go to the window, and see what the Saxon slaves wanted at this time of night with their rascaille cow-horns! But when the sacrist reported that he saw a great bark lying in the river, and many armed men standing at the edge of the moat (in the darkness the sacrist took sundry stumps of willow-trees for warriors), the man of Angers became alarmed, and all Ivo Taille-Bois' kindred became alarmed, and quitting the blazing fire and their good wine, they all ran to the windows of the hall to see what was toward.

As they were a ruleless, lawless, unconsecrated rabble, who knew not what was meant by monastic discipline, and respect, and obedience, they all talked and shouted together, and shouted and talked so loud and so fast that it was impossible for any Christian man to be heard in answer to them. But at length the pseudo-prior silenced the gabble for a minute, and said, "Saxons, who are you, and what do you want at this hour, disturbing the repose of holy men at a holy season?"

Even this was said in Norman-French, which no man understood or could speak, except Hereward and the dark stranger who had attended him hither. But the Lord of Brunn gave out in good round French, "We are Saxons true, and true men to King Harold, and we be come to pull you out of this good nest which ye have defiled too long!"

"Get ye gone, traitors and slaves!" cried the false prior from Angers; "ye cannot cross our moat nor force our gates, and fifty Norman lances are lying hard by."

"False monk, we will see," quoth the Lord of Brunn. "Now, Saxons, your blast-horns again; blow ye our second signal!"

The horn men blew might and main; and before their last blast had ceased echoing from an angle of the walls, another horn was heard blowing inside the house, and then was heard a rushing and stamping of heavy feet, and a clanging of swords in the hall, and a voice roaring, "Let me cleave the skull of two of these shavelings for the sake of Wybert the wright!"

"Thou art cold and shivering, Girolamo," said Hereward; "but step out of that quagmire where thou art standing, and follow me. We will presently warm ourselves at the fireside of these Frenchmen." Girolamo followed the Lord of Brunn to the front of the house; and they were scarcely there were the drawbridge was down, and the gate thrown open.

"Well done, Ralph of Spalding," said Hereward, who rushed into the house followed by the score of armed men. But those who had descended from above by the spiral staircase had left nothing to be done by those who ascended from below. The false prior and all his false fraternity had been seized, and had been bound with their own girdles, and had all been thrown in a corner, where they all lay sprawling the one on the top of the other, and screaming and begging for Misericord. The brother of Wybert the wright had given a bloody coxcomb to the prior, and one of Hereward's soldiers had slit the nose of a French monk that had aimed at him with a pike; but otherwise little blood had been shed, and no great harm done, save that all the stoups of wine and all the wine-cups had been upset in the scuffle. The brother of Wybert begged as a favor that he might be allowed to cut the throats of two of the false monks; but the Lord of Brunn, so fierce in battle, was aye merciful in the hour of victory, and never would allow the slaying of prisoners, and so he told the good man of Spalding town that the monks must not be slain; but that, before he had done with them, they should be made to pay the price of his brother's blood; nay, three times the price that the Saxon laws put upon the life of a man of Wybert's degree.

"I would give up that bot for a little of their blood!" said Wybert's brother. But, nevertheless, he was obliged to rest satisfied; for who should dare gainsay the young Lord of Brunn?

Girolamo of Salerno, who understood nought of the debate between Hereward and the brother of Wybert, thought that the intrusive monks ought to be put into sacks and thrown into the river, inasmuch as that the Normans, when they conquered Salerno, threw a score of good monks of that town and vicinity into the sea; but when he delivered this thought unto the Lord Hereward, that bold-hearted and kind-hearted Saxon said that it was not the right way to correct cruelties by committing cruelties, and that it was not in the true English nature to be prone to revenge. All this while, and a little longer, the false alien monks, with their hands tied behind them, lay sprawling and crying Misericord: howbeit, when they saw and understood that death was not intended, they plucked up their courage and began to complain and reprove.

"This is a foul deed," said one of them, "a very foul deed, to disturb and break in upon, and smite with the edge of the sword, the servants of the Lord."

"Not half so foul a deed," quoth Hereward, "as that done by Ivo Taille-Bois, the cousin of ye all, and the man who put ye here, and thrust out the Saxon brotherhood at the dead of night, slaying their cook. Ye may or may not have been servants of the Lord in the countries from which ye came, but here are ye nought but intruders and usurpers, and the devourers of better men's goods."

Here the prior from Angers spoke from the heap in the corner, and said, "For this night's work thou wilt be answerable unto the king."

"That will I," quoth the Lord of Brunn, "when bold King Harold returns."

"I will excommunicate thee and thy fautors," said the intrusive prior.

"Thou hadst better not attempt it," said Hereward, "for among my merry men be some that know enough of church Latin to make out the difference between a Maledicite and a Benedicite; and I might find it difficult to prevent their cutting your weazens."

"Yet would I do it by bell, book and candle, if I could get the bell and candle, and read the book," said the intrusive prior.

"Thou hadst better not attempt it," said two or three voices from the heap; but another voice, which seemed buried under stout bodies and habits and hoods, said, "There is no danger, for our prior cannot read, and never had memory enough to say by heart more Latin than lies in a Credo. Beshrew you, brothers all, bespeak these

Saxons gently, so that they may give us leave to go back into Normandie. If I had bethought me that I was to play the monk in this fashion, Ivo Taille-Bois should never have brought me from the plough-tail!"

When the Lord of Brunn and Girolamo of Salerno had done laughing, the Lord Hereward said, "Let this goodly hall be cleared of this foul rubbish. Girolamo, see these intruders carried on board the bark and thrown into the hold. We will send them to my Lord Abbat at Ely, that they may be kept as hostages. But tell the shipmen not to hurt a hair of their heads."

When the alien monks understood that they must go, they clamored about their goods and properties. This made Hereward wroth, and he said, "When ye thrust out the good English monks, ye gave them nought! Nevertheless I will give ye all that ye brought with ye."

Here the voice that had spoken before from under the heap said, "We all know we brought nothing with us—no, not so much as the gear we wear! Therefore let us claim nothing, but hasten to be gone, and so hope to get back the sooner into Normandie."

But the prior and the sacrist and divers others continued to make a great outcry about their goods, their holy-books, their altar vases, their beds and their bed-clothes; and as this moved Lord Hereward's ire, he said to his merry men that they must turn them out; and the merry men all did turn them out by pulling them before and kicking them behind: and in this manner the unlettered and unholy crew that Ivo Taille-Bois had thrust into the succursal cell of Spalding were lugged and driven on shipboard, and there they were made fast under the hatches. As soon as they were all cleared out of the convent, Lord Hereward bade his Saxons put more fuel on the fire, and bring up more wine, and likewise see what might be in the buttery. The brother of Wybert the wright knew the way well both to cellar and buttery; and finding both well filled, he soon re-appeared with wine and viands enough. And so Hereward and his men warmed themselves by the blazing fire, and ate and drank most merrily and abundantly: and when all had their fill, and all had drunk a deep health to Hereward the liberator, they went into the monk's snug cells, and so fast to sleep.

On the morrow morning they rose betimes. So featly had the thing been done overnight, that none knew it but those who had been present. The good folk that yet remained in Spalding town, though so close at hand, had heard nothing of the matter. Hereward now summoned them to the house; but having his reasons for wishing not to be known at this present, he deputed one of his men to hold a conference with them, and to tell the few good men of Spalding that the hour of deliverance was at hand, that their false monks had been driven away, and that Father Adhelm and their true monks would soon return: whereat the Spalding folk heartily rejoiced. In the present state of the road, or rather of the waters, there was no fear of any Norman force approaching the succursal cell. Therefore Lord Hereward ordered that much of his munition of war should be landed and deposited in the convent: and leaving therein all his armed men with Girolamo of Salerno, he embarked alone in the lightest of his barks, and went up the river as far as the point that was nearest to Brunn.

There, leaving the bark and all the sailors, and taking with him nought but his sword and his fen-staff, and covering himself with an old and tattered seaman's coat, he landed and struck across the fens, and walked, waded, leaped, and swam, until he came within sight of his own old manor-house and the little township of Brunn. It was eventide, and the blue smoke was rising from the manor-house and from the town, as peacefully as in the most peaceful days. Hereward stopped and looked upon the tranquil scene, as he had done so many times before at the same hour in the days of his youth, when returning homeward from some visit, or from some fowling in the fens; and as he looked, all that had since passed became as a dream; and then he whistled and stepped gaily forward, as if his father's house was still his own house, and his father there to meet and bless him.

But, alack! his father was six feet under the sod of the churchyard, and a fierce Norman was in the house, with many men-at-arms. Awakening from his evening dream, and feeling that the invasion of England was no dream—the bloody battle of Hastings no dream—the death of his father no dream—and that it was a sad reality that he was a dispossessed man, barred out by force and by fraud from his own, the young Lord of Brunn avoided the direct path to the manor-house, and struck into a narrow sloppy lane which led into the township. As he came among the low houses, or huts, the good people were beginning to bar their doors for the night. "They will open," said Hereward, "when they know who is come among them!" He made straight for the abode of one who had been his foster brother; and he said as he entered it, "Be there true Saxon folk in the house?"

"Yea," said the man of the house.

"Then wilt thou not be sorry to see Hereward the Saxon and thy foster-brother;" and so saying he unmuffled himself and threw off his dirty ship cloak; and his foster brother fell at his feet, and kissed his hand, and hugged his knee, and said, "Is it even my young Lord Hereward?" and so wept for joy.

"It is even I," said the young Lord of Brunn; "it is even I come back to get mine own, and to get back for every honest man his own. But honest men must up and help.

Will the honest folk of Brunn strike a blow for Hereward and for themselves? Will the town-people, and my kith and kindred and friends in the old days, receive and acknowledge me?"

It was the wife of the foster-brother that was now kneeling and clasping Hereward's knee, and that said, "The women of Brunn would brand every catiff in the township that did not throw up his cap and rejoice, and take his bill-hook and bow in his hand for the young Lord of Brunn!"

Every one of the notables was summoned presently; and they all recognized Hereward as their true lord and leader, vowing at the same time that they would follow him into battle against the Normans, and do his bidding whatever it might be. Many were the times that Hereward was forced to put his finger upon his lip to recommend silence; for they all wanted to hail his return with hearty Saxon shouts, and he wanted to avoid rousing the Normans in the manor-house for the present. The welcome he received left him no room to doubt of the entire affection and devotion of the town-folk; and the intelligence he gleaned was more satisfactory than he had anticipated. Raoul, a Norman knight, and, next to Ivo Taille-Bois, the most powerful and diabolical of all the Normans in or near to the fen-country, held the manor-house, and levied dues and fees in the township; but many of those who dwelt in the neighborhood, and who had held their lands under the last quiet old Lord of Brunn, had never submitted to the intruder, nor had Raoul and his men-at-arms been able to get at them in their islands among the fens and deep waters.

There was John of the Bogs, who had kept his house and gear untouched, and who could muster a score or twain of lusty hinds, well-armed with pikes and bill-hooks and bows; there was Ralph of the Dyke, the chamberlain of the last Lord of Brunn, who had beaten off Raoul and his men-at-arms in a dozen encounters; there were other men, little less powerful than these two, who would be up and doing if Lord Hereward would only show himself, or only raise his little finger. The manor-house was well fortified and garrisoned; but what of that?

For Lord Hereward it should be stormed and taken, though it should cost a score or twain of lives. Here the young Lord of Brunn told them that he hoped to get back his house without wasting a single drop of the blood of any of them, inasmuch as he had practiced men of war not far from hand, together with engines of war proper for sieges. He bade them spread far and near the news of his return: he begged them to do this cautiously, and to remain quiet until he should come back among them; in the meanwhile they might be making such preparations for war as their means allowed. To-morrow night it would be the full of moon; and as soon as the good town-folk should see the moon rising over Elsey Wood they might expect him and his force. And now he must take a short repast and a little sleep, so as to be able to commence his return to the Welland river before midnight.

Long before midnight Hereward was on his way; but he travelled with much more ease than he had done in coming to Brunn, for his foster-brother and two other trusty men carried him in a boat the greater part of the way.

Being again at Spalding, the approaches to which had been curiously strengthened, during his short absence, by Girolamo of Salerno, Hereward sent off one of the barks for Ely to convey the news of his first success and the prisoners he had made to the Lord Abbat, and to bring back the good prior of Spalding to his own cell; he left one bark moored below Spalding to watch the lower part of the river, and prevent any but friendly boats from ascending (there was little danger of any Norman coming this way; but a good commander like the Lord of Brunn leaves nothing to chance, and neglects no precaution); and with the three other barks and Girolamo and twenty of his armed men he began to move up the river on the following morning. Ten men were left to hold the succursal cell, and protect the township of Spalding; and all such war-stores as were not immediately required were left in the convent.

The three barks were to be moored near to the point of debarkation, so as to prevent any communication between Crowland and Spalding, it being very expedient to keep the intrusive monks at Crowland ignorant of what had passed and what was passing. True, these unholy Norman friars were feasting and keeping their Christmas, and were little likely to move out at such a season, or to take heed of anything that was happening beyond the walls of their own house: but Hereward, as we have said, neglected no precaution; and therefore it was that the Lord of Brunn was ever successful in war.

When he and his troops landed at the bend of the river that was nearest to Brunn, it was made visible to all, and not without manifest astonishment, that Girolamo of Salerno could do many wondrous things. Under his direction light and shallow skerries and boats made of wicker-work, and lined with skins, had been prepared; and while these were capable of carrying men and stores across the deeper streams that lay between the bend of the Welland and the town of Brunn, they were so light that they could easily be carried on the men's shoulders. A catapult and another engine which Hereward had purchased in Flanders were taken to pieces in order to be carried in these boats and skerries; the more precious parts of the munition of war which Girolamo had made with his own hands before embarking for England were most carefully wrapped up in many cloths and skins, so that even in that wettest of countries they could not be wetted. There was one small package, a very small package was it, of which the dark stranger took especial care, carrying it himself, and telling Hereward that with its contents he could open the gates of the strongest of houses.

Notwithstanding the weight of their arms, and of the other burdens they had to bear from one stream or mere to another, the whole party pushed steadily forward across the more than half-inundated fens; and although some of the men, not being native fen-men, were not practiced in such travelling, and although some of them could not swim, they all reached in safety a broad dry dyke near to the back of the township of Brunn a good hour before the full moon began to rise over Elsey-Wood. Having seen everything safely landed, Hereward walked alone into the town, going straight to the house of his foster-brother. But before he got into the rambling street he was accosted by three tall Saxons, who said, "Is it our Lord Hereward?"

"Yea; and are ye ready to be stirring? Have ye collected a few true men that will strike a blow for the houseless Lord of Brunn?"

"Thou shalt see, my Lord," said one of the three, who was no less a man than John of the Bogs, and clapping his hands thrice, three score and more Saxons armed with bows and bills, and some of them with swords and battle-axes, started forth from behind so many alders and willow-trees; and at that moment the broad full moon showed her bright, full face over the bare trees of Elsey-

Wood. The men had been well taught, and so they did not rend the air with a shout which might have startled the Normans in the manor-house; but every man of them, whether freeman or serf, knelt at Lord Hereward's feet, and kissed his hand.

The score of armed men and all that had been brought with them from Spalding were soon carried into town. A supper was already, and smoking on the table of Lord Hereward's foster-brother. Every man was welcomed as one amongst brethren, albeit these simple-minded men of Brunn started and looked askance when they saw the dark stranger with the hooked nose and fiery eyes; and much they marveled all when they heard the young Lord of Brunn talking with this stranger in an unknown tongue.

"Wouldst thou have possession of thine house to-night or to-morrow morning?" said Girolamo. "At the hazard of burning a part of it I could gain thee admittance in less than half an hour by means of my Greek fire."

"I would not have a plank of the dear old place burned," said Hereward. "I would rather delay my entrance till the morning."

"Then this must be a busy night," replied the dark man.
And a busy night it was; for lo! in the morning, when Raoul the Norman knight awoke from the deep sleep which had followed his heavy overnight's carouse, and looked forth from his chamber in the tower over the gateway of the manor-house, he saw what seemed another and a taller tower on the opposite side of the moat; and what seemed a bridge of boats laid across the moat; and in the tower were archers with their bows bent, and men-at-arms with swords and battle-axes. Raoul rubbed his eyes, and still seeing the same sight, thought it all magic or a dream. But there was more magic than this, for when he called up his sleepy household, and

his careless and over-confident men-at-arms, and went round the house, he saw another bridge of boats leading to the postern-gate at the back of the house, and beyond that bridge he saw a catapult with a score of armed men standing by it. But look where he would, there were armed men; the manor-house was surrounded, and surrounded in such fashion that there could be no egress from it, and small hope of defending it. The despairing Norman knight, therefore, went back to his tower over the gateway, and called a parley.

"What would ye, O Saxons?" said Raoul; "know ye not that ye are breaking the king's peace? Who is your leader, and what wants he?"

"I am their leader and lord," quoth Hereward, speaking from that marvelous wooden tower which Girolamo had caused to be raised; "I am their leader and the Lord of Brunn, and all that I want is to get possession of my house and lands. So come forth, Norman, and fear not! Thou and thy men shall have quarter and kindly treatment. But if ye seek to resist, or let fly so much as one arrow upon these my good people, by all the saints of old England I will hang ye all on one gibbet."

"What shall we do in this strait?" said Raoul to his seneschal.

"Take terms and surrender," quoth the seneschal; "for the house cannot be defended against the host that is come against it, and against the engines of war that are raised against it. Three butts of that catapult would shiver the postern gate; that tower in front commands the battlements; the bridges of boats will give access to every part of the walls. This could not be done in one short night, except by magic; but magic is not to be withstood by sinful men-at-arms, and our chaplain is gone to feast with the monks of Crowland. Moreover, oh Raoul, we have consumed nearly all our provisions in our own feastings, and so should starve in a day or two if we could hold out so long—but that is impossible."

"But," said Raoul, "be there not some twenty or thirty Norman lances no farther off than in the town of Stamford?"

"But they cannot cross the wide watery fens; and if they were here they could not charge among these accursed bogs."

"'Tis all too true," quoth Raoul, "and therefore must we surrender."

The Norman knight spoke again to Hereward, who stood on the tower, looking like the good soldier and great lord that he was; and Raoul bargained to give immediate admittance to the Saxons, if the Saxons would only grant life and liberty to him and his garrison, with permission to carry off such arms and property as were their own.

"Life and security of limb ye shall have," said Hereward, "and liberty ye shall have likewise when good King Harold comes back and peace is restored; but, in the meantime, I must have ye kept as hostages, and sent to Ely to do penance for your sins: your arms must remain with us who want them; but an ye brought any other property with ye beyond the clothes on your backs, it shall be restored upon your solemn oaths that ye did not get it by robbery here in England!"

"These are harsh terms," muttered Raoul; "but, Saxon, thou art no knight."

"I soon shall be one," quoth Hereward; "but that is nought to thee. So come out of mine house, and save me the trouble of hanging thee. Come out, I say, ye Norman thieves, and give me up mine own!"

And Raoul, seeing nothing better for it, pulled down a flag which some too confident wight had raised over the battlements; and the drawbridge being let down, and the front gate opened, he and all his Normans came forth and laid down their armor and their arms at the feet of Hereward the Saxon.

Even thus did the young Lord of Brunn get his own again.

A Norman carousal

CHAPTER IX.

ELFRIC THE EX-NOVICE, AND GIROLAMO OF SALERNO, PREPARE TO PLAY AT DEVILS

A feast was prepared in the great hall of the manor-house, and the young Lord of Brunn was about sitting down to table with his kinsmen and the good friends that had rallied round him in the hour of need, when Elfric arrived at Brunn from the house of the Ladie Alftrude at Ey. To look at Lord Hereward's glad countenance as he talked in a corner of the hall with the new comer, one would have thought that he had won a fairer house and a wider domain than those of his ancestors of which he had repossessed himself in the morning.

And for that matter he had won or was winning his way to a better house and greater estate; for had not the fair young heiress of Ey sent again to tell him that she abided by her troth-plight, and looked for him to come and rescue her from that burthensome and dishonoring protection of the Normans under which she had been living! The retainers of her father's house, and all the hinds and serfs, were devoted to her, and ready to receive the young Lord of Brunn as their own liege lord and deliverer.

Her friends and neighbors had all been consulted, and would assemble in arms and meet Lord Hereward at any hour and place that it might suit him to name. Save some few men-at-arms that were at Crowland to protect the intrusive Norman monks, there was no Norman force nearer to Ey than Stamford. The season of the year and all things were favorable for recovering the whole of the fen-country, and for driving the invaders from every country in the neighborhood of the fens.

After putting a few questions to Elfric, such as lovers usually put to their pages when they come from seeing their ladie-loves, Hereward asked what force there might be in Crowland Abbey. Elfric said that there might be one knight and from ten to fifteen men-at-arms; but then all the monks that had been so recently brought over from France were fighting men, at a pinch; and these intruders were from thirty to forty in number, and well provided with weapons and warlike harness. The young man also bade Lord Hereward reflect that the great house at Crowland was not like the cell at Spalding, but a lofty and very strong place, and built mostly of stone and brick. Elfric too had learned that Crowland was well stored with provisions, so that it might stand a long siege.

"And yet," said the Lord of Brunn, "it is upon the great house of Crowland that I would fain make my next attempt; and great in every way are the advantages that would follow the capture of that strong and holy place, and the immediate restoration of the true Saxon Lord Abbat and his dispossessed brethren."

"My silly head hath been venturing to think of this," said Elfric, "and I very believe that with the aid of Girolamo and with a little of that blue fire and stinking smoke which he hath the trick of making, I could drive knight, men-at-arms, and monks all out of the abbey without any loss or let to our good Saxons."

"Why, what wouldst do?" said Hereward.

"Only this, my lord. I would make the Normans believe that all the blubber-devils of Crowland were come back to earth to drive them from the house."

"I see, yet do not fully comprehend," said Lord Hereward; "but we will talk of these things with Girolamo to-night, when this my first feast as Lord of Brunn is over, and when every Saxon shall have seen that the hospitality of mine ancestors is not to know decrease in me."

And late that night, when Hereward's first and most bountiful feast was over, and when his guests had betaken themselves to the town of Brunn, or to their beds or to clean hay and rushes in the manor-house, Elfric and Girolamo followed Hereward to his inner chamber, and consulted with him about the best means of driving out the French from Crowland. First crossing himself—for although he feared not man, he had a lively dread of all manner of goblins and demons—the Lord of Brunn said, "Elfric, thou mayest now tell us about thy Crowland devils."

"You wist well, my lord," said Elfric, "for who should know it better, that in the heathenish times the whole of the isle of Crowland and all the bogs and pools roundabout were haunted day and night, but most at night, by unaccountable troops and legions of devils, with blubber-lips, fiery mouths, scaley faces, beetle heads, sharp long teeth, long chins, hoarse throats, black skins, hump shoulders, big bellies, burning loins, bandy legs, cloven hoofs for feet, and long tails at their buttocks. And who so well as your lordship knoweth that these blubber-fiends, angered at that their fens and stinking pools should be invaded, allowed our first monks of Crowland no peace nor truce, but were forever gibing and mowing at them, biting them with their sharp teeth, switching them with their filthy tails, putting dirt in their meat and drink, nipping them by the nose, giving them cramps and rheum's and shivering agues and burning fevers, and fustigating and tormenting not a few of the friars even to death! And your lordship knows that these devils of Crowland were not driven away until the time when that very pious man Guthlacus became a hermit there, and cut the sluices that lead from the fetid pools to the flowing rivers. Then, in sooth, the devils of Crowland were beaten off by prayer and by holy water, and the horrible blue lights which they were wont to light upon the most fetid of the pools, ceased to be seen of men."

"All this legend I know full well," said the Lord of Brunn, explaining it to Girolamo of Salerno, who crossed himself many times as he heard the description of the very hideous Crowland devils.

"All that dwell in the fen-country know the legend," continued Elfric; "the house of Crowland is full of the legend, and the usurping Norman crew must know the legend well, and in the guilt of their conscience must needs tremble at it! The devils are painted in cloister and corridor; their blue lights are painted, as they used to appear to our first good monks; and the most pious anchorite Guthlacus is depicted in the act of laying the evil ones. If a Saxon saint laid them, these Norman sinners have done enough to bring them back again; and it can only be by the bones of our saints and the other Saxon relics that lie in the church of Crowland, that the devils of Crowland are prevented from returning. Now all that I would do is this,—I would haunt the house and the fens roundabout with sham devils, and so make these Norman intruders believe that the old real blubber-fiends were upon them! I do not believe they would stand two days and nights of such a siege as I could give them, if your lordship would but consent and Girolamo lend his aid."

"But were it not sinful for christened Saxon men to play at devils?"

"Assuredly not, when playing against devils like these Normans, and for a holy end, and for the restoration of such good men and true Saxons as my Lord Abbat of Crowland and his expelled brotherhood."

Hereward put the question, as a case of conscience, to Girolamo, as *vir bonus et sapiens*, a good man and learned; and Girolamo was of opinion that, as the wicked often put on the semblance of saints to do mischief, the good might, with certain restrictions, be allowed to put on the semblance of devils to do good. His patron Hereward, he said, would give him credit for being a true believer, and a devout, though weak and sinful, son of the church, yet would he think it no sin to play the part of a Crowland devil, or to give to Elfric the benefit of his science in making ghastly blue lights, or in causing flames to appear on the surface of the stagnant waters, or in fact in doing anything that might be required of him in order to scare away the Normans. Hereward had still some misgivings, but he yielded to the representations of Elfric and the exceeding great earnestness of Girolamo; and when he dismissed them for the night he said, "Well, since you will have it so, go and play at devils in Crowland. Only have a care that ye be not taken or slain, and be back to this house as soon as ye can; for if Crowland cannot be taken, we must try and blockade it, and proceed to Ey to collect more strength."

"I have good hope, my lord," said Girolamo; "for with my white magic I can do things that will carry terror to the hearts of these untaught Normans; and then this young man Elfric hath ever succeeded in all that he hath attempted: he already knoweth enough of my language (thanks to the little Latin he got as a novice) to make out my meaning and to act as my interpreter to others. He tells me that even should the devil experiment fail, he can assure our retreat, with scarcely any chance of danger."

"Then go, Girolamo, and take with thee such men and boats and other appliances as thou mayest need. But have a care, for I have work on hand that cannot be done without thee; and if I lose Elfric I lose the nimblest-witted of all my Saxons. So good night, and may the blessed saints go with ye both, although ye be dressed in devils' skins!"

"Brother devil, that is to be," said Elfric to the Salernitan, "there be bulls' hides and bulls' horns in the out-houses; and good coils of iron chain in the kitchen, to do the clanking."

"Boy," said Girolamo, "thou hast but a vulgar idea about demons! Dost think I am going to make jack-pudding devils, such as are gazed at wakes and country fairs? No, no; I will give you devils of another sort I guess. But leave all that to me, and apply your own mind to the means of getting into the house at Crowland or of establishing a correspondence therein, so that the Normans may be devil-ridden inside as well as outside."

"And do thou, great master Girolamo, leave that to me," said Elfric, "for I know some that are within the house of Crowland that would face the real devil and all his legions for the chance of driving out the French abbat and friars; and if I myself do not know every dark corner, every underground passage, and every hiding-hole in and about the house, why there is no one living that hath such knowledge."

Here the two separated. The young Saxon lay down on some rushes near the door of Lord Hereward's chamber, and pulling his cloak over his face was soon fast asleep: the Salernitan, who had a chamber all to himself, sat up till a late hour among the packages and vessels he had brought with him: and yet was he ready to start on his journey for Crowland at the first glimpse of day. Those who entered his room in the morning, just after he was gone, smelt a strong smell of sulphur: and, sorely to Girolamo's cost, some louts remembered this smell at a later season.

CHAPTER X.

THE HOUSE AT CROWLAND

Compared with Crowland, Ely was quite a dry place: there the abbey church and conventual buildings stood upon a hill and on firm hard ground; but here all the edifices stood upon piles driven into the bog, and instead of a high and dry hill, there was nothing but a dead wet flat, and unless in those parts where the monastery and the town stood the ground was so rotten and boggy that a pole might be thrust down thirty feet deep.

Next to the church was a grove of alders, but there was nothing else roundabout but water and bogs, and the reeds that grow in water. In short this Crowland, both in the situation and nature of the place, was a marvel even in the fen-country; and, certes, it was different from all places in any other part of England. Lying in the worst part of the fens, it was so enclosed and encompassed with deep bogs and pools, that there was no access to it except on the north and east sides, and there too only by narrow causeways. Even in the summer season the cattle and flocks were kept at a great distance, there being no pasture-land upon which they could be placed without danger of seeing them swallowed up; so that when the owners would milk their cows they went in boats, by them called skerries, and so small that they would carry but two men and their milk-pails.

There was no corn growing within five miles of Crowland. The greatest gain was from the fish and wild-ducks that were caught; and the ducks were so many that the Crowland fowlers could at times drive into a single net three thousand ducks at once; and so the good people called these pools their real corn-fields. For this liberty of fishing and fowling they paid yearly to the Lord Abbat a very round sum of money: and, we ween, the abbat and the monks had ever the choice of the best fowls and fishes they caught. That holy man Guthlacus, who had laid the Crowland devils, and who had cut the sluices that led from the fetid pools to the flowing rivers had also made the causeways which gave access to the town and monastery.

These narrow but solid roads of wood and gravel ran across the deepest marshes, and had willows and alders growing on either side of them: they were marvelous works for the times; and do we not see in our own day a pyramidal stone on the causeway leading to the north, inscribed with the name of Guthlacus? Much had this beatified anchorite done to alter the face of the country; yet many of the foulest pools remained and could not be purified.

The town was separated from the abbey by a broad stream, and three other streams or water-courses flowed through the town, separating the streets from each other; the streets were planted with willows; and the houses raised on piles driven into the bottom of the bog; and the people of one street communicated with the people of another street by means of light flying-bridges or by means of their skerries. A bold people they were, and hardy and dexterous withal, for their lives were spent in hazardous fowling and fishing, and in toiling over measureless waters and quagmires. Fenners must be bold and expert men, or they must starve.

Moreover the folk of Crowland town were very devout and constant in their worship of the Saxon saints and had a laudable affection for their dispossessed Saxon monks and Lord Abbat: although in the time of King Edward, of happy memory, when they knew not what real sorrow or trouble was, they would at times murmur to my Lord Abbat's chamberlain about the money they were called upon to pay, and at times they would even quarrel lustily with the purveyors of the house about eels and wild-ducks, pikes and herons, and such like trivialities. But the usurping abbat from France had already nearly doubled their rents and dues, and for every fish or fowl that the Saxon purveyors had claimed, the Norman purveyors laid their hands upon a dozen. Ye may judge, therefore, whether the good folk of Crowland town did not abhor the Norman monks and wish them gone.

In turning away the good Lord Abbat and all his obedientiarii or officials, and all his superior monks, the intruders had left in the house a few inferior monks, and about half a score of servientes and lay-brothers to hew their wood and draw their water. And they had so overwrought these Saxon laics, and had so taunted and vilipended them that the poor hinds, one and all, wished them in the bottomless pit.

On the night after Lord Hereward's feast at Brunn and the fifth night from the festival of the Nativity, Alain of Beauvais, the intrusive abbat, was feasting in the hall with his Norman friars, who had never passed through a novitiate, and with his Norman men-at-arms, who were neither more nor less godly than his monks. One or two of the English laics were waiting upon these their lords and masters; the other lay-brothers were supposed to be gone to their straw beds. Alain the pseudo-abbat, being warm with wine, was talking in the manner of all Frenchmen about dames and demoiselles, and was telling his company what a sweet lady it was that broke her heart when he first left Beauvais to seek his fortune with Duke William. Just at this juncture of time there came into the hall an invisible devil in the essence of a stink. It was such a stench as mortal nose had never smelt before—it was so intense, so foul and diabolical, that no mortal man could bear it long! Alain the pseudo-abbat, putting both his hands to his nose, said, "Notre Dame de la misericord! what smell is this?" They all put their hands to their nostrils, and roared "What stink is this?"

Before the English lay-brothers could make any answer, the foul smell, which kept growing stronger, was accompanied by a terrible rumbling noise:—and then there came most violent gusts of wind, which extinguished all the lamps, cressets, torches, and candles; and then, upon the darkness of the hall, there burst a livid, ghastly, blue light, and above and below, from side to side, the hall seemed filled with streaming blue flames, and still that atrocious stench grew stronger and stronger!

Abbat, monks, men-at-arms, and all, rushed out of the hall, some crying that it was the eve of the Day of Judgment, and some roaring that it must be the devils of Crowland come back again. Outside the hall, in the darkened corridor (and by this time there was not a single lamp left burning in any part of the house, but only the altar-lights in the church) they ran against and stumbled over other Frenchmen who were running up from the inferior offices and from the stables, for they had all and several been driven away by blue lights and foul smells; and every mother's son of them believed that the Crowland devils had been sent to dispossess them and drive them back to Normandie.

The corridor was long and straight, but as dark as pitch; some fell in their flight and rolled the one over the other, and some stood stock still and silent as stocks, save that their knees knocked together and their teeth chattered; and some ran forward howling for mercy, and confessing their sins to that hell-darkness. But, when near the end of the long dark passage, a French monk and a man-at-arms that ran the foremost of them all fell through the flooring with a hideous crash, and were heard shrieking from some unexplored regions below, that the fiends had gotten them—that the devils of Crowland were whirling them off to the bottomless pit! The pit or fetid pool into which these two evil-doers were thrown was not bottomless, though deep; yet I wist nothing was ever more seen either of that monk or of that man-at-arms. As these piercing shrieks were heard from below, the Normans roared in the corridor—some blaspheming and cursing the day and hour that they came to England, others praying to be forgiven, with many a Libera nos! and Salve! and others gnashing their teeth and yelling like maniacs. But some there were that made no noise at all, for they had swooned through excess of fear.

And now there came an exceeding bright light from the chasm in the floor through which the monk and the man-at-arms had fallen; but the light, though bright, was still of a ghastly blue tinge; and by that light full twenty devils, or it might be more, were seen ascending and descending to and from the flaming pit, or chasm in the floor. Some of these fiends had blubber-lips, beetle heads, humped shoulders, and bandy legs, and were hirsute and black as soot; others of them were red and altogether shapeless; others were round and yellow; but all their visages were most irregular and frightful, and they had all long tails tipped with fire, and flashes of red, green, and yellow flames came out of the mouths of every one of them.

As for hoarse throats, no voices could be hoarser and more dreadful than the voices of these lubber-fiends as they went up and down the pit, like buckets in a well, or as they roared in the dark cavities under the passage, and beneath the very spot where the Normans lay huddled. The intrusive abbat tried to say a *De profundis*, but the words stuck in his throat, not being very familiar with that passage.

By degrees that exceeding bright light from the chasm in the floor died away, leaving the corridor as black as Erebus. "And we could but get to the church door," said one of the false monks, "we might be safe! Will no man try?—Is there no brave man-at-arms that will adventure along this passage and see whether we can cross that chasm and get out of it?" The men-at-arms thought that this was a reconnaissance to be more properly made by monks, who were supposed to know more about the devil and his ways than did plain soldiers: nevertheless several of them said they would adventure, if they had but their swords or their pikes with them. But they had all left their weapons in their several lodgings; and so, not one of them would budge.

The darkness continued, but the voices which had been roaring below ground ceased. At last Alain of Beauvais, fortifying himself with such short prayers and Latin interjections as he could recollect, and crossing himself many score times, resolved to go along the dark passage and try whether there could be an exit from it. Slowly he went upon his hands and knees, groping and feeling the floor with his hands, and now and then rapping on the floor with his fist to essay whether it was sound. Thus this unrighteous intruder went on groping and rapping in the dark until he came close to the edge of the chasm.

Then a quivering blue light shot out of the pit, and then—*monstrum horrendum*! a head, bigger than the heads of ten mortal men, and that seemed all fire and flame within, rose up close to the intrusive abbat's nose, and a sharp shrill voice was heard to say in good Norman French, "Come up, my friends, from your *sombre abodes!* Come up and clutch me my long while servant and slave

Alain of Beauvais!" The intrusive abbat rushed back screaming, and fell swooning among the swooned. Again the long corridor was filled with that intense and intolerable blue light, and again the blubber fiends ascended and descended like buckets in a well, and again the horrible noise was heard below, and the devil that spoke the good Norman French was heard shouting, "Devil Astaroth, art thou ready? Devil Balberith, hast thou lit thy fires on the top of the waters? Devil Alocco; are thy pools all ready to receive these Norman sinners? Fiends of the fen, are your torches all prepared? Fire fiends; are ye ready with your unquenchable fires? Incubuses and succubuses, demons, devils, and devilings all, are ye ready?" And the hoarse voices, sounding as if they came from the bowels of the earth, roared more fearfully than before; and one loud shrill voice, that sounded as if close to the mouth of the pit, said in good Norman French, "Yea, great devil of Crowland, we be already!"

"'Tis well," said the other voice, "then set fire to every part of this once holy building, over which the sins of these Norman intruders have given us power! Fire it from porch to roof-tree, and if they will seek to abide here, let them perish in the flames, and be buried under the cinders and ashes."

"If the devil had spoken Saxon," said one of the monks, "I should have known nought of his meaning, but since he parleys in Norman, it is not I that will neglect his warning!" And rushing back into the hall where they had so lately been feasting, and bursting open one of the windows, this well-advised intruder leaped from the window into the stinking moat. As when a frighted ram is seized by the horns and dragged by the shepherd hind through the brake, all the silly flock that could not move before follow him one by one, even so did our Norman monks and men-at-arms follow the first monk through the window and into the foul moat! Such as had swooned were brought, if not to their senses, to the use of their legs and arms, by the renewal of that exceeding bright light, or by the pinches and twitches of their comrades, which they took for pinchings of the devil—roaring accordingly. But in a wondrously short space of time every one of the intruders was outside of the house, and was either sprawling in the foul moat, or wading through muck and mud towards the firm, dry causeway. There was great peril of drowning or of being suffocated in the bogs; nor were they yet free from the supernatural terrors, for ghastly blue fires were burning on the surface of sundry of the deeper pools, and there was an overpowering stench of sulphur.

Not one of them doubted but that the lights were from hell; yet, truth to say, those blue flames showed them how to avoid the deep pools in which they might have been drowned, and how to find their way to the causeway; for the moon had not yet risen, and except when illuminated by these unearthly lights the fens were as dark as chaos. When they had floundered a long while in the mud and fen-bogs, they got to the firm and dry causeway which the holy Guthlacus had made for the use of better men. They were so exhausted by the fatigue, fright, and agony of mind they had undergone, that they all threw themselves flat upon the narrow road, and there lay in their soaked clothes, and shivering in the cold winds of night. They were still so near to Crowland that they could see bright lights, with nothing blue or unearthly about them, streaming from the windows of the abbey and from almost every house in the township, and could very distinctly hear the ringing of the church bells and the shouting of triumphant voices.

"The like of this hath not been seen or heard," said Alain of Beauvais; "the serfs of Crowland are in league with the devils of Crowland! The Saxon rebels to King William have called the demons to their assistance!"

"Nothing so clear," said one of the men-at-arms, "but let my advice be taken. The moon is rising now, therefore let us rise and follow the road that lies before us, and endeavour to get out of these infernal fens to the town of Huntingdon or to the castle at Cam-Bridge, or to some other place where there be Normans and Christians. If the men of Crowland should come after us, Saxons and slaves as they are, they may drive us from this causeway to perish in the bogs, or cut us to pieces upon the narrow road, for we have not so much as a single sword among us all!"

"We have nothing," groaned Alain of Beauvais.

"Aye," grunted one of his friars, "we brought little with us and assuredly we take less away with us! We be poorer than when we came and drove the English abbat out of his house with nought but his missal and breviary."

"But we men-of-war depart much poorer than we came," said one of the soldiers; "for each of us brought a good stout English horse with him, and arms and armor—and all these are left to the devils of Crowland; and we shall all be laughed at for being devil-beaten, though how men-at-arms can contend with demons I cannot discover. But hark! what new din is that?"

The din was a roar of voices proceeding from Crowland town. It soon came nearer, and still nearer; and then the hurried tramping of many feet, and the tramp of horses as well as of men, were heard along the causeway; and, as the moon shone out, the head of a dense moving column was seen on the narrow road and sundry skerries or light skiffs were seen gliding along the canals or broad ditches which ran on either side the causeway; and shouts were heard of "Hereward for England! Hereward for England!" Hereupon the Normans all rose from the cold ground, and began to run with all the speed and strength that was left in them along the narrow road, the hindmost hardly ever ceasing to cry "Misericordia," or "Have pity upon us, gentle Saxons!"

But run as they would, the cry of "Hereward for England" was close behind them; and the horses, being put into a trot, broke in among them. More than one of the men-at-arms had the mortification of being knocked down and ridden over by a Crowland man mounted on his own war-horse; several of the monks got fresh immersions in the canals. Had the Saxons so disposed, not a Norman of all that company would have escaped with his life, for they were all as helpless as babes in their swaddling-clothes. But Hereward of the true English heart had conjured Elfric and the Salernitan to shed as little blood and destroy as few lives as possible; and Girolamo well knew that the terror and panic these fugitives would carry into whatsoever Norman camp or station they went would do far more good to the good cause than was to be done by dispatching or by making prisoners of this score or two of obscure rogues.

Thus Elfric, who led the van on a stately horse, called a halt when he had carried his pursuit to some three miles from Crowland abbey. "And now," said he, "with the permission of good Guthlacus, we will cut such a trench as shall prevent these robbers from returning to Crowland. So dig and pull away, ye lusty fenners and nimble boys of Crowland that lately made such good sham devils! Dig away for one good hour by this bright moonlight, and to-morrow ye may make the trench broader and deeper by daylight! Oh, Guthlacus, we will repair thy good work when the good times come back again, and when honest men may walk along the road in peace, without any fear of Norman cut-throats!"

Two score and more lusty hinds came forward with axes and spades and mattocks; and within the hour a trench was dug quite broad and deep enough to stop the march of any heavily armed man or war-horse. The Saxons then returned to Crowland, and as they went they sang in chorus a joyous war-song, and shouted "Hereward for England!"

Girolamo the Salernitan, who had remained in the abbey with the Saxon lay-brothers, had put the house so completely in order and had so cleansed it of the foul odors he had made by his art, and had so sweetened it with frankincense brought from the church, and with barks and fragrant spirits taken from his own packets, that no man could have conceived that anything extraordinary had taken place. Save that the good Lord Abbat and his cloister monks were missing, the whole house looked just as it did before the Normans broke in upon it and drove away the Lord Abbat and his brethren. Honest and merry English voices rang again through hall, corridor, and cloister, instead of Norman speech that whistles in the nose; and Saxon saints were once more invoked instead of the unknown saints of France.

Other men had been busy in the house besides the Salernitan and his assistants. No joyful occurrence ever took place among the Saxons without its being noted by a feast;—provided only that such good Saxons had wherewith to feast upon. The Normans had gone off in much too great a hurry to think of taking anything with them. In the buttery remained, among other rich drinking-horns, all carved and ornamented with silver, that famed horn which Witlaf, king of Mercia, had given from his own table to Crowland monastery, in order that the elder monks might drink there out on festivals, and in their benedictions remember sometimes the soul of the donor. It was a mighty large horn, such as became a great king: and it was an ancient custom of the house that when any new Lord Abbat came they filled the horn with strong wine, and offered to him to drink, and if he happened to drink it all off cheerfully, they promised to themselves a noble Lord Abbat and many good years in his time.

Now for this high festival the subcellarer brought forth this ancient and royal drinking-horn, which held twice the quantity of our modern horns; and in order that there might be no delay in filling it, the good subcellarer caused to be brought up from below an entire cask of wine, and as soon as the cask was in the refectory the head of it was stove it. Old Robin the cook, who had been pastor and master in the art culinary to that good cook of Spalding, had so bestirred himself, and had put so many other hands and feet in motion, that there was a good supper ready for all of the house, and all of the town, and all of the vicinage of Crowland who had been aiding in the good work of disseizing, now so happily accomplished; and by the time Elfric and his friends got back to the monastery, the feast was ready.

The thin and dark Salernitan, being but a puny eater and no drinker, and not fully versed in our vernacular, partook only of three or four dishes and of one cup of wine; and then went straight to the bed which had been prepared for him. The homely Saxons felt a relief when he was gone. They sent the wine round faster, and began to discourse of the wonders they had done and seen. Elfric gave thanks to the lay-brothers of the house without whose aid the sham devils of Crowland could never have gotten within the house.

"And how suitably attired!" said Roger the tailor.

"Yet what nimble devils we were!" said Orson the smith.

"What wizards! what tails! That thin dark stranger made the wizards; but it was I that made the tails, and proud am I of the work! How they twisted! How lism they were! How I switched mine about by pulling the strings under my jerkin!"

"I wish," said Hob the carpenter, "that thou hadst not switched thy devil's tail into mine eye as I was coming up after thee through the trap-door. That trap-door was a good device, and it was all mine own; for who went and cut away the beams just at the right time but Hob?"

"All did well," said Elfric, "but there were some that did wondrously. Colin Rush, thou madest a very pretty nimble devil! Hugh, thy roar was perfection! Joseph the novice, thou wast so terrible a devil to look upon, that although I dressed thee myself, I was more than half afraid of thee!"

"And I," responded Joseph, "was wholly terrified at thee, master Elfric! nor can I yet make out how thou didst contrive to throw about all that fire and flame, through eyes, mouth, and nostrils, without burning thy big wizard. Hodge the miller set fire to his big head and burned it to pieces, and so could do nothing but stay below in the cellar and help in the roaring."

"And not much did I like that dark underground place," quoth Hodge: "and when the lights were all out, and goodman Hugh, groping his way in the dark, caught my tail in his hand and pulled it till it nearly came away from my breech, I 'gan fancy that the Crowland devils were angered, and that some real devil was going to haul me off! I wot that the roar I then gave was quite in earnest! My flesh still quivers, and ice comes over my heart as I think of it!"

"Then melt thine ice with good warm wine," said Elfric: pushing him a cup: "I thought thou hadst known that all the Crowland devils had been laid for aye by the good

Guthlacus, and that thou hadst had nothing to fear whilst engaged in so good a work and all for the service of thy liege lord the abbat, and for the honor and service of the church and the liberties of England. Did I not besprinkle thee with holy water before thou didst don thy devil-skin?"

"For my part," said another, "what most feared me was that awful stench! I was told, that as a devil I must not cough, but help coughing I could not as I stirred up the pan over the charcoal fire, and kept throwing in the foul drugs the dark stranger gave me to throw in. In sooth I neither frisked about nor hauled myself up by the rope over the trap-door; nor did I howl, nor did I help to carry the blue links and torches; but the stinking part did I all myself, and I think I may be proud of it! Not to defraud an honest man and good artisan of his due, I may say it was Hob the carpenter that bored the holes through the floor so that the incense might rise right under our Norman abbat's nose; but for all the rest it was I that did it. That hell-broth still stinks in the nose of my memory. Prithee, another cup of wine, that I may forget it."

"Well," said old Gaffer the tithing-man of Crowland, "we have done the thing, and I hope it hath been honestly done; and without offence to the saints or to the beatified Guthlacus."

"Never doubt it," quoth Elfric: "the Norman spoilers and oppressors are gone to a man, and as naked as they came. I, the humble friend and follower of my Lord Hereward the liberator, am here to dispense hospitality to-night; your own Lord Abbat will be here in a few days; and the dread of our demons of the fens and Crowland devils will make the invaders run from all the fen country. So much good could not have come out of evil; if the means employed had been unlawful or in any way sinful, we should have failed, and never have met with such easy and complete success."

"Nevertheless," continued Gaffer, "the things which I have seen fill me with doubt and amaze. Whoever saw the like before? Fire burning upon the top of water, flames not to be quenched by water from below nor by water from above! Smoke and flames not of their natural colors, but blue, and green, and scarlet, and bright yellow! and the light from these flames so dazzling and so ghastly! In truth I wot not how this can be done by mortal man!"

"Nor wot I," said Elfric; "but this I know full well, that there was no magic or sortilege in the preparation, and that the stranger is as good and devout a Christian as any that dwells in the land. Many are the things which I have seen done by the hand of man that I cannot understand; but am I therefore to think that the evil one hath a finger in them? I have carried on my back, and have handled with mine own hands, the liquids and the substances which have been used, and yet have felt neither cramp nor any other ache. And plain homely things those substances and liquids do appear to be—the quietest and dullest trash until mixed together and compounded. Girolamo, who hath studied in the schools in foreign parts, even as our young clerks studied at Cam-Bridge before the detestable Normans came and built their donjon there, calls this art of compounding by the name of Chemeia, or Chimia, and he says that things much more wondrous are to be done by it.

Further, he says, that his own proficiency has been acquired by long fasting and diligent study, by prayers to heaven and votive offerings to the saints. Methinks it was better to give God credit for these inventions and combinations, and for the wit and ingenuity of man, than to be always attributing them to the devil, as our uninformed clowns do. But these last words the ex-novice spoke under his breath. And this also do I know—the stranger sprinkled his powders with holy water, and prayed the prayers of our church all the while he was doing his preparations."

"But what makes him look so grim and black, and so wild about the eyes," said the old cook.

"Nothing but sorrow and anxiety, sun and climate," replied Elfric. "In the country of the south where he was born there be no blue eyes or flaxen heads of hair; and the Normans drove him from his home and seized his house and lands, even as they are now doing with Englishmen; and he hath known long captivity and cruel torture, and hath wandered in the far climates of the East where the hand of the Arab is lifted against every man."

"Well," said Hob the carpenter, "two things are clear—the Normans are gone from Crowland, and we have gotten their wine butts. And, therefore, I submit to this good company that we should leave off talking and be jolly. Goodman Hodge, pass me down the cup."

Crowland Abbey

CHAPTER XI.

THE LINDEN-GROVE AND LADIE ALFTRUDE

The restored Lord of Brunn, having done so much in a few days, made full report thereof unto the good Lord Abbat and the great prelates and Saxon thanes that had made the isle of Ely and the Camp of Refuge their homes. Right joyous was the news; and prudent and unanimous were the counsels which followed it. The Abbat of Crowland and the Prior of Spalding, and such of their monks as had gone with them or followed them to Ely to escape from the oppression of Ivo Taille-Bois, now, without loss of time, returned to the banks of the Welland.

The abbat and the prior were soon comfortably re-established in their several houses; the rest of the expelled monks came flocking back to their cells, and the good Saxon fen-men began to renew their pilgrimages to the shrines. Many pilgrims too came from the countries bordering on the fens; and while some of these men remained to fight under the Lord of Brunn, others going back to their homes carried with them the glad intelligence that the Camp of Refuge was more unassailable than it had ever been, and that a most powerful Saxon league was forming for the total expulsion of the Normans from England.

Besides his own dependence and the chiefs of his own kindred, many Saxon hinds, and not a few chiefs of name, began now to repair to Hereward's standard. There came his old brother in arms Winter of Wisbech, who had never touched the mailed hand of the conqueror in sign of peace and submission; there came his distant relative Gherik, who bore on his brow the broad scar of an almost deadly wound he had gotten at Hastings; there came Alfric and Rudgang, and Sexwold and Siward Beorn, that true Saxon soldier who had formerly been a companion to Edgar Etheling in his flight, and who had come back from Scotland because he could not bear to live in ease and plenty while his country was oppressed.

Not one of these Saxon warriors but would stand against three Normans on foot! Hereward afterward gave proof, and more times than once, that he could keep his ground against seven! As for the hungry outlandish men the Conqueror was bringing from all the countries in southern Europe, to help him to do that which he boasted he had done in the one battle of Hastings, they were not men to face any of our lusty Saxons of the old race; but they fell before them in battle like reeds of the fen when trampled upon. But the skill and craft of these alien men were great: many of them were drawn from Italy, though not from the same part of that country which gave birth to Girolamo; and therefore were the services of the Salernitan the more valuable; and therefore was it that the young Lord of Brunn had need of all his own strategy, and of all the inborn and acquired qualities which made him the foremost captain of that age.

Ivo Taille-Bois, whom some did call the devil of the fens, was not in the manor-house of the Ladie Lucia, near unto Spalding, when Hereward first came to claim his own, and to turn out his false monks. Being weary with living among bogs and marshes, and having occasion to consult with the Norman vicomte who held command at Stamford, Ivo had gone to that town, some few days before the feast of the Nativity, and had carried with him his Saxon wife and her infant child, leaving none in the moated and battlemented house save a few servants, and some ten or twelve armed Normans.

The house was strong and difficult of access; but if it had not been for the respect due to the Lady Lucia, the kinswoman of his own Ladie Alftrude, Hereward, on his gaining possession of Spalding, would have made a rough attempt upon it: and such was the temper of the Saxons within the house, that doubtlessly they would have played into his hands. For several days the Normans remained wholly ignorant of the great things which had been done in the succursal cell, at Brunn and at Crowland, for they could not venture outside the walls of the manor-house, and even if there had been no danger in their so doing, the inundated state of the country, and the cold wintry weather, offered few temptations to rambling. At length the passing of many skerries across the fens, and the frequent passage of larger boats, crowded with people, on the broad and not distant Welland, and the triumphant shouts that were occasionally heard from the banks of the river, caused the men-at-arms to suspect that some insurrection was a-foot.

They thanked their stars that the moat was so broad, the house so strong, and the store-house so well stored, and they went on sleeping like dormice, or like squirrels, in the topmost hollow of an oak, whose root is deep under the wintry waters. They could not trust any Saxon messenger to Stamford; and therefore it was not from his garrison in the manor-house, but directly from Alain of Beauvais and others of that unholy crew, that the fierce Ivo learned all that had happened upon or round about his wife's domains. Some of the herd were seized with fever and delirium—the effects of fear and fatigue and wet clothes—and they did not recover their senses for many a week; but Alain and such of them as could talk and reason, related all the horrible circumstances of their expulsion and flight, of the onset of the devils of Crowland, and of the close and self-evident league existing between Beelzebub and the Saxons.

All this was horrible to hear; but Alain of Beauvais pronounced a name which was more horrible or odious to Ivo Taille-Bois than that of Lucifer himself:—this was the name of Hereward the Saxon—of Hereward the Lord of Brunn, which the men of Crowland town had shouted in their ears as the Norman monks were flying along the causeway. Partly through the tattle of some serving-women, and more through the confidence of his wife, who did not hate her Norman lord quite so much as she ought to have done, Ivo had learned something of the love passages between Hereward and the Ladie Alftrude, and something also of the high fame which Hereward had obtained as a warrior: and he gnashed his teeth as he said to himself in Stamford town, "If this foul game last, my brother may go back to Normandie a beggar, and I may follow him as another beggar, for this Saxon churl will carry off Lanfranc's rich ward, and besiege and take my house by Spalding, and the devil and the Saxon people being all with him, he will disseize me of all my lands!

But I will to the Vicomte of Stamford, and ask for fifty lances to join to my own followers, and albeit I may not charge home to Spalding, I can ride to Ey and carry off the Saxon girl before this Hereward takes her. Great Lanfranc must needs excuse the deed, for if I take her not, and give her to my brother, the Saxon rebel and traitor will take her. I was a dolt and wife-governed fool ever to have let her depart from mine house after that christening feast. But haply now my brother is here! The instant we get her he shall wed her. We will carry a ring with us to Ey for that purpose!"

While Ivo Taille-Bois was thus making up his wicked mind in Stamford town, the good Lord Hereward was advancing with one hundred brave Saxons from his fair house at Brunn to the fairer and statelier house of the Ladie Alftrude at Ey, having dispatched Elfric the ex-novice before him to make his way straight, and to appoint a place of meeting with his ladie-love, and a place of meeting between his friends and retainers, and her retainers and the friends of her house. Now from Brunn to Ey is a much longer distance than from Stamford to Ey; but while the Normans were obliged to keep to the roundabout roads and to make many preparations beforehand (for fear of the fenners), the Englishmen, aided by skerries, and whatever the country people could lend them, struck directly across the fens.

And in this wise it befell that Lord Hereward got a good footing within the Ladie Alftrude's domain many hours before Ivo Taille-Bois and his brother could get within sight of the manor-house of Ey. On the bank of a river which flowed towards the Welland, and which formed the natural boundary of her far-extending lands, the hundred chosen warriors of the Lord of Brunn were met and welcomed by fifty armed men of the Ladie of Ey, and by fifty or sixty more brave men from the neighboring fens, furnished with long fen-poles, bill-hooks, and bows. While these united warriors marched together towards the manor-house in goodly array, and shouting "Hereward for England!" the young Lord of Brunn, attended by none but Elfric, who had met him by the river, quitted the array and strode across some fields towards the little church of the township which stood on a bright green hillock, with a linden grove close behind it.

It was within that ivied church that the heir of Brunn and the heiress of Ey had first met as children; and it was in that linden-grove that the bold young man Hereward had first told Alftrude how much he loved her. And was it not within that grove, then all gay and leafy, and now leafless and bare, that Hereward had taken his farewell when going to follow King Harold to the wars, and that the Ladie Alftrude had reconfirmed to him her troth-plight? And was it not for these good reasons that the Saxon maiden, who loved not public greetings in the hall, amidst shouts and acclamations, had appointed the linden-grove, behind the old church, to be the place where she should welcome back Hereward to his home and country.

The church and the linden-grove were scarce an arrow-flight from the manor-house. The noble maiden was attended by none but her handmaiden Mildred. When the young Lord of Brunn came up and took the Ladie Alftrude by the hand, that noble pair walked into the grove by a path which led towards the little church. For some time their hearts were too full to allow of speech: and when they could speak no ear could hear them, and no mortal eye see them. With Elfric and the maid Mildred it was not so. They stopped at the edge of the grove, and both talked and laughed enough—though they too were silent for a short space, and stood gazing at each other. It is said that it was the maiden who spoke first, and that she marveled much at Elfric's changed attire.

"Master novice," she said, "where are thy gown and thy cowl? When last I saw thee thou wast habited as a wandering glee-man; and now I see thee armed and attired even like a man-at-arms. What meanest this? Is thy war-dress to serve only for an occasion, like thy minstrel cloak? Tell me; art thou monk, minstrel, or soldier? I thought thy novitiate was all but out, and that thou wast about to take thy vows."

"No vows for me," said Elfric, "but vows to serve my country, and vows to love thee, oh Mildred! I was not meant to be a cloister-monk—albeit, if the Normans had not come into the fen country, and I had never been sent on the business of the Spalding cell to the house of thy mistress, and had never seen thee, fair Mildred, I might in all possibility have submitted quietly to the manner of life which had been chosen for me. But these accidents which have happened have made me feel that I love fighting better than praying, and loving much better than fasting. My superiors have all come to the same conclusion, and have liberated me, and have given me to the brave and bountiful Lord Hereward to be his page and sword-bearer, and whatsoever he may please to make me."

Maid Mildred tried to check her tongue, and to look composed or indifferent; but not being well practiced in the art of concealing her feelings, she set up a cry of joy, and then falling on her knees she inwardly and silently thanked heaven that Elfric was not to be a monk, or one that could not be loved by her without sin. Perhaps the ex-novice understood what was passing in her mind; and perhaps he did not: for when he raised her up by her hand, and kept her hand closed within his own, and looked in her bright blue eyes, he said, "Mildred, art thou glad, indeed, at this my change of condition? Art thou, indeed, happy that I should be a soldier, fighting for the good English cause, and a sword-bearer constantly in attendance on the brave and bountiful Lord of Brunn, to go wherever he goes, and to dwell with him in mansion and hall, when the battle is over and the camp struck; or wouldst thou have me back in the house at Spalding, and a monk for all my days?"

"It seemeth to me that when devout and learned men have opined that thou art fitter for a soldier than for a monk, it is not for a weak unlettered maid like me to gainsay it. In sooth thou lookest marvelously well in that soldier jerkin and baldric; and that plumed cap becomes thy merry face better than the hood. Thou carriest that sword too by thy side with a better grace than ever thou didst carry missal or breviary. But—but—alack and woe the while!—soldiers get killed and monks do not! Elfric, thou wert safer in thy cell."

"No, Mildred, these are times when war rages in the convent as in the tented field. No house is safe from intrusion; and where I was, Norman should never intrude without finding at the least one bold heart to defy him and oppose him. A young man of my temper would encounter more danger in the cloisters than on the field of battle, and would perish unnoticed by the world, and without any service to his country. But as a soldier and follower of Hereward our great captain, I may aid the liberties of the Saxon people, and if I fall I shall fall, the sword in my hand, fighting like a man, with the broad green earth under me, and the open blue sky above me! I shall not die pent in cloister like a rat in his hole! and men will remember me when I am gone as the slayer of many Normans....

But turn not so pale, be not discomfited, my merry Mildred, at this thought of death! Of the thousands that go forth into battle the greater part always return, and return unscathed, whether they have been victorious or vanquished; but if victorious, the less is their loss. Death turns aside from those who fear him not, or are too busy and too earnest in a just cause to think about him. The brave live when the cowards perish: the dread carnage falls upon those who run away, or who are deaf to the voice of their leader. Our cause is just, and will be protected and blessed by heaven. We fight only for our own—for our own country, our own king, our own ancient laws and usages, our own church. The Lord Hereward is as politic as he is brave; he is famed even beyond seas as one of the greatest of commanders; and with such a cause and such a leader, upheld and followed, as they must be by all honest and stout-hearted Englishmen, we cannot fail of victory. And when these Norman robbers shall be driven forth of the land, and good King Harold restored, there will be no more war, and no more danger."

Mildred felt comforted, and they spoke no more of war. Elfric related all his wondrous adventures, and described all that he had seen in foreign lands when he was in quest of the Lord of Brunn, the maiden listening to him with wide-open, wondering eyes. Next he told her how ingeniously he had played the devil at Crowland, and driven away the Norman shavelings; and at this Mildred laughed out right merrily, saying that she would like to have seen it, and yet would not like to have seen it, and asking him what sort of wizard he had worn, and what had been his complexion as a devil.

Elfric told her that he would appear to her, and frighten her as a devil some night soon, if she did not give him one kiss now; and so Mildred laughed a little, and blushed a little, and said nay a little, and then let the bold youth take what he asked for. It is weened and wotted by some that there had been kisses under the hood before now; but now the cucullus had given way to the cap, and there was no harm in it. All this talk and dalliance by the edge of the linden-grove occupied much time, yet the Ladie Alftrude and the Lord Hereward did not reappear; and much as Elfric loved his master, and Mildred her mistress, they did not think the time long, nor wish for their reappearing.

Both, however, spoke much of the bold lord and the fair lady, and in settling their matters for them (as handmaidens and pages will aye be settling the loves and marriages of their masters and mistresses), they in a manner settled their own lots.

The Lord of Brunn and the Ladie Alftrude, so long torn asunder, must soon be united forever by holy church—that was quite certain; Elfric would never quit his lord—that was quite certain; Mildred could never leave her lady—that was equally certain; and from this they derived the consequent certainty that he, Elfric, and she, Mildred, must henceforward have a great deal of each other's company. Further than this they did not go; for just as Elfric was about to propound another proposition, Lord Hereward and the Ladie Alftrude came forth from the grove, and took the direct path towards the manor-house, smiling each upon the youth and upon the maiden as they passed them. The ladie's countenance was happy and serene, although her eyes showed that she had been weeping; the Lord Hereward had a clear, open, joyous face at all seasons, but now he seemed radiant with joy all over him: and as thus they went their way to the near house, followed by the young soldier and the young handmaiden, there were four of the happiest faces that ever the sun shone upon.

When they came to the good old Saxon house, where lowered drawbridge and open gate betokened the Saxon hospitality and the absence of all fear about Norman intruders, there was a universal throwing of caps into the air, with another loud and universal shouting of welcome to the Lord of Brunn; and every man, woman, and child there, whether a relative or retainer of the one house or of the other, whether a vassal to the young lord or to the young lady, coupled the names of the twain as if they were to be indissolubly joined, and still cried, "Long life to

Lord Hereward and the Ladie Alftrude! Long life to the Ladie Alftrude and to Lord Hereward! God bless the bravest and fairest of the Saxons!" The impatience of these good people had been great, for great was their curiosity and great their appetite: they had all been longing to see, side by side, the long-separated and re-united pair, and the feast had been ready in the hall for the space of one hour or more.

It proved a much merrier feast than that given by Ivo Taille-Bois at the christening of his son; and if Elfric had sung well there, he sang much better here. Sundry kinsmen and kinswomen of the Ladie Alftrude, who had long journeys to make, and who had not been able to arrive before, arrived during the festivity; and, during the same season of joy, sundry scouts and messengers came in, and spoke either with the Lord of Brunn or with his sword-bearer; for Hereward in the act of being very merry could be very wise, and he could think of fighting at the same time that he was thinking of love: he had sent scouts into many parts, and other good Saxons that were living near Cam-Bridge, or Huntingdon, or Stamford, or other Norman stations, were now beginning to send messengers to him with all the information that could be procured, and with all the good suggestions they had skill to offer, for all good men fixed their hopes upon him.

After communing for a short time with one of these trustworthy messengers, Hereward gave a merry peal of laughter, and said aloud, "So this Ivo Taille-Bois is coming hither to seek my bride! He shall be welcome! Let him come."

CHAPTER XII.

THE MARRIAGE AND THE AMBUSCADE

It was agreed on all sides that too much happiness had been lost already in their long separation, and that Alftrude and Hereward ought now to be married as quickly as possible; the great heiress whose lands were so coveted could be safe only under the protection of a warlike lord and devoted husband; and who was there in the land so brave and likely to be so devoted as the Lord of Brunn, who had known and loved her from his youth, and who had gotten her troth-plight? If the ladie remained single, and the fortune of war should prove for a season unfavorable, the Normans, by mixing fraud with force, might carry her off, as they carried off and forcibly wedded other English heiresses; but if she were once united to Hereward, even the Normans might hesitate ere they broke the sacred tie of the Church. Time was not needed for wooing, for there had been good and long wooing long ago; and but for the Normans would not Hereward and Alftrude long since have been husband and wife? Thus reasoned all the kinsmen and kinswomen of the Ladie Alftrude; and yielding to their good advice, the Saxon heiress consented that her good old household priest should prepare the little church on the hill by the linden-grove, and that the wedding should take place on the morrow.

Hereward was urged by a pleasant spirit of revenge to be thus urgent; for Ivo Taille-Bois was coming on the morrow with his men-at-arms and with his brother

Geoffroy, that unmannerly and unlucky wooer; and so the Lord of Brunn would fain bid them to his marriage feast, if so it might be. But Hereward kept this pleasant thought to himself, or explained it to none but Elfric and Girolamo of Salerno. The morning after that happy meeting in the linden-grove was a bright winter's morning. The sun rarely shines so bright in the summer time in the fen country.

The little church was ready, the good old English priest was robbed and at the altar; the path leading from the manor-house to the church, in lack of flowers, was strewed with rushes, and the serfs of the Ladie Alftrude were ranged on either side of the path; the lady herself was attired as became a bride (a Saxon bride in the good old time before our fashions were corrupted); her fair young kinswomen, who were to stand by her side at the altar, were dressed and ready, and all other persons and things were ready about two hours before noon. There was music and there were fresh shouts of joy in the hall and outside of the manor-house when Lord Hereward stepped forth with his blushing bride on his arm and headed the gay procession.

But though gay, the attendance was not so great as it might have been, for a great many of the armed men were not there, and even the sword-bearer and the Salernitan were both absent. Maid Mildred thought it very strange and very wrong that Elfric should be away at such a happy juncture; but the truth is that Elfric and Girolamo, and many of the fighting men, had something else to do. The goodly procession soon reached the church porch, and then all entered that could find room without overcrowding their betters. But most of the armed men who had followed the procession either remained in the porch or stationed themselves on the hill side outside the church. It was noticed afterwards that these bold men often looked to their weapons, and that all the hinds and serfs that had been standing by the pathway had bills and bows, or long fen-poles loaded and spiked with iron. The household priest had scarcely said the Benedicite ere the alert Elfric came running up the hill and through the linden-grove and into the porch, and up to his lord's side in the body of the church; and when Elfric had whispered a few words Hereward said, "Alftrude, let thy heart rejoice! I have caught as in a trap the villains that would have wronged thee! Saxons, all rejoice, and remain here, and move not until I return!" And so bowing to the priest, and praying his patience, the Lord of Brunn strode out of the church, leaving the fair ladie of Ey looking all astonishment and somewhat pale. Behind the church Elfric helped the lord to his armor and arms. While putting on his mail, Hereward said, "Are they well in? Art thou sure that thou hast caught this Ivo and his brother?"

"Well in!" said Elfric; "as many as we let come over the bridge are in up to their chins, and Ivo and his brother came on first!"

"It pleaseth me well," quoth Hereward, as he ran down the hill followed by his sword-bearer; "it pleaseth me right well! I did not expect the two caitiffs quite so soon; but since they are come, I vow by every saint that ever spoke the Saxon tongue, that they shall be witnesses to my marriage, and after they shall be bidden to my wedding feast!"

"I wish them a good appetite," said Elfric.

A scant mile beyond the church hill and the linden-grove there ran a narrow but very deep stream, which was crossed by an old wooden bridge. All persons coming from Stamford must pass this river; and Hereward had been properly advised of all Ivo's intentions and of all his movements. Girolamo had been hard at work over-night upon the bridge, and by his good science the timbers of the bridge were so cut into pieces and put together again, that he could allow any given number of persons to cross, and then by a simple operation disjoint the bridge and pull it to pieces so that no more should pass. To contain the water within its bed some broad embankments of earth had been made in very old times near to the bridge; and under cover of these embankments nearly all the armed Saxons had been mustered by Lord Hereward at a very early hour in the morning, yet not until divers other traps and pitfalls had been prepared for the Normans. As the Lord of Brunn and the Ladie Alftrude were walking from the manor-house to the church, the good men lying in ambush by the river side discovered a great troop pressing along the half-inundated road towards the bridge.

These Normans had not been able to get their horses across the fens, and therefore were they all coming on afoot, cursing the bogs and pools and making a loud outcry when they ought all to have been silent. Girolamo and Elfric, who were holding some coils of rope in their hands behind the embankment, presently heard Ivo Taille-Bois say to his brother, "Vive Notre Dame, the wooden bridge is standing! The fools have not had wit enough to see that it ought to be cut down! Set me down this Hereward for an ass! Come on Geoffroy, this detestable foot march is all but over. Behind that hill and grove stands thy manor-house, and therein thy bride."

"We shall soon see that," said Elfric to himself, "and thou shalt soon see whose bride the Ladie Alftrude is."

This while Girolamo was peeping at the head of the Norman column; and he kept peeping until Ivo Taille-Bois and his brother Geoffroy and some half-score men-at-arms came upon the bridge and fairly crossed it. And then, as the rest of the diabolical band were about to follow, Elfric gave a shrill whistle, and tugged at his rope, and other good Saxons pulled hard at other ropes, and in the twinkling of an eye the bridge fell to pieces, and Ivo and his brother and such as had followed them remained on this side of the bridge, and the rest of the Normans remained on the other side of the bridge. And then a score of horns sounded lustily along the ambuscaded line, and fourscore well-armed Saxons vaulted from their wet lair to the top of the embankments, and set up a shout, and sent such a flight of arrows across the river as put the Normans on the other side to a rapid flight along the causeway.

Ivo and his brother and the rest that had crossed the bridge ran along the inner bank of the river followed by hearty laughter and a few sharp arrows from the Saxons; but they had not gone far when what seemed hard and dry ground broke in under their feet, and let them all drop into a quagmire or pool, one not quite so foul as some of those by Crowland Abbey, but still foul enough. It was not until he saw them safely deposited in this place that Elfric went in search of his master; and as he went off for the church he enjoined the Saxons, in Lord Hereward's name, to do the Normans no further hurt.

Now, as the Lord of Brunn strode down from the hill towards the river side, and as the Saxons on the embankment shouted, "Hereward for England!" Ivo Taille-Bois, all in his woeful plight, looked hard at the Saxon warrior, and as Hereward came nearer Ivo said, "Peste! Brother Geoffroy, but this Hereward is the very man that shivered my shield with his battle-axe and unhorsed me at Hastings. And I had thought he had been so near I would not have come with thee on thy accursed wooing!"

"Brother Ivo," said Geoffroy, "it is thou that hast brought me into this evil with thy mad talk about Saxon heiresses.

But let us confess our sins, for our last moment is at hand. My feet are sinking deeper and deeper in the mud: I can scarcely keep my mouth above the surface of this feculent pool!"

When the Lord of Brunn came up to the edge of the pool with Elfric and Girolamo, and all his merry men who had been standing on the embankments, and who could no longer see the Normans who had fled from the opposite side of the river, the Norman men-at-arms that were floundering in the pool with their leader set up a cry about misericord and ransom; and even the great Taille-Bois himself called out lustily for quarter; while his brother, who was a shorter man, cried out that he would rather be killed by the sword than by drowning, and piteously implored the Saxons to drag out of that foul pool no less a knight than Geoffroy Taille-Bois.

"Verily," said Elfric, who understood his French, "verily, Master Geoffroy, thou art in a pretty pickle to come a-wooing to the fairest and noblest maiden in all England."

"That is he!" said the Lord of Brunn, who at first took more notice of Geoffroy, nay, much more notice than he took of Ivo; "and I believe that if he were in better case, and a Saxon, and no Norman, he would not be a very dangerous rival."

"Hereward of Brunn," said Ivo, whose teeth were chattering with cold, if not with fear; "Hereward the Saxon, an thou be he, bid thy churls draw us from this pool, and I will settle with thee the terms of ransom. Thou canst not wish that we should be smothered here; and if thou art a soldier, thou wilt not put to the sword two knights of name, who have been most unfairly entrapped by a set of boors."

"Ivo Taille-Bois the Norman, an thou be he," said Hereward, "I wish neither to drown nor to slay thee by the sword; at least not at this present; but I would fain humble thy pride and arrogance, and give thee some reason to remember thy foul attempt to seize and force the will of a noble maiden whom thou believedst to be defenseless!"

"As for being entrapped by boors," said Girolamo of Salerno, "thou art mistaken, oh Taille-Bois! in that, for I, thine equal, laid the trap into which thou art fallen."

"And foul designs deserve foul traps," said Elfric.

"I know not what design thou layest to my charge," said Ivo. "I am true liege man to King William, the lawful heir of King Edward, of happy memory: the heiress of these lands is in the king's peace and under the protection of the primate Lanfranc; and I, the Vicomte of Spalding, hearing that there were troubles in these parts, was coming only to place the lady in security."

"Aye, such security as the wolf giveth to the lamb," said Hereward. "But Ivo, add not more guilt and dishonor to thy soul by lying! The intent of thy coming, and the object for which thou hast brought thy brother with thee, are as well known to me as to thyself. Ye Normans be all too talkative to keep a secret, and if King Harold had Saxon traitors that betrayed him, so have ye men in your camps and in your stations that think it no sin to betray you Normans. Have a heed to it, Ivo! And bethink thyself in time that all Saxons be not as dull-witted as thou imaginest."

Geoffroy Taille-Bois, greatly encouraged by the Lord of Brunn's assurance that death was not intended either by drowning or by the sword, spoke out as boldly and as clearly as the chattering of his teeth would allow, and said, "Saxon, methinks that thou talkest at an unfair vantage, and that we might settle the matter of ransom the sooner if we were on dry land."

"'Tis well thought," replied Hereward, "for I have small time to lose in parley. This is my wedding day, Sir

CONQUEST OF THE ISLE OF ELY

Geoffroy. My bride, the Ladie Alftrude, is in the church, and the priest is waiting for me with open book at the altar. My humor is that thou and thy brother shall be witnesses to our marriage ceremony. Come, my good Saxons, drag me this pond, and pull out those big Norman fish!"

A score of Saxons instantly threw strong fishing-nets and coils of rope across the pool. The men-at-arms, seeing that quarter was to be given, gladly caught hold of the ropes, and so were landed; but the mention of the marriage, and of Hereward's humor to have them both present at it as witnesses, had so filled the minds of Ivo and his brother with trouble and shame, that they caught neither at the ropes nor at the nets, seeming to prefer tarrying where they were to going up to the church. The Lord of Brunn waxed impatient; and making a sign to Elfric, that nimble sportsman threw a noose over the surface of the pool, and threw it with so good an aim that he caught Geoffroy round the neck; and then giving his coil a good tug, which brought the head of the unlucky rival of his master under water, Elfric shouted, "Come out, thou false Norman, come out, and to the wedding, or be drowned or hanged—I care not which."

Geoffroy, thus hardly entreated, waded, and struggled to the brink as best he could, and was there pulled out all covered with mud, or with the green mantle of the pool. Ivo, apprehending a rope round his own neck, caught hold of one of the nets that the shouting and laughing Saxons kept throwing at him, and he too was dragged out of the water, all bemired or green, and almost breathless.

Such of the men-at-arms as had kept their weapons had laid them at the feet of Lord Hereward, in token of unconditional surrender. Geoffroy, the unlucky wooer, had no weapon to give up, having left his sword in the pool; but his brother Ivo had his broad blade at his side, and when called upon to surrender it, he made a wry face and said that a knight ought to surrender only to a knight, meaning hereby to taunt the Lord of Brunn with his not having been admitted into the high military confraternity.

"Ivo," said Hereward, "I told Raoul, that dispossessed usurper and robber, and I now tell thee, that I shall soon be a knight, meaning that I shall be one according to usage and rites and ceremonies. True knighthood is in the heart and soul of man, and not in the ceremonies. Were I not already a truer knight than thou, I would hang thee and thy brother to these willow-trees, and butcher thy men here, even as too many of ye Normans have butchered defenseless Saxon prisoners after surrender. Give up thy sword, man, or it may not be in my power to save thee from the fury of my people! Give up thy sword, I say!"

Ivo began a long protest, which so incensed Elfric and Girolamo that they drew their own blades; but the Lord of Brunn bade them put up their weapons, and then said to the proud Norman knight, "Traitor and spoiler as thou art, talk no more of dark stratagem and treachery! A people, struggling for their own against numerous and organized armies, must avail themselves of the natural advantages which their soil and country, their rivers and meres, or mountains, may afford them.

No stratagem is foul: the foulness is all in the invaders and robbers. Armies are not to be bound by the rules of thy chivalry. Until my forces be both increased and improved, I will risk no open battle, or adventure any number of my men in an encounter with the trained troops from Normandie, and from nearly all Europe besides, that have been making a constant occupation and trade of war for so long a season. This I frankly tell thee; but at the same time I tell thee to thy teeth, that if I and thou ever meet on a fair and open field, I will do thee battle hand to hand for that sword which thou must now surrender. Norman! I would fight thee for it now, but that the field is not fair here—but that these rough fen-men would hardly allow fair play between us—but that this is my wedding-day, and the priest and my bride are waiting. Man, I will brook no more delay—give me thy sword or die!"

Ivo Taille-Bois stretched out his unwilling arm, and holding the point of his sword in his own hand, he put the hilt of it into the hand of the English champion, who threw it among the heap of Norman swords that lay at his back. At this new mark of contempt, Ivo muttered, "Was ever knight treated in so unknightly a manner! Must I really be dragged to the church by these dirty clowns?"

To this my Lord Hereward replied, "Did ever knight engage in such unknightly deed! Yea, Ivo, and thou, Geoffroy, likewise, I tell ye must to the church; and if ye will not go but upon compulsion, these honest men and clean shall drag ye both thither."

"Then," said Geoffroy, speaking mildly, "permit us at least to wipe this mud from our hose, and this green slime from our coats."

"It needs not," said the Lord of Brunn, with a laugh; "thine hose are not as dirty as the motive which brought thee hither, and thine head is as green as thy coat. So close up, my men, and let us march."

The Lord Hereward, however, did not prevent Ivo from rubbing himself down with the skirt of a coat appurtenant to one of his men-at-arms. As for Geoffroy, Elfric would not permit a Norman to approach him; and when he would have stopped by the hill-side to rub himself against a tree, as our fen swine use when they would clean themselves from the mud of the marshes, Elfric or some other zealous Saxon got between him and the tree and pushed him forward.

In this wise—the Normans groaning and distilling, and the Saxons laughing and shouting—the whole mixed party ascended the hill and came to the church. The Lord Hereward's absence from the church had been but short—it had not lasted an hour in all—yet were the priest and the goodly company assembled growing very impatient, and the Ladie Alftrude very much alarmed, albeit she was a maiden of high courage, as befitted one who lived in troublous times, and she had been opportunely advised that the Lord Hereward had only gone to an easy triumph.

But bright, though bashfully, beamed her blue eye when Hereward appeared in the porch. But who were these two forlorn Norman knights walking close behind him with their heads bent on their breasts and their eyes on the ground? Ha, ha! sweet Ladie Alftrude, thine own eye became more bashful, and thy blush a deeper red, when thou didst see and understand who those two knights were, and why they had been brought into the church! The dames and damsels of the company all stared in amaze; and the Saxon priest, still standing with open book, started and crossed himself as he looked at Ivo Taille-Bois and his brother Geoffroy.

"They be but two witnesses the more," said bold Hereward. "We will tell thee at the feast how proper it is that they should be here; but now, good priest, go on with that which their arrival interrupted. Elfric, make space here near the altar for our two unbidden guests. Dames, come not too near them, for they be very cold strangers!"

The marriage ceremony then went on to its happy completion, Ivo Taille-Bois and his brother Geoffroy grinding their teeth and groaning inwardly all the while: and even thus was it made to come to pass that those who would have carried off the Ladie Alftrude were forced to be witnesses to her union with her old and true love.

CONQUEST OF THE ISLE OF ELY

It was a tale for a minstrel; and a pretty tale Elfric made of it, at a later date, to sing to his four-stringed Saxon lyre. "And now," shouted the bountiful Lord of Brunn, as they all quitted the church, "now for the wassail-bowl and the feast in hall! Ivo Taille-Bois, and thou, Geoffroy, much as thou wouldst have wronged us, we bid thee to the feast— the Ladie Alftrude and I bid thee to our marriage feast!"

"Throw me rather into thy dungeon," said Geoffroy.

"Enough of this farcing," said Ivo. "Hereward the Saxon, name the terms of the ransom, and let us be gone from thy presence. Ladie Alftrude, remember that I am thy cousin by marriage."

"Methinks," replied Alftrude, "that thou oughtest to have remembered that same fact before coming with thy men-at-arms against me."

But, after saying these words, the gentle and kind-hearted Saxon bride, stepping aside from the throng, spoke for a while in Lord Hereward's ear; and after that the Lord of Brunn, who was radiant with joy as ever was knight that sat with King Arthur at the Round Table, turned to Ivo and Geoffroy, and said, "Unwilling guests mar a feast. Since ye will not come willingly, ye need not come at all. A Saxon manor-house hath no dungeon in it or near it, and at present I have no wish to keep ye in duress. Saxon chiefs were ever generous on their happy days, and when shall I find a day as happy as this? I will ask no ransom, for thou, Sir Geoffroy, art but a pauper; and thou, oh Ivo, albeit thou callest thyself Vicomte of Spalding, thou wilt soon find thyself as moneyless and as landless as thy brother! I will ask for no vows or promises, for well I ween ye would break them all. I will only ask of thee, oh Ivo, that if we twain meet on some field of battle, thou wilt not turn from me! Thy half score men-at-arms we will send to the Camp of Refuge, that they may be exchanged for a like number of Saxon prisoners; but for thyself, and for thy brother, I say get ye gone, and tell your Normans in Stamford town, aye, and in London city, all that you have seen and heard this day, and all that they may expect if they come to make war in the fen country."

"How can we get gone? The bridge is broken, and we cannot cross that cursed river," said Ivo.

"Thy Saxon boors will murder us on the road," said Geoffroy.

"Not on our lands; not within the bounds of Ladie Alftrude's domains. Elfric, Girolamo, conduct these Norman knights across the river, and send a few good men to escort them to the edge of the fen country. Let not a drop of blood be spilt, nor so much as a hair of their head be injured. It were of ill omen that blood should be shed on this day. There will be a time for that hereafter. Come; make good speed, for the feast will be but dull until Elfric returns."

"But wilt thou not give us back our swords, that we may defend ourselves with them in case of attack?" said Ivo.

"No, no," quoth the Lord of Brunn; "we must keep the swords to show that ye have been here-about—that ye have been our surrendered prisoners. As for self-defense, ye had better not think of that until ye get back to Stamford town. Ye must trust to my escort, and to the respect and obedience paid to me by all this fen country. If our fenners were to fall upon ye, it is not your brace of swords that would be of any use."

"Then I say again we shall be murdered on the road," said Geoffroy.

"And I again say nay," quoth the Lord of Brunn. "I tell ye again, that ye shall have safe escort to the edge of the fens, and that not a hair of your head shall be injured—provided only ye do not insult homely honest folk by calling them foul names, or by otherwise treating them discourteously, for if ye offend in that way the Saxon blood may boil up and cause my orders to be forgotten. So now go!—and if I cannot say Fare ye well for aye, I say May ye fare well as far as Stamford, and until we meet on a fair field, where thou and I, Sir Ivo, may prove which is the better man or the better knight."

As the two Normans walked off the ground, they looked so crestfallen and woe-begone that the Ladie Alftrude quite pitied them, and chided her maid Mildred for so loudly laughing at them and pointing the finger of scorn at them. But others wanted this chiding as much as Mildred, seeing that every Saxon maid and every Saxon matron present were laughing and tittering at Geoffroy Taille-Bois' unlucky wooing, and his damp and dismal case.

The marriage feast in the hall was sumptuous and most joyous. It was enlivened and lengthened by tricks of jugglery and legerdemain, by the recitation of tales, legends, and romances, and by lays sung to musical instruments, for although the notice given had been so short, many jugglers and minstrels had hurried to Ey from different parts of the fen country. In nearly all the rest of broad England the art of the Saxon minstrel was now held in scorn; and the minstrel himself was oppressed and persecuted, for his tales and songs all went to remind the Saxon people of their past history, of their heroes and native saints, and of their past independence.

But this persecution had driven many towards the eastern coasts, and thus it was that the fen country and the Camp of Refuge as much abounded with Saxon minstrels as with dispossessed Saxon monks. Of those that flocked in troops to the manor-house at Ey, to sing at the marriage feast, it may be judged whether they did not exert their best skill on so solemn an occasion! Loudly and nobly did they sing Athelstane's Song of Victory, which related how Athelstane the King, the Lord of Earls, the rewarder of heroes, and his brother Edmund of the ancient race, triumphed over the foe at Brunanburg, cleaving their shields and hewing their banners; how these royal brothers were ever ready to take the field to defend the land and their homes and hearths against every invader and robber; how they had made the Northmen sail back in their nailed ships, on the roaring sea, over the deep water, after strewing the English shore with their dead, that were left behind to be devoured by the sallow kite, the swarth raven, the hoary vulture, the swift eagle, the greedy goshawk, and that grey beast the wolf of the weald.

And as the minstrel sang, the drinking-horn, capacious as became the hospitality of that old Saxon house, was handed quickly round by page and waiting-man, who carried great vessels in their hands, and filled the dark horn right up to its silver rim with mead, or wine, or pigment, every time that they presented the horn to gentle or simple.

Hereward and Alftrude

CHAPTER XIII.

HOW LORD HEREWARD AND HIS LADIE LIVED AT EY

Even when the marriage festival was over it was a happy and a merry life that which they led in the good Saxon manor-house, and discreet and orderly withal. It being the wolf-month of the year (Januarius), when the days are still short and the nights long, Hereward and the Ladie Alftrude, together with the whole household, rose long before it was daylight. Before attending to any household or other duties, prayers were said in the hall by Alefric, the good mass-priest, all the servants of the house and all the indwelling serfs being present thereat.

Some short time after prayers the first of the four meals of the day was served by torch or candle-light, and the lord and ladie broke their fast; and when they had finished the meal the door of the house was thrown open, and the poor from the neighboring township, or the wanderers that had no home, were admitted into the house, and the lord and lady with their own hands distributed food among them, and while they distributed it the mass-priest blessed the meat and said a prayer. And this being over, they went forth at early-dawn to the little church on the hill behind the linden-grove and there heard mass.

The ladie then went home to attend unto domestic concerns, and the lord went forth with his hawks and proper attendants to hawk by the river, or he took forth his hounds (of that famous breed of English dogs which hath been famed in all times, and as well for war as for hunting, and which hath been so much coveted by foreign nations that already it beginneth to disappear from this land), and he called together the freemen of the vicinage that loved the sport, and such of the serfs as were best practiced in it, and went well armed with venabula or hunting-spears into the fens and covers to hunt the hart and hind, or the wild goat, or the wild bull of the fens, or the wild boar, or the grey wolf, which was not yet extinct in these parts of England.

It was a good law of King Canute, which said that every free man in England might hunt in his own woods and grounds, and hunt as much as he list, provided only he interfered not with the royal parks and demesnes. But the Norman princes, not content with spreading their parks all over the country, and with seizing upon the lands of the church and the poor to make them great hunting-grounds and deer-parks, established cruel laws therewith, so that whosoever slew a hart or a hind should be deprived of his eyesight; and Duke William forbade men to kill the hart or the boar, and, as our Saxon chronicler saith, he loved the tall deer as if he were their father! and likewise he decreed that none should kill so much as a hare, and at this the rich men bemoaned and the poor men shuddered. Old England will not be England until these un-Saxon laws be entirely gone from us!

From this good sport Lord Hereward returned to the house about an hour before the sun reached the meridian, and then was served the abundant dinner in the hall; and the not stinted dinner in the kitchen for the churls and serfs followed the dinner in the hall. If the weather was fine, the lady as well as the lord went out in the afternoon to hawk, or to fish, or to see the pleasant and profitable sport of their expert fenners who snared the wild fowl, or took the animals of the chase by means of fovea or deep pitfalls which they cunningly dug in the ground in the likeliest places, and still more cunningly concealed by laying across them sticks, and twigs, and moss, and turf. As the sun set they returned again to the house and sang in concert with all the household the Ave Maria or they went into the little church and heard the full service of Vespers.

Upon these duties of religion there followed a slight merenda or afternoon's drinking, or refection between dinner and supper; and then Elfric or some other skillful wight made music in the hall by playing upon the harp and singing; or Alefricus, that learned clerk, brought down a book and read in it, or the freedmen and elders of the township gathered round the cheerful hearth with the lord and ladie, and related tales and legends of the old times, or took counsel with Hereward as to the future. If a Saxon gleeman came that way he was ever welcome; and these evening hours were often made to pass away the more pleasantly by the arrival of such a stranger, who, mayhap, could sing a new song, or tell an unheard tale, or give some little intelligence of what was passing in the upland country and in the world beyond the fens.

No Saxon chief of fame ever stinted the bard; and whether he went south or north, east or west, the minstrel found every hall open to him, and had but to speak his wants and to raise his grateful voice, and all and more than he wanted was given unto him. When he entered a house they brought him water to wash his hands and warm water for his feet, or they prepared for him the warm bath, which was ever offered in good Saxon houses on the arrival of an honored and welcome guest—and where was the guest that could be more welcome than the bard? So dearly did the Lord of Brunn love the sound of the harp that it was his occasional custom now, and his constant custom in after-life, to place a harper near his bedchamber to amuse and solace him upon occasion, and for the exhilaration of his spirits and as an excitement to devotion. And it was because Hereward so loved minstrels, and pious and learned men of the Saxon stock, that his friends and adherents were so numerous while he was living, and his deeds so faithfully recorded and lovingly preserved when he was dead. Thus music and talk brought on the hour for supper; and after supper the good mass-priest said prayers in the hall to gentle and simple; and then, when a good watch had been set, all of the household went to their beds and prayed to lead as happy a life on the morrow as that which they had led to day: for, whether serfs, or free-born men, or manumitted churls, all were happy at Ey, and most kindly entreated by lord and ladie twain; in such sort that what happened in other houses, as the running away of serfs, or the putting collars round their necks and gives to their legs to prevent their running away, never happened here or at Brunn.

And if they lived thus happily and orderly for these few days at Ey, when danger was close at hand, and when they might be said to be living in the midst of perils and uncertainties, I wist their rule was not changed at a later time of their lives, when Hereward and Alftrude came to dwell in safety and tranquility at the noble old house at Brunn.

But during these few tranquil days at Ey the young bride's mind was at times clouded by the thought that her husband must soon leave her to contend with the pitiless Normans, and to rush into all the hazards of war; and, Saxon-hearted as she was, this afflictive thought, being aided by the gentleness of her nature, which ever revolted at bloodshed, made her long for a peace upon almost any terms, not even excepting that of submission to the Norman dominion. "My Hereward!" said the Ladie Alftrude, "it is now more than four years since the banner of King Harold was laid low, and yet blood hath never ceased flowing in England! When will this cruel war come to an end? Oh, Hereward, why wilt thou leave me again, and so soon? What art thou fighting for?"

"Sweet Alftrude," quoth the Lord of Brunn, "I am fighting for my country, for the Saxon church, and for mine own inheritance! A man can hardly have more to fight for!"

"But, Hereward; is not all the country, save this most fenny part of it, quietly submitting to the Conqueror! Doth not Lanfranc the archbishop give assurance that no lasting usurpation of the goods of the church is contemplated, and that it is his wish and intention only to improve the Saxon church and the great and rich Saxon houses of religion by bringing over from foreign parts some more learned priests, and more learned and more active monks? And are not these broad lands enough for thee and me? Nay, frown not! And might not thine own lands at Brunn be secured if thou wouldst submit and take the peace of the Norman ruler? Forgive me if I err, as the error all proceeds from the love I bear thee and the dread I have of losing thee. England, we are told, was happy under the dominion of Canute the Dane, and what was King Canute in England but a conqueror? And if Englishmen were happy under one foreign conqueror, might they not be happy under another?"

"Not so, sweet Alftrude. Canute was contented to govern according to the old Saxon laws. When he gave some new laws, they were the freest and best that were ever given until those of Edward the Confessor, and they were given with counsel of his Witan, a free and honored assemblage of Saxon lords and Saxon bishops, Saxon abbats and priests, and Saxon eldermen. And in those dooms or laws King Canute, speaking with and for the Saxon Witan, said that just laws should be established, and every unjust law carefully suppressed, and that every injustice should be weeded out and rooted up from this country; and that God's justice should be exalted; and that thenceforth every man, whether poor or rich, should be esteemed worthy of his folk-right, and have just dooms doomed to him. And likewise did Canute, in these dooms, which were conceived in the mild Saxon spirit, raise his voice and set his face against death punishments and all barbarous penalties.

'And we instruct and command,' said he, 'that though a man sin and sin deeply, his correction shall be so regulated as to be becoming before God and tolerable before men; and let him who hath power of judgment very earnestly bear in mind what he himself desires when he thus prays—Forgive us our trespasses as we forgive them that trespass against us. And we command that Christian men be not, on any account, for altogether too little, condemned to death, but rather let gentle punishments be decreed, for the benefit of the people; and let not be destroyed, for little God's handiwork, and his own purchase which he dearly bought.'

Thus said King Canute in his dooms, and in his day's men in power were made to act according to those mild laws. But how is it now, under the Normans? My gentle-hearted bride, I would not wring thy heart and bring tears into thine eyes, but is it not true that for any wrong done or offence given—nay, for the allowable deed of defending their own, and standing up for their country, Saxons of all degrees are butchered like sheep in the shambles, or are put to slow and horrible deaths, or are mutilated in the limbs, or have their eyes put out, as if it were no sin to spoil and destroy God's noblest handiwork? Nay, is not the life of a Saxon held as a thing of less price than the life of a small deer? By our old laws, if the greatest thane in the land slew but the poorest serf or lowliest churl, he made bot for it; but now, and even in those parts of England where the war hath ceased, if the meanest Norman soldier kill twenty Saxon serfs or slay a Saxon lord, no heed is taken of it. The Saxons have no redress except that which they may find in their own swords. Even in London city, there is one law for the Saxons and another law for the Normans.

If a Saxon be accused of murder or robbery he is bound to justify himself according to our ancient custom, by compurgation, and by the ordeal of red-hot iron or boiling water; but if a Frenchman be accused of the like crime by a Saxon, he vindicates himself by duello or single combat, or simply by his oath, according to the law of Normandie. King Canute said, 'Let the free people of England manage their own townships and shires, and learn to govern themselves; let no man apply to the king unless he cannot get justice within his own hundred; let there be thrice a-year a burgh-gemot, and twice a-year a shire-gemot, unless there be need oftener; and let there be present the bishop of the shire and the elderman, and there let both expound as well the law of God as the law of man.'

But William the Norman alloweth not of these free things; William the Norman consulted not the Witan of the nation, but governed the country through a Norman council. When he was coming back from his pilgrimage to Rome, King Canute sent a long letter to Egelnoth the metropolitan, to Archbishop Alfric, to all bishops and chiefs, and to all the nation of the English, both nobles and commoners, greeting them all, and telling them all that he had dedicated his life to God, to govern his kingdoms with justice, and to observe the right in all things. 'And therefore,' said he, 'I beg and command those unto whom I have entrusted the government, as they wish to preserve my good will, and save their own souls, to do no injustice either to rich or to poor: and let those who are noble, and those who are not, equally obtain their rights according to their laws, from which no departure shall be allowed either from fear of me, or through favor to the powerful, or to the end of supplying my treasury, for I want no money raised by injustice.' But what saith this Norman William? He saith, 'Get me all the money ye can, and heed not the means!' And hath he not extorted money by right and by unright?

And have not his greedy followers done worse than he in the land? And are they not building castles everywhere to make robbers' dens of them? And have they not made beggars of the rich, and miserably swinked the poor— aye, even where resistance was none after Hastings, and where the Saxons prostrated themselves and trusted to the promises and oaths pledged by William at Westminster and Berkhampstead, that he would govern the land according to our old laws? For the church, my sweet Alftrude, I see not that it is to be improved by thrusting out peaceful monks and priests of English birth, and by thrusting in turbulent fighting priests, who speak not and comprehend not the tongue of the English people. Better men may come hereafter; but, certes, it is but an ungodly crew which, as yet hath followed Duke William, and Lanfranc, the whilom Abbat of Caen, into England!

Touching my poor house and lands at Brunn, it is not by a mean submission to Duke William that I should ever keep them from Raoul the Norman plunderer that had seized upon them. They must be kept at the sword's point, and at the sword's point must these thine own good house and lands be maintained. The protection of Lanfranc, given to the noble maiden and heiress of Ey, will not be extended to the wife of Hereward of Brunn, whom Normans call a rebel and an outlaw. Oh Alftrude, the wife of a soldier like me, and in a war like this, hath need of a soldier's heart within her own bosom!"

"And I will find it or make it there, mine own Hereward! I knew the danger, and all the risk, and thou thyself toldest me of it all before I became thine. As I live and love thee, and by all the saints to whom I pray for better times, I was thinking less of myself than of thee when I spoke that which I have spoken. Thou knowest the state of these great matters better than a poor woman can know them, albeit I can understand the difference between Canute the Dane and William the Norman. If submission will not avail, or if submission is dishonoring"....

"It were in the lowest degree base and dishonorable; for although I came over into England at thy summons, it was to fight, and not to submit; and I have since so pledged my faith to the Abbat of Ely and to all the good lords in the Camp of Refuge, that I would rather perish in these the first days of my happiness than forego or wax cold in the good cause."

"Then fight on, mine own brave Hereward! And come what may, I will never murmur so that I be near to thee; and whether we live in plenty at Ey or at Brunn, or wander through the wild fens poorer and more unprovided than is the poorest churl that now dwelled within these gates, thou shalt hear no complaint from me. Let not the wide seas, and evil tongues, and false tales divide us evermore, and I shall be happy."

"And with such a bride, and such a wife, I shall be invincible. Cheer up, my own Alftrude! If submission will bring down utter ruin as well as utter shame, a bold and persevering resistance, and an unflinching hand-to-hand fight with the enemy, may bring her old laws and liberties back to England, and bring to us glory and happiness, and a peaceful and honored life in after-times. I would be a peaceful man, even now, if so I might, and if I had less to fight for; for, albeit, I love the art and stratagems of war, and the rapture that is given by the well-contested combat, I love not much blood, and never could get myself to hate any man or parties of men, for any length of time. Were their rule less cruel and tyrannical to the English people, and were my good friends and allies secured in their lives, honours, and properties, I could sit down quietly and in good fellowship with these same Norman knights; nay, I would not refuse a seat on my hearth to Ivo Taille-Bois, or even to his brother Geoffroy."

"Name not that ugly name," said the Lady Alftrude, blushing a little. And here the discourses ended. The gentle lady had strengthened her heart with the great love that was in it, so as to bear whatsoever might befall her as the mate of Lord Hereward, the last champion of the Saxon liberties.

While the lord and lady talked this above stairs, there was something of the like discourse below stairs between the waiting-woman and the sword-bearer; for maid Mildred, merry as she was, could not but feel that Elfric was running a course of great peril, and that peace and tranquility would be a blessed thing, if it could only be obtained. Albeit the young sword-bearer spoke not so knowingly of the old Saxon laws, and the dooms of King Canute, and of Witans and Gemots, as did his lord, he found sufficiently good arguments to show that the war was a just and unavoidable war; and that while everything was to be hoped from bravery, there was nothing to be gotten by a timid submission. There was another consideration:—"But for this war," said Elfric, "I must have become a monk! I am now a soldier and liege-man to Lord Hereward, and ready, as soon as the lord and ladie permit, to be thy loving husband, oh Mildred of Hadenham!"

CHAPTER XIV.

HEREWARD IS MADE KNIGHT

Before the marriage festival was well ended, the festival of the Epiphany arrived. The Lord of Brunn could not go to Ely; but he was now in constant correspondence with the good Lord Abbat and the prelates and lay nobles there; and in sending off his last Norman prisoners, he had sent to tell the abbat that he must hold him excused, and that he would eat the paschal lamb with him, hoping before the Easter festival to have gained many more advantages over the Normans. The returning messenger brought Hereward much good advice and some money from Ely.

Among the many pieces of good counsel which the Abbat Thurstan gave was this, that the young Lord of Brunn should lose no time in getting himself made a lawful soldier or knight, according to the forms and religious rites of that Saxon military confraternity which had been authorized by the ancient laws of the country, and which had existed long before the Normans came into England with their new-fashioned rules and unholy rites.

The great lay lords at Ely and in the Camp of Refuge had all been initiated, and their swords had been blessed by Saxon priests; and as all these knights and lords had agreed in appointing Hereward to the supreme command, it behooved him to be inaugurated in the Saxon knighthood; otherwise there would be a mark of inferiority upon him, and people might proclaim that he was not a lawful soldier. Now the young Lord of Brunn had thought well of these things before, and had been reminded of

CONQUEST OF THE ISLE OF ELY

them by the taunting Normans. Any Lord Abbat or other prelate could perform the rites. The Abbat of Crowland had now returned to his house, and would rejoice to confer the honor upon Hereward; but Hereward's own uncle, and by his father's side, was Lord Abbat of Peterborough; and not only was it more suitable that the rites should be performed by him and in his church, but also was it urgent that the young Lord of Brunn should march speedily upon Peterborough in order to rescue his kinsman and the Saxon monks that yet lived under his rule from the oppression and tyranny of the Normans. This uncle of Hereward and Lord Abbat of Peterborough, whose secular name was Brand, had been sundry times plundered and maltreated, and now expected every day to be dispossessed.

Brand had not long been Lord Abbat, and he had put on the Peterborough mitre, of silver gilded, at a time of the greatest trouble. His predecessor the Abbat Leofric had gone forth with the English army of King Harold; and, after Hastings, he had sickened, and returning unto Peterborough, he had died on the night of Allhallows mass: God honor his soul! In his day were all bliss and all good at Peterborough. He was beloved of all. But afterwards, as we shall see, came all wretchedness and all evil on the minster: God have mercy on it!

All that he could do had been done by good Leofric's successor. Abbat Brand had given a large sum of money to Duke William, in the view of keeping the house and convent free from molestation. Always a rich and always a bountiful man had been the uncle of Lord Hereward; and while yet a cloister monk and one of the obedientiarii, he had given to the monastery many lands, as in Muscham, Schotter, Scalthorp, Yolthorp, Messingham, Riseby, Normanby, Althorp, and many other parts. Judge ye, therefore, whether the brothers of Peterborough were not largely indebted to Abbat Brand, and whether Abbat Brand was not the proper man to confer Saxon knighthood on his nephew. After the disastrous journey of Ivo Taille-Bois and his brother to Ey, the news of which was rumored all over the country, Brand had dispatched an intelligencer to his bold nephew, and had sent other messengers to his neighbors, and to all the good Saxon people that dwelt between Peterborough and Stamford. He had beseeched Hereward to march to his rescue and to the rescue of his house; and Hereward, like a duteous nephew and loving kinsman, had sent to promise that he would be with him with good two hundred armed men on the octave of the Epiphany.

But, before going for Peterborough, the young Lord of Brunn had much to do in the way of collecting men and arms, strengthening the house at Ey and the house at Brunn, and the abbey of Crowland, and the succursal cell at Spalding; and much time he spent with Girolamo of Salerno in devising war stratagems, and in planning the means by which the whole fen country might be rendered still more defensible than it was, as by the cutting of new ditches, the making of sluices and flood-gates, movable bridges, and the like.

The men-at-arms, left by Ivo Taille-Bois to guard the manor-house near to Spalding, becoming sorely alarmed, and despairing of finding their way across the fens, sent a Saxon messenger to the returned Prior of Spalding, with an offer to surrender the house to the soldiers of Lord Hereward, if the good prior would only secure them in their lives by extending over them the shield of the church. The conditions were immediately agreed to: a garrison of armed Saxons took possession of the moated and battlemented house, and the Normans were sent as war prisoners to Ely. Hereward gave orders that all due respect should be paid to the house, and to all other the goods and chattels of the Ladie Lucia; for albeit that ladie was forcibly the wife of Ivo, she was cousin to Alftrude and relative to King Harold, and her heart was believed to be wholly Saxon. As Brunn was a house of greater strength, and farther removed from that skirt or boundary of the fen country upon which the Normans were expected to collect their strength, Hereward removed his bride to Brunn, and there he left her in the midst of friends and defenders; for his followers were now so numerous that he could keep his promise with his uncle Brand without leaving his bride exposed to danger, and without weakening one of the sundry posts he had occupied, as well along other rivers as upon the banks of the Welland.

By the octave of the Epiphany, being the thirteenth day of the Wolf-month, or kalends of January, and the day of Saint Kentigern, a Saxon abbat and confessor, the Lord of Brunn was at the Abbey of Peterborough with more than two hundred well-armed Saxons! And on that very night—a night of the happiest omen—was begun his initiation in the old abbey church. First, Hereward confessed himself to the prior, and received absolution. After this he watched all night in the church, fasting and praying. At times a cloister monk prayed in company with him; but for the most part he was left alone in the ghostly silence of the place, where light was there none save the cressets that burned dimly before the effigies of his patron saint. But while he knelt there, Elfric his faithful sword-bearer stood guard outside the door of the church, whiling away the time as best he could, by calling to mind all the legends and godly stories connected with the Peterborough Abbey and its first founders, and specialiter that marvelously pretty miracle which Saint Chad performed in the presence of his recent convert King

Wolfere. Which miracle was this, according to the faithful relation of Walter of Whittlesey, a monk of the house: One day, after praying a long while with King Wolfere in his oratory, the weather being warm, Saint Chad put off his vestment and hung it upon a sunbeam, and the sunbeam supported it so that it fell not to the ground; which King Wolfere seeing, put off his gloves and belt, and essayed to hang them also upon the sunbeam, but they presently fell to the ground, whereat King Wolfere was the more confirmed in the faith. In the morning, at the hour of mass Hereward placed his sword upon the high altar; and when mass had been said, and he had confessed himself and been absolved again, the Lord Abbat took the now hallowed sword and put it about Hereward's neck with a benediction, and communicating the holy mysteries, finished the simple and altogether religious ceremonial: and from thenceforward Hereward remained a lawful soldier and Saxon knight.

In the good Saxon times men were never so vain and sinful as to believe that a knight could make knight, or that any lay lord, or even any sovereign prince or king, could give admittance into the confraternity of knights by giving the accolade with strokes of the flat of the sword upon the shoulders and with the tying on of spurs and hauberks, and the girding on the sword, and such like vanities.

These things were brought in among us by the Normans; and being brought in, our knights lost their religious character, and ceasing to be the defenders of the church, and the protectors of all that wanted protection, they became unhallowed oppressors, depredators, barefaced robbers, and the scourges of their kind. And it was so at the very first that these Normans did affect to contemn and abhor our old Saxon custom of consecration of a soldier, calling our Saxon knights in derision priest-made knights and shaveling soldiers, and by other names that it were sinful to repeat.

The good Abbat Brand had now nothing more to fear for his shrines and chalices. Every Norman that was in Peterborough, or in the vicinage of that town, fled to Stamford; and the Lord of Brunn, with the help of the Salernitan, strengthened the abbey, and made good works to defend the approaches to it, even as he had done at Crowland and elsewhere. Happy was Abbat Brand, and hopeful was he of the deliverance of all England; but he lived not long after this happy day, and when he was gone cowardice and treachery invaded his house, and monks who had lost their English natures made bargains and compacts with the Normans, and brought about many calamities and shames, as will be seen hereafter.

If Brand had lived, or if Hereward could have remained at Peterborough these things would not have happened, and disgrace would not have been brought down upon a convent which for four hundred and more years had been renowned as the seat of devotion, hospitality, and patriotism. But the Lord of Brunn could not stay long on the banks of the Nene, his presence being demanded in many other places. Between the octave of the Epiphany and the quinzane of Pasche, Hereward recovered or liberated twenty good townships near the north-western skirts of the great fen-country, fought and defeated Norman troops in ten battles, and took from them five new castles which they had built. A good score of Norman knights were made captive to his sword; but he had not the chance to encounter either Ivo Taille-Bois or his brother.

As the paschal festival approached, Hereward received various urgent messages from the Abbat of Ely. These messages did not all relate to the coming festivity, and the promise of the Lord of Brunn to be the Lord Abbat's guest: while Hereward had been beating the Normans, and gaining strength on the side of Peterborough and Stamford, the Normans had been making themselves very strong at Cam-bridge, and were now threatening to make another grand attack upon the Camp of Refuge from that side.

Abbat Thurstan therefore required immediate assistance, and hoped that Hereward would bring with him all the armed men he could. Moreover, jealousies and heart burnings had again broken out among the Saxon chiefs, who had all pledged themselves to acknowledge the supreme authority of the Lord of Brunn. If Hereward would only come, these dissensions would cease. Other weighty matters must be discussed; and the discussion would be naught if Hereward were not present. Thus strongly urged, Hereward left his young wife in his house at Brunn, and taking with him nearly three hundred armed men, he began his march down the Welland in the hope of raising more men in that fenniest of the fen-countries, which lies close on the Wash, and with the intention of crossing the Wash, and ascending the Ouse in ships and boats. It grieved him to leave the Ladie Alftrude, and much did it grieve Elfric his sword-bearer to quit maid Mildred; but Hereward thought that his wife would be safe in his strong house at Brunn, and Elfric was made happy by the assurance that as soon as they came back again he should be allowed to marry Mildred. The Ladie Alftrude had shed a few tears, and her handmaiden had made sundry louder lamentations; but the lady was full of heart and courage and hope, nor did the maid lament out of any fear.

When the Lord of Brunn moored his little fleet of barks, and raised his standard on the shores of the Wash, many more good fen-men came trooping to him, as he had expected. Many came from Holland. And how did they come? They came marching through the mires and waters upon high stilts, looking all legs, or, at a distance, like herons of some giant breed. Voyagers have related that in that sandy country which lies along the Biscayan gulf, and between Bordeaux and Spain, men and women and children all walk upon high stalking poles or stilts, as the only means of getting across their soft, deep sands; and here, in the most marshy part of the fens, men, women, and children were trained to use the same long wooden legs, not to get over dry loose sand, but to get over water and quagmire, and broad and deep ditches.

These stilted men of Holland, who were all minded to go help in the Camp of Refuge, threw their stilts into Lord Hereward's bark; which was as if men of another country should throw away their legs, for without these stilts, we ween, there was no walking or wayfaring in Holland: but the thing was done to show that they were devoted to the good cause and put an entire trust in the victorious Lord of Brunn, and that they would go with him, legs, arms, and hearts, wherever he might choose to lead them.

At Lynn, on the other side of the Wash, still more Saxons joined Lord Hereward's army, some of them coming in boats, and some marching by land. Ha! had there been but five Herewards in England, England would have been saved!

It was on the eve of the most solemn, yet most joyous festival of Pasche, or on the day of the month Aprilis, in the year of grace one thousand and seventy-one, that the Lord of Brunn, arrived with his host at the great house of Ely, to the inconceivable joy of every true Saxon heart that was there. Pass we the welcome and the feast, and come we to the councils and deliberations in the Aula Magna of the house. On the third day after the paschal Sunday all the Saxon lords and chiefs, prelates and cloister-monks, met early in the morning, or immediately after prime, and ceased not their deliberations until the dinner hour. On one great point there was no difference of opinion—the victorious Lord of Brunn was to hold supreme command over all the troops and bands, of whatsoever description, collected in the Camp of Refuge, and have the entire management of the war wherever it should be carried. On other heads of debate opinions were very various, but the greatest divergence of all was upon the question whether the Danes should or should not be invited again to the assistance of the Saxons. When all had spoken on the one side or the other, and with much vehemence of speech, the Lord of Brunn, who had been forced to correct his taciturn habits, and to speak on many occasions at greater length than he had ever fancied he should speak, rose and said—

"Prelates and chiefs, ancients and younger men, if one so young as myself may deliver opinions in this assemblage, I would say let us take heed ere we tamper any more with Denmark. The woes of the Anglo-Saxons first began when the Danes crossed the seas in their nailed ships and came among them first to rob and plunder, and next to seek a settlement in this fat and fertile land of England. Our rubric is filled with Saxon martyrs butchered by the Danes. This noble house of religion where we now consult was plundered and burned by the Danes; and the Danes slew all the ancient brotherhood of the house, and did the foulest things upon the tombs of the four Saxon virgins and saints—Saint Etheldreda, Saint Sexburga, Saint Ermenilda, Saint Withburga. I am lately from the Abbey of Peterborough, where I read upon the monumental stones the names of the good Saxon abbats and monks of that house that were murdered by the Danes.

The same thing happened at Crowland, and at fifty more religious houses. The Danes have been the great makers of Saxon martyrdoms. The worst famed of our Saxon kings are those who submitted to them or failed in conquering them; the name of King Alfred is honored chiefly for that he defeated the Danes in an hundred battles, and checked their rapacity and blood-thirstiness."

"Oh, Hereward of Brunn!" said the bishop of Lindisfarne, "this is all true; but all this happened when the Danes were unconverted Pagans."

"But good my Lord Bishop of Lindisfarne," quoth the Lord of Brunn, "let us note well the conduct of the Danes since they have been Christian men, and we shall find as Saxons that we have not much to praise them for. Had it not been for the unmeet alliance between Lord Tostig and the strangers, and the invasion of Northumbria and York, and the need King Harold lay under of breaking that unholy league, and fighting Tostig in the great battle by Stamford Bridge, King Harold would never have been worsted at the battle of Hastings, for his armed forces would have been entire, and fresh for the fight, instead of being thinned as they were by that first bloody combat, and worn out by that long march from York unto Hastings."

"It was an army of Norwegians that fought King Harold by Stamford Bridge," said the Prior of Ely.

"I fought in that battle," quoth Hereward, "and know that it was a mixed army of Danes and Norwegians, even like most of the armies that, for two hundred years and more, devastated this land and the kingdom of Scotland. But let that pass. Those armies came as open enemies: let us see the conduct of an army that came as friends. Only last year the good Saxon people from the Tyne to the York Ouse were deserted in the hour of success and victory by an army of Danes, commanded by the brothers of the King of Denmark, who had been invited into the country by the suffering Saxons, and who had sworn upon the relics of saints not to leave this land until it was clear of the Normans. The two royal Danes took the gold of the son of Robert the Devil and the harlot of Falaise, and thereupon took their departure in their ships, and left the Saxons, with their plan all betrayed, to be slaughtered in heaps, and the whole north country to be turned into a solitude and desert, a Golgotha, or place of skulls."

"This is too true," said the Bishop of Durham; "and terrible is all this truth!"

"But," said the Bishop of Lindisfarne, "the King of Denmark's brothers are not the King of Denmark himself. We hear that the king is incensed at what those brothers did, and that he hath banished them from his presence and from the land of Denmark, and that he hath sworn by the rood that he will send four hundred keels across the ocean, and take himself the command of the army."

"Yet even if he come," quoth the Lord of Brunn, "he may prove as faithless and as greedy for gold as his brothers; or he may set up his pretended right to the throne of King Harold, our absent but not lost lord, and in that case we shall find that the Saxon people will fall from our side; for if they are to be cursed with a new and foreign master, they will not overmuch care whether his name be William of Normandie or Svend of Denmark."

"Assuredly not quite so," said the Prior of Ely, who opposed Hereward the more because the Lord Abbat Thurstan was disposed to agree with him; "assuredly not quite so, my Lord of Brunn, for there hath been large admixture of Danish blood in our Anglo-Saxon race, and Danes and English sprang, ab origin, from nearly one and the same great hive of nations in the north."

"And so also do these North men, or Normans," said Hereward, "only they have more affinity to Danes and Norwegians than to us; and while the Danish pirates were ravaging the coasts of England, Rollo, the North man, ravaged the coasts of France, and gained a settlement and sovereignty, and gave the name of Normandie to the country which has now sent forth these new conquerors and devastators upon England. Trace back our blood to the source, and I, and the Lord Abbat Thurstan as well as I, and many other true Englishmen, natives of the English Danelagh, may be called half Danes; but a man can have only one country, and only one people that he can call countrymen, and these admixtures of blood in parts and parcels of England will not be considered by the English people at large; and let it be Danes, or let it be Normans, it will be the same to them."

"But," said the Abbat of Cockermouth, "the Danes be now very poor, and their king will not be able to raise an army sufficiently strong to aim at any great thing by himself."

"And therefore is it," quoth the Lord of Brunn, "that come king or come king's brothers, they will get what they can from us poor Saxons as the price of their assistance, then get all the gold they can get from the Normans as the price of their neutrality, then betray all such of our secrets as they possess, and then embark and sail away for their own country, leaving us in a far worse plight than before. I say, let us not send for them, or ask their aid at all! If a people cannot defend themselves by their own swords, they will never be defended at all. If England cannot be saved without calling in one foreign people to act against another, she will never be saved. If this king of Denmark comes this year he will act as his kinsmen did last year, and we shall rue the day of his coming. Wherefore, I say, let us pray for the speedy return of King Harold, and let us keep what little store of gold and silver we possess to nurture and pay our own native soldiers, and to purchase in the Netherlands such munition and warlike gear as we may yet need; but let us not waste it by sending into Denmark."

"Were our enemies less numerous and powerful," said one of the chiefs, "we still might hope to stand our ground, in this wet and difficult corner of England, alone and unaided!"

"We shall be the better able to stand our ground against any foe if we be on our guard against false friends, and keep our money and our own counsels," said Abbat Thurstan. "Lord Hereward hath reason for all he saith; take my word for it he is right."

But there were many there that would not take my Lord Abbat's word, and that would not be persuaded by the arguments of the Lord of Brunn; and in an inauspicious hour it was determined to send an embassage from the lords and prelates in the Camp of Refuge to the king and lords and free rovers of Denmark, to implore their aid and assistance, and to present them with a sum of money, as the earnest of a large future reward. The strong money-box at the shrines of Ely church, wherein the pilgrims deposited their offerings, was now in reality broken open and emptied; at which some of the unworthy members of the house who had most opposed Hereward and their Lord Abbat went about whispering and muttering, in the corners of the cloisters, and even among the townsfolk of Ely, that sacrilege had been committed.

Yet was the total sum thus procured so very disproportionate to the well-known appetites of the Danes for money, that a collection was made in the Camp of Refuge, and even Jews were secretly invited from Norwich and St. Edmundbury in order to see whether they could be tempted to advance some money upon bonds: and here were raised fresh whisperings and murmurings about impiety, together with severe censures on Abbat Thurstan for want of uniformity or consistency of conduct, seeing that he had formerly been the sworn foe to all the Israelites whom the Normans had brought over in their train; and that, nevertheless, the convent were now sending for the Jews to open accounts and dealings with them.

It suited not these back-biters to remember that they themselves, in determining that the aid of the Danes should be required, had agreed that money should and must be sent to them; and that when Abbat Thurstan said there was but very little money in the house, they themselves had recommended sending for the Israelites who made a trade of usury. All points connected with the unhappy business had been decided, after the public discussions in the hall, by the members of the house in close chapter, wherein the Lord Abbat had only given his vote as one. But these unfaithful monks and untrue Englishmen hoped to make people believe that their opinions had been overruled, and that Thurstan was answerable for everything.

It was also noticed—although not by the abbat and the monks that were faithful unto him, and that were never allowed to hear any of the whisperings and murmurings—that several of those who had most eagerly voted for calling in the assistance of the Danes shrugged their shoulders whenever men mentioned the expected invasion of the fen country and the new attack on the Camp of Refuge, and spoke of the Norman as a power too formidable to be resisted by the English, or by any allies that the English could now procure.

CHAPTER XV.

THE CASTLE AT CAM-BRIDGE AND A BATTLE

When the Normans first came into England, the town of Cam-Bridge, or Grant-Bridge, was not the stately town which we have seen it since, nor was it the flourishing place which it had been in the time of the Saxon Heptarchy. According to the Venerable Bede, Sebert, or Sigebert, King of the East Angles, by the advice of Felix the Bishop, instituted within his kingdom a school for learning, in imitation of what he had seen in France; and this school is believed to have been fixed on the very spot where the town of Cam-Bridge now stands.

Others there are who say that a school had flourished there in the time of the Romans, and that Sebert, or Sigebert, only restored this school in the year of our Lord six hundred and thirty. Certain it is that from a very early time Cam-Bridge was the residence of many students, who at first lived in apartments, hired of the townspeople, and afterwards in inns or hostels of their own, where they formed separate communities, of which each was under its own head or principal.

But in the fiery distraction of the Danish invasion of England, when abbats and monks and religious women were slaughtered at the feet of their own altars, and churches and abbeys and monasteries consumed, the pagan flames fell upon this quiet seat of learning, and left nothing behind but ashes and ruins. After this the place lay a long time neglected. There are some who write that when, about the year of grace nine hundred and twenty, King Edward, surnamed the Elder, and the eldest son and successor of Alfred the Great, repaired the ravages of the Danes at Cam-Bridge, he erected halls for students, and appointed learned professors; but these facts appear to be questionable, and it is thought that, although learning would no more abandon the place than the waters of the river Cam would cease to flow by it, the scholars were in a poor and insecure condition, and were living not in the halls or colleges of stately architecture, but under the thatched roofs of the humble burghers, when the blast of the Norman trumpets was first heard in the land.

At that sound all humane studies were suspended. The town and territory round it were bestowed upon a Norman chief, and Norman men-at-arms were quartered in the houses which had lodged the students. But it was not until the third year after the battle of Hastings, when Duke William became sorely alarmed at the great strength of the Saxons, gathered or still gathering in the neighboring Isle of Ely, that Cam-Bridge felt to their full extent the woes attendant on wars and foreign conquest. Then it was made a great military station, and a castle was built to lodge more soldiers, and command and control the town and all the vicinity. Just beyond the river Cam, and opposite to the little township, there stood, as there still stands, a lofty barrow or mound of earth, overgrown with green sward, and looking like those mounds which the traveler observes by Salisbury plains, and on the plain where the ancient city of Troy once stood.

This great cone was not raised and shaped by nature. The common people, who will be forever betraying their ignorance, said that the devil had made it, for some ridiculous purpose; but learned men opined that it had been raised by the ancient Britons for some purpose of defense, or as some lasting monument to the great dead. When the Romans came and conquered the country, they had made an entrenched camp round about this mound, and had built a tower or guard-house upon the top of the mound; but these works had either been destroyed by the Danes or had been allowed to fall into decay and into ruin through the too great negligence of the Saxons. Now from top of this green hillock, looking across rivers and meres and flat fens, where the highest tree that grew was the marsh-willow, a good eye could see for many miles and almost penetrate into the recesses of the Isle of Ely and the Camp of Refuge.

The old Roman road or causeway, called the Ermine Street, which led into the heart of the fen country, ran close under the mound and a little outside the trenches of the Roman camp. Seeing all the advantages of the spot, as a barrier for the defense of the country behind the Cam, and as an advanced position on the side of the country, and as a place of arms wherein might be collected the means of attacking the indomitable Camp of Refuge, the Normans cleared out the broad ditches which the Romans had dug, and which time and accident or design had filled up, restored the double circumvallation of earthen walls or embankments, erected a strong castle within, and raised the Julius, or keep or main tower of the castle, upon the summit of the mound, where the old Roman tower or guard-house had stood.

They had not been allowed to do all this work without many interruptions and night-attacks of the daring people of the neighboring fens, or by the bold Saxons who had fled for refuge into the Isle of Ely. But when the work was finished the Normans boasted that they had bitted and bridled the wild Saxon horse of the fens. For some time past knights, and men-at-arms, and bowmen, and foot-soldiers, drawn from nearly every country in Europe to aid the son of Robert the Devil in conquering the little island of England, had been arriving at the entrenched camp and castle of Cam-Bridge; whither also had come from the city of London and from various of the towns and ports which had quietly submitted to the strangers, great convoys of provisions and stores of arms and armor and clothes; and all these aliens had been telling such of the English people as could understand them, and had not fled from the town, that they were going to assault the great house at Ely and the Camp of Refuge, and hang all the traitors and rebels they might find there, upon the willow trees.

Nothing, however, could be undertaken in the land of marshes and rushes until the rainy season should be over and the waters somewhat abated. Now it happened this year that the rains ceased much earlier than was usual, and that the summer sun, as if impatient for empire, began to rule and to dry up the wet ground long before the season of spring was passed. There fell very little rain after the quinquane of Pasche, but after the feast of Saint Walburga the Virgin there fell no rain at all, and the weather became uncommonly dry and hot.

It was pleasant to the eye to see the waters of the Cam, the Ouse, the Welland, the Nene, the Witham, and the other rivers retiring as it were into their natural beds, and flowing very smoothly and clearly towards the great Wash; to see green meadows re-appear where pools and meres had been, and flocks and herds beginning to graze where boats and skerries and men walking upon tall stilts had been seen but a few weeks before; to see, as far as the eye could reach, a beautiful green prospect, with rich pastures, gliding rivers, and adornments of woods and islands. But if this was pleasant to the eye, it was not conducive to the security of the Saxon chiefs. On the vigil of Saint Bede the Venerable, priest and confessor, which falls on the twenty-seventh of the decades of May, Eustache of Ambleville, a Norman captain of high repute, who had come over with William and the first incomers, and had fought at the battle of Hastings, arrived at Cam-Bridge with more soldiers, and with orders from William to take the entire command of all the forces collected in the camp and castle. Eustache was so confident of an easy victory that he would not allow himself to think of the possibility of any defeat or reverse.

As he looked from the top of the keep towards Ely, he said, triumphantly, "The waters are gone, and I am come. The Camp of Refuge is no more! In three days' time we shall be feasting in the hall of this rebellious abbat, who hath so long defied us!" The other knights that were to follow him in this adventure were just as confident as Eustache of Ambleville, and the men-at-arms were already calculating how they should divide the spoil that was to be made at Ely. Little did they think how the shrine-boxes had all been emptied! Less still did they think of the great loss of goods they themselves were going to sustain!

Much did these Normans pretend to despise our Saxon fathers for their ignorance of the stratagems of war, and for their general dullness: and yet it must be confessed that they themselves gave very many proofs of ignorance and dullness, as well as of great negligence, the fruit of the unwise contempt in which they held their adversaries. Before the arrival of Eustache some few of the Normans had ridden along the causeway as far as they could conveniently go on horseback, but for the state of the country beyond their ride they trusted to mere report, taking no pains whatever to inform themselves accurately. They had all been told of the extraordinary deeds which Hereward had performed, but they gave the whole merit of these exploits to Crowland devils and other fiends and goblins that were not to be feared in summer weather or in daylight. They had been told that the Lord of Brunn was a well-skilled commander, but they would not believe that any Saxon whatsoever could be a great soldier. Instead of being cautious and silent as to their intended attack, they had been loudly proclaiming it on every side. Certes, Duke William was a knowing soldier himself, and one that did great things in war, being cautelous and discreet; but, wherever he was not, his chiefs in command did not much. It was rather for the sake of avoiding the heat of the day than for any other reason that Eustache resolved to begin his march at midnight.

He did not think of surprising the Saxons, and, as for being surprised by them, he scornfully laughed at the notion. He wished, he said, that the rebels and traitors should know that he was coming, in order that they might collect all their forces in the camp, and so afford him the opportunity of destroying them all at one blow. His chief fear was that Hereward the Saxon would flee from the mere terror of his name.

On the midnight which followed the feast of Saint Bede the Normans began to issue from their castle and camp. There shone a bright moon along the causeway where they formed their array. First went a great troop of horse with lances and long pennants floating from them. Next went a body of archers bearing long bows and quivers well stocked with long arrows. Then followed a large and miserable company of Saxon serfs and hinds, who had been forcibly impressed into the service, and who were laden like beasts of burthen, carrying stores and provisions on their backs, and hurdles, and planks, and other pieces of timber, by means of which these too confident Normans hoped to be able to cross every ditch, stream, and river.

After this unhappy company there marched another band of archers; and then there went another and still greater body of horse; and in the rear of all were more bowmen. As the raised road was very narrow the horsemen marched only two abreast, and the footmen only three abreast; and thus, as the total number of the army was great, the line was very long and thin; and the knights riding in the rear would seldom either hear or see what was passing in the van.

Yet merrily and thoughtlessly they went on singing their Norman war-songs, their bridles ringing sharp and clear in the cool night air as if to accompany the music of their songs, and their bright lance-heads glinting in the moonlight: thus merrily and thoughtlessly until the van came abreast of Fenny Ditton, where the road or causeway was flanked on either side by a broad deep ditch or canal, and by a long belt of thick growing willows and alders. But here Eustache, and the other knights that rode in the van, heard a loud voice shouting in very good Norman-French—

"Halt, horse and foot! No farther to-night! Saxons true do forbid your advance!"

And, well-nigh at the same moment those knights and soldiers that rode in the rear heard another loud voice shouting—"Halt, Normans! Halt ye must, but ye shall not get back to Cam-Bridge unless ye can swim the ditch."

It seemed as though some hollow willow-trees had spoken, for neither in front nor rear was there a man seen. But presently the loud voices spoke again, and a still louder voice was heard about mid-way between the two, and all the three voices cried—

"Saxons, your bow-strings to your ears, and next a charge for England and Lord Hereward!"

As soon as these words were heard in the center, the Saxon serfs, whom the Normans had impressed, threw the provisions and stores they carried right across the broad ditches; threw down the hurdles and beams and timber on the road, and then, with a wild yell, rushed into the water and swam across to the covering of the trees. But in the center those trees were all alive before these men reached them, and no sooner were they seen to be safe than a rush was made towards the ground which they had abandoned.

All fen-men swim, but to make their passage the quicker light bridges were laid across the ditches, and moving from the right-hand side of the road and from the left-hand side two bodies of Saxons, well-armed with bows and billhooks, established themselves on the causeway just where Eustache's long line was broken. In vain did the Normans nearest to it think of closing up that fatal gap; the Saxon serfs had so thrown about their timber on the road that they could not cross it without falling or stumbling.

The Saxons, who had just got into the gap, making themselves shields of the hurdles, fought fiercely with bill and bow, and their comrades behind the willow trees smote the thin Norman lines on both sides with their arrows. Eustache of Ambleville, without seeing or knowing that his army was cut in twain, went charging along the causeway with his van, the Saxon arrows rattling on their steel jackets all the while; for here, as in the center and rear, every tree that grew on either side the road covered some Saxon bowman.

But short was Eustache's career, for he found the causeway cut away before his horse's feet, and a trench much broader than any horse could leap, cut across from ditch to ditch; and beyond this trench was a good barricade formed of felled trees, after the fashion used by that true Saxon the late Lord Abbat of Saint Alban's: and from behind that breastwork and across the trench there came such a flight of arrows and spears and javelins, and other missiles, that neither Eustache nor any of his people could stand it. Then the trumpet in the van sounded the retreat. The Norman knight, commanding in the rear, had sounded the retreat before this, and finding that he could not force his way forward, he had begun to retrace his steps towards Cam-Bridge Castle: but this rearward knight had not gone further in arrear than Eustache had careered in advance ere he found the road broken, and a barricade of freshly cut willow trees laid across it with bowmen and billmen behind it.

Horsemen and archers being mixed, as in the van, the rear turned back again along the causeway, as if determined to drive the Saxons from off the road and so unite themselves with the van from which they were severed; and thus van and rear were moving in opposite directions—were rushing to meet and hustle against each other on that narrow way, even as waves beat against waves in a mighty storm. Their meeting would have been very fatal; but they could not meet at all, for the Saxons that had made the great gap had been reinforced from either side; they had made barricades of the timber, and they plied with their sharp archery the heads of both the Norman columns, while other Saxons assailed those columns on their flanks, and still another band throwing a flying-bridge over the chasm, where Eustache had been made to halt, and turn back, charged along the causeway, still shouting, "Hereward for England! Pikes, strike home, for the Lord of Brunn sees ye!"

And foremost of all those pikes was the Lord Hereward himself, who shouted more than once, "Stop, Eustache! Run not so fast, Eustache of Ambleville! This is not the way to the Camp of Refuge!"

Broken, confused beyond all precedent of confusion, disheartened, assailed on every side, and driven to desperation, the Normans began to leap from the fatal narrow causeway into the ditches, where many of the heavily-armed men and divers knights were drowned. Some surrendered to Lord Hereward on the road, and were admitted to quarter. Others were killed in heaps; and the rest, succeeding in crossing the ditches, and in getting through the willow groves, ran for their lives across the open country towards Cam-Bridge.

Dry as the season was, there were still many bogs and morasses in those plains, and into these many of the panic-stricken fugitives ran and sank up to their necks. As Girolamo, the Salernitan, led one of the parties of Saxons in pursuit, he muttered to himself in his own tongue, "Those Normans in English bogs look like so many Mariuses in the marshes of Minturnum!"

Those were the most fortunate that sank where the sedges grew thick, or the bulrushes concealed them. Those who showed their heads above the bog were for the most part slain by spears or arrows. In all, not one-third of the force, which Sir Eustache had led forth a few hours before with so much pride and confidence, got back alive to the camp and castle at Cam-Bridge: all the horses had been drowned or suffocated, or wounded, and rendered useless, or killed or taken. Provisions, stores, and all the implements of the army had been lost; and, although Eustache of Ambleville had escaped with life, he had left his standard behind him in the hands of the Lord Hereward, who, after this signal victory, returned in triumph, and with his *spolia opima*, to Ely Abbey, where the monks in the choir sang *"Te Deum Laudamus."*

As for Eustache of Ambleville, he soon quitted the command of the post at Cam-Bridge, and cursing the Fen Country, as a place where knights and horses were of no use, he made the best haste he could back to London city.

For many a long day the Normans left at Cam-Bridge would not venture outside the walls of their castle.

It boots not to tell of what became of that other Norman force collected in Huntingdon for the invasion of the isle of Ely. Was it not overthrown and totally discomfited at Fenny Stanton? And was not this, and were no other victories gained by the Saxons from the Camp of Refuge, recited in the songs in praise of Lord Hereward, which the Saxon people now began to sing about the streets of our cities and great towns, even in the hearing of their Norman oppressors?

Attack in the fen!

CHAPTER XVI.

THE TRAITOROUS MONKS OF PETERBOROUGH

But the Lord of Brunn could not be everywhere. While he was gaining great victories on the southern side of the Fen Country, the Normans were gaining strength in the north, and were receiving the aid of cowards and traitors. Brand, the uncle of Lord Hereward, and the good Lord Abbat of Peterborough, who had ever labored to keep his convent true to their own saints and to their own country, was now lying by the side of the abbats, his predecessors, under the stone-flooring of the abbey-church; and with him had died all the English spirit of the place.

The monks began to murmur, for that they were called upon to contribute to the sustenance of the Saxon fighting men that had been left to guard their house; and for that they had been called upon to send some small matter of gold and silver for the use of the brave Saxons that were maintaining the liberties of England in the Camp of Refuge.

Having, by their own representations and entreaties, brought about the removal of nearly every bowman and billman that Hereward had left behind him, these monks next began to turn up their eyes, and say that they had no armed strength wherewith to withstand the Normans, and that therefore it were better to make terms with Ivo Taille-Bois, and cease all connection and correspondence with the Lord of Brunn and that faction. But happily even at Peterborough, when the good Abbat Brand was dead, not all the monks were traitorous. Some of them made haste to inform their late abbat's nephew, and the hope and stay of England, of what was passing; and the Lord

CONQUEST OF THE ISLE OF ELY

Hereward made haste to apply some remedy to this foul disorder.

Great had been the wrath excited among the Normans by that last great act of Abbat Brand's life—the Saxon knighthood of Lord Hereward. Duke William had sworn by the splendor of God that the abbat should rue the day on which he had given his benediction to the sword of a rebel; but a greater than kings had saved good Brand from this kingly fury. When he knew that he was dead, William named as his successor that terrible Norman, the Abbat Torauld of Fescamp, who always wore a coat of mail under his rochet, and who wielded the sword and battle-axe much oftener or much more willingly than he carried the crosier.

This terrible Torauld had been wont to govern his monks even in foreign parts as captains govern their turbulent soldiery; and whenever any opposition was offered to him, it was his custom to cry, "Come hither, my men-at-arms!" and upon men-at-arms he always depended for the enforcing of his ecclesiastical discipline. Where he ruled there were few penances except such as were inflicted with his own hand; for he was a very choleric man, and would smite his monks and novices over their fleshiest parts with the flat of his heavy sword, and tweak their noses with his sharp steel gloves, and strike them over their shaven crowns with his baton. Terrible as a man, and still more terrible as an abbat, was this same Torauld of Fescamp!

Monks crossed themselves, and said Libera nos, whenever his name was mentioned. Now Duke William told this terrible Torauld that as Peterborough was so near to the turbulent Fen Country, and so little removed from the Camp of Refuge, it was a place well suited to an abbat who was so good a soldier, and that a soldier rather than an abbat was wanted to preside over that abbey.

And Torauld was farther told, by Ivo Taille-Bois, who was roaring, like a bear bereft of her cub, for the loss of the manor-house at Spalding, that on arriving at Peterborough he must take good care to disinter the Abbat Brand, and throw his body upon the dung heap; that he must well scourge the monks for their past contumacy, and make a quick clutch at such treasure as might yet remain within the house, seeing that the Norman troops were greatly distressed by reason of their poverty, and that, notably, he, the Vicomte of Spalding, had not a denier.

"Factum est," said Torauld, "consider all this as done."

And in order that it might be done the more easily, Ivo Taille-Bois superadded one hundred and forty men to those that the fighting abbat brought with him, thus making Torauld's whole force consist of one hundred and sixty well-armed Frenchmen. At the head of this little army, with sword girded round his middle and with battle-axe tied to his saddle-bow, the monk of Fescamp began his march from Stamford Town. As soon as the disloyal monks heard that he was coming, they drove away by main force the very few Saxon soldiers that remained about the house, and began to prepare sackcloth and ashes for themselves, and a sumptuous feast for the Abbat Torauld, hoping thereby to conciliate him, and make him forget the bold doings of my Lord Abbat Brand.

But before that uncanonical abbat and his men-at-arms could get half way to Peterborough, the Lord Hereward, who had been duly apprised of all these late proceedings and intentions, arrived at the abbey with Elfric his swordbearer, and about three-score fighting men; and before the monks could make fast their gates he was within the house. There be some who do say that the entrance was not got without a fight, and that some of my Lord

Hereward's people set fire to a part of the monastery; but I ween there was no fighting or beating of monks until Torauld, that very stern man, got possession of the house, and that there was no fire until a time long after the visit of the Saxons, when the monks of Peterborough, being disorderly and drunken, set fire to the house themselves by accident. The Lord of Brunn made straight for the house which King Etheldred of happy memory had built for the Lord Abbats. A building it was very large and stately; all the rooms of common habitation were built above-stairs, and underneath were very fair vaults, and goodly cellars for sundry uses; and the great hall above was a magnificent room, having at the upper end, in the wall, very high above the floor, three stately thrones, whereon were seated the effigies of the three royal founders, carved curiously in wood, and painted and gilt.

In this hall stood Hereward and his merry men. Little did the monks wot of this visit. They thought the Lord of Brunn was many a league off, fighting in the fens; and when he came among them like one dropped from the clouds, and they saw in his honest, plain-speaking face that he was angered, the traitors began to blush, and some of them to turn pale; and when this first perturbation was over, they began to welcome him in the very words of a speech they had prepared for the welcoming of Torauld. But Hereward soon cut their speech short, and asked the prior of the house what was become of the twenty men he had left there for the protection of the house. The prior said that the men had behaved in a riotous manner, eating and drinking all the day long, and had deserted and run away because they had been reproved.

"It likes me not to call a priest a liar, but this is false!" said the Lord of Brunn; "thou and thy French faction have driven away those honest men; and here be some of them to speak for themselves, and to tell thee, oh prior, how busy thou hast been ever since the death of my good uncle (peace to his soul!) in preparing to make terms with the French—in preparing to welcome the shaven cutthroat that is now a-coming to rule over this house!"

The men stood forward, and the loyal part of the monks (alas! that they were so few) stood forward also, and told the traitors to their faces all that they had been doing. The prior and the chamberlain, the refectorarius and the rest of the officials, then began to excuse themselves on the plea of their weakness, and on the plea of the great danger in which they stood.

"You confess, then," said Hereward, "that you cannot of yourselves defend this house and its shrines?"

"Of a surety we confess it," said the prior; "nor is this house to be held against the Normans even with a garrison of armed men. Peterborough is not Ely, good my lord! There Saxon monks may hold their own; but here it cannot be done."

"So ho!" quoth Hereward, "this is where I would have thee! and therefore, oh prior, since thou canst not keep thy gilded crosses and silver vessels, thy chalices and pateras, thy drapery and rich church hangings, and as all these things and all other the property of this house will fall into the hands of the Norman thieves if they are not removed, I will and must carry them all off to Ely, where thou allowest they will be in safe Saxon keeping."

"Wouldst thou despoil the temple of the Lord? Wouldst thou rob the shrines of Saxon saints?" said the sacrist.

"My Lord of Brunn, thou darest not do the deed," said the prior.

"It is not for thee, false monk! To set the limits to my daring, when my conscience sanctions that which I am doing, and when the cause of my country urges it to be done," said Hereward.

"I will excommunicate thee as a sacrilegious robber," said the prior.

"Archbishop Stigand, the true primate of England, will excommunicate thee as a traitor to his country and traitor to his church," quoth the Lord of Brunn. "But I have little time to waste in words. Come, my merry men, be stirring! pack up all the plate, and all the hangings, and everything that we can carry with us."

"They shall not have the keys," said the chamberlain or treasurer of the house.

"We have them already," quoth Elfric, who had been led to the chamberlain's cell by one of the true Saxon monks. "We have the keys already, and so have we the engraven seals of silver gilt. The sigillum of so good a man as Abbat Brand shall never be used by so bad a man as Torauld. See! Here it is, my lord!" And so saying Elfric handed the good massive seal to his master, who kissed it as though it had been a relic, and then put it in his bosom.

"This is sacrilege! This is the worst of thefts," roared the prior. "This is done in the teeth of the law, and in outrage of the gospel. Sinful young man, knowest thou not the old Saxon law which saith, Sevenfold are the gifts of the Holy Spirit to the church, and seven are the degrees of ecclesiastical states and holy orders, and seven times should God's servants praise God daily in church, and it is very rightly incumbent on all God's friends that they love and venerate God's church, and in grith and frith hold God's servants; and let him who injures them, by word or work, earnestly make reparation with a sevenfold bot, if he will merit God's mercy, because holiness, and orders, and God's hallowed houses, are, for awe of God, ever to be earnestly venerated?"

"I know that good Saxon law," said Hereward, "and bow my head in reverence to it! I earnestly venerate this hallowed house and all houses that be hallowed, and all the shrines that belong to them. I do not rob, but only remove to safe keeping what others would rob; and, for any mischief that may be done to the goods of this house by such removal, I will myself make bot, not seven but seventy-fold, whenever England shall be free, and Harold restored to his throne."

"Dreams!" said the prior—"thy King Harold lies six feet deep in Waltham clay!"

"Unmannered priest, thou liest in thy throat for saying so! King Harold is alive, is safe in some foreign land, and at his own good time will be back to claim his own. But come he back or come he not back, the Normans shall not have the spoil of this house. They have spoiled too many hallowed houses already! Look at Saint Alban's! Look at Saint Edmund's-bury! and at York and Durham and Lindisfarne, and all other places, and tell me how they have respected Saxon saints and the property consecrate of our monasteries!"

"Leave that to us," said the chamberlain.

"I tell thee again I will leave nought for the Normans!" quoth Lord Hereward. And while he was speaking, his merry men all, aided and assisted by the honest monks, who revered the memory of Abbat Brand, were packing; and before the prior could finish a maledicted which he began, all the gold and silver, all the linen and silks and embroidered hangings, and all the effigies of the Saxon saints, and all the silver-gilded plates from their shrines, were carefully made up into divers parcels, for facility of carriage, and the relics of the saints were packed up in coffers. Ywere, an un-Saxon monk of the house, had succeeded in concealing the testaments, mass-hackles, cantel-copes, and such other small things, which he afterwards laid at the feet of the French abbat; but Hereward's people had gotten all the things of great value: they had climbed up to the holy rood, and had taken away the diadem from our Lord's head, all of pure gold, and had seized the bracket that was underneath his feet, which was all of red-gold: they had climbed up the campanile, or belfry, and had brought down a table that was hid there, all gold and silver; they had seized two shrines of gold and nine reliquaries of silver, and fifteen large crucifixes of gold and of silver; and, altogether, they had so many treasures in money, in raiment and in books, as no man could tell another.

The prior now sniveled and said, "Lord Hereward, my Lord of Brunn, wilt thou then leave us nothing to attract pilgrims to our shrines? Thou mightest as well carry off the house and the church, as carry these things away with thee!"

"Our house will be discredited and we shall starve!" said the sacrist. "Lord of Brunn, leave us at least the bones of our saints!"

"Once more," said Hereward, "once more and for the last time I tell ye all that I will leave to the Norman spoilers and oppressors nought that I can carry. If I could carry away the house and the church and the altars, by Saint Ovin and his cross, by Saint Withburga and her blessed and ever-flowing well, I would do it!—but only to bring them back again when this storm shall be passed, and when every true Saxon shall get his own."

Then turning to Elfric, Hereward said, "Where is the sacrist's register of all these effects and properties?"

Elfric handed a very long scroll of parchment to his lord. This parchment had been placed in the hands of Elfric by the sub-sacrist, one of the honest party, and the parchment contained, in good Saxon writing, a list of the treasures, even as they had been left on the day of the death of the good Abbat Brand.

"Now write me at the bottom of this scroll a receipt and declaration," said the Lord of Brunn to the sub-sacrist.

"Say that I, Hereward the Saxon, have taken away with me into the Isle of Ely, and unto that hallowed house of the true Saxon Abbat Lord Thurstan, all the things above enumerated. Say that I have removed them only in order to save them from the thievish hands of the Normans, or only to prevent their being turned against ourselves—say that I swear by all my hopes of life eternal to do my best to restore them uninjured so soon as the Normans are driven out of England; and say that I will make bot for every loss and for every injury. Mortal man can do no more than this."

The sub-sacrist, maugre the threats and maledictions of his superior the sacrist, and of the prior and refectorarius, and all the upper officials, quickly engrossed on the parchment all that the Lord of Brunn wanted; and Hereward, being himself a scholar and penman, signed it with his name. Next he called for signatures of witnesses. Girolamo of Salerno wrote a sic subscribitur, and wrote his signature, and Elfric, who had improved as much in learning as in the art of war, did the same. Some others made the sign of the cross opposite to their names that were written for them; but upon the whole it was a good receipt, and solemn and well witnessed. The Lord of Brunn handed the parchment to the prior, bidding him to take care of it, and show it to his new abbat Torauld as soon as that Frenchman should arrive with his one hundred and sixty men-at-arms; but the prior cast the parchment upon the ground, saying that the house was impiously spoiled—that nothing would ever be gotten back again—that nothing was left in the house but woe, nakedness, and tribulation.

"Oh prior!" said Hereward, and he smiled as he said it—"oh untrue and un-Saxon prior! The savory odors that come upwards from thy kitchen tell me that there is something more than this. By saint Ovin! It is not Torauld of Fescamp and his men-at-arms that shall eat this thy feast! Elfric, see those viands served up in the refectory, and we will eat them all, be they cooked or uncooked, done or underdone."

"My Lord," responded Elfric, "the roast meats be done to a turn, the boiled meats and the stewed meats, and fowl and fish be all ready. The cook of this house of Peterborough, being no caterer for Normans, but a Saxon true, and one that hath owed his promotion to thine uncle, of happy memory, the Abbat Brand, hath seen to all these things, and hath advanced the good dinner by an hour or twain."

"Then for love of mine uncle's nephew, let him dish up as quickly as may be! Elfric, what say thy scouts? Where be the Frenchmen now?"

"Good ten miles off, my lord; so do not over-hurry the meal."

"Prior, sacrist, chamberlain, traitors all!" said Lord Hereward, "will ye do penance with us in eating of this feast which ye had prepared for Norman stomachs?"

"The wrath of the Lord will overtake thee for this ribaldry! Oh, Hereward of Brunn, we will not break bread with thee, nor sit at the table with such as thou art."

"Then stay here where ye are, and munch your dry bread to the odor of our roast meats," said the young Lord of Brunn.

And so, leaving the false monks under guard of some of his merry men, Hereward with the true monks went straight to the refectory and fared sumptuously; and then, like the bounteous lord that he was, he made all his followers, of whatsoever degree, eat, drink, and be merry; and so heartily did these true Saxons eat and drink, that of that same feast they left nothing behind them for Torauld of Fescamp and his hungry Normans. And when it was time to get gone, and they could drink no more,

Elfric and sub-sacrist went down to the cellars and set every cask running, to the end that there should not be a drop of wine or a drop of ale or a drop of mead to cool the throats of the disappointed Frenchmen.

Then the Lord of Brunn and his merry men all took their departure from the abbey of Peterborough, taking with them the chalices and pateras, the crosses and candelabra, the shrine-plates and the reliquaries, the diadems and the tables, the linens, the silks, and hangings, and everything that was worth taking, and everything that Torauld of Fescamp and his men-at-arms most wanted to find and seize. And thus did the great house of Peterborough cease to be called the rich and begin to be called miserably poor, *de aurea erat pauperrima.*

Judge ye the wrath of that terrible false French abbat when he came to the house at Peterborough, and heard and likewise saw all that had been done! First he pulled at his own hair, and next he snatched at the prior's head and tore his hair away by handfuls. He would not believe one jot of the tale that was told him about Hereward's forcible entry and seizures; he would believe nothing but that they were all in league with the rebels and robbers of the fens, even as they had been when Abbat Brand blessed the sword of Hereward and made him knight, and took into his house a garrison of armed Saxons.

The more they protested and vowed, the more he disbelieved them; and this first conference between these untrue Saxon monks and their choleric Norman abbat ended in Torauld's shouting, "Come hither, my men-at-arms, and fustigate these liars!" And while the men-at-arms beat the commoner monks and the lay-brothers of the house, Torauld himself tweaked the noses of the superiors with his gauntleted hand, and drawing his heavy sword, he applied the flat of it to the prior, the sacrist, the chamberlain, the refectorarius, and all the rest of the officials, beating them all even as he used to belabor his monks and novices in Normandie. But the true English members of the house did not share in this pain and humiliation, for the sub-sacrist and every one of them that was a good Saxon had gone off with Lord Hereward more than an hour before. When he grew tired of this his first hard lesson in ecclesiastical discipline, Torauld caused the prior and the sacrist and every monk that had stayed behind, to be thrown into the dungeon of the house, and there he kept them two days and two nights without food and drink.

Some few of the new Lord Abbat of Peterborough's men-at-arms thought, that instead of fustigating the English monks, they ought to have followed Hereward and the English soldiers, and have made an effort to recover the good things they had carried off; but Torauld, who was bold only where there was no chance of resistance, would not venture a pursuit after an alert and most daring enemy into a difficult country; and so he swore to his people that the Saxon robbers must have been gone, not one, but more than three hours before his arrival; that instead of counting sixty men, they were six hundred strong at the very least.

Whether they were sixty or six hundred, none of the men-at-arms who knew anything concerning the fenny country were at all eager for the pursuit, albeit they all imagined that the treasure which Lord Hereward had carried off with him from the abbey was great enough to pay for a king's ransom.

Thus the new Norman Abbat and his unpriestly and ungodly men entered upon possession of the ancient abbey of Peterborough: but feast that day was there none.

CHAPTER XVII.

HEREWARD GOES TO BRUNN AND IS DISTURBED THERE

From Peterborough the Lord of Brunn made one good march across the fen country to Crowland, where he saluted the good Abbat and brotherhood, who had put their house into excellent order. And having tarried for a short season with the trusty monks of Crowland, he went down the river Welland unto Spalding, where he embarked the treasure which he had taken, and sent Girolamo of Salerno to have charge of it and see it safely delivered to the Lord Abbat of Ely.

Having done all this, and having seen that the river Welland and the country about Crowland and Spalding were well guarded; Hereward went across the country to Brunn to visit his fair wife, whom he had not seen since the quinquaine of Pasche. Elfric went with him, and in this manner there were two happy meetings. The old manor-house at Brunn had been beautified as well as strengthened under the eye of the Ladie Alftrude; and the old township, being ridded of the Normans, was beginning to look peaceful and prosperous as it used to do in the happy times of the good Lord Leofric of blessed memory.

The unthinking people were already forgetting their past troubles, and beginning to imagine that there would be no troubles for the future, or that, come what might the Normans would never get footing again in the fen country. Elfric was not an unthinking young man, but his love for Maid Mildred caused him to take up the notion of the townsfolk. He thought he might soon turn his sword into a reaping-hook, and that it was already time for keeping the promise which his master had made to him. Mildred said nay, nay, but in a manner which sounded very like yea, yea. Lord Hereward said, "Wait awhile; ye are both young, and this war is not over. Beyond the fens the Normans are still triumphant, and the Saxons confounded and submissive. Elfric, there is work to do, and short is the time that I can abide here."

The ex-novice quietly submitted himself to the will of his lord; and for a short season he lead a very easy, happy life, hawking or fishing in the morning, with Hereward and the ladie, and rambling in the eve with Mildred in the wood which lay near the house. One fine summer eve, about fifteen days after their coming to Brunn, Elfric and Mildred went rather farther into the wood than it had been usual for them to go; and reaching the bank of a clear little stream, they sat down among the tall rushes, and after talking and laughing for a while they became reflective and silent, and gazed at the stream as it glided by, all gilded and enameled by the setting sun.

They had not sate thus long when Elfric was startled by some distant sound, which did not reach the ear of Mildred, for when he said, "What noise is that?" she said she heard none. But Elfric was quite certain he had heard a noise afar off, and a sound of a rustling among the willows and fen-trees. "Well," said Mildred, "it will be the evening breeze, or the fen-sparrows, or mayhap the marsh-tits tapping the old willow-trees to hollow out their nests."
"There breathes not a breath of air, and this is not the season in which the marsh-tit makes its nest in the old willows," said Elfric. "But hark! I hear the sound again, and... ah! what is that?... By St. Ovin's cross! I see afar off a

something shining in the red sunbeams that looks like the head of a Norman lance! See! look there, behind those trees at the foot of yon hillock!"

The maiden looked, and although at first she saw nothing, she soon turned pale, and said, "In truth, Elfric, I see a spear, and another, and now another. But now they move not! They disappear."

"Mildred," said the young man, "run back to the manor-house with thy best speed, and tell Lord Hereward what thou hast seen!"

"But wilt thou not go with me? I almost fear to go alone through the wood."

"The path is straight and dry," said Elfric; "there is no danger: but I must go forward and discover what be these new comers, who are coming so stealthily towards the wood and the manor-house, and who bring lances with them and sound no horn."

"But there will be peril for thee, oh Elfric, unarmed and all alone as thou art."

"Fear not for that, my Mildred; I will crawl through the rushes and keep this winding stream between me and these strangers. But fly to the house, and if thou chancest to meet any of Lord Hereward's people, bid them hasten home and look to their arms."

"Alas!" quoth Mildred, "when will this fighting be over?" and having so said, she flew like a lapwing towards the house, while Elfric disappeared among the sedges and bulrushes.

"Lances so near the wood!" said Hereward, "and no notice given! Our guard at Edenham must have fallen asleep!"

"Or mayhap they be gone to Corby," said Mildred, "for to-day is Corby wake."

"Or it may be," said Hereward, "that thou and Elfric are both mistaken—albeit his good eyes are not apt to deceive him."

Before the Lord of Brunn had time to assemble his people, Elfric was back to speak for himself, and to give more certain and full notice of what was toward. He had gone near enough not only to see, but also to hear. The force was a great Norman force led on by Ivo Taille-Bois and Torauld of Fescamp, who hoped to take Hereward by surprise, and to recover from him the treasure which he had seized at Peterborough; for, being robbers themselves, they made sure that he meant to keep the treasure for himself.

"What be their numbers?" said the Lord of Brunn.

"Two hundred men-at-arms," responded Elfric.

"Bring they any of their great siege-tools?" asked Hereward.

"None, my Lord. They carry nothing but their arms, and even with that burthen they seem sorely fatigued. They are covered with our fen mud, and are all swearing that they should have been forced to travel without their horses."

"Then," said Hereward, "although Girolamo be away, we can hold good this house and laugh at their attempt to take it. Call in all the good folk of the township, and then up drawbridge, and make fast gates!"

"Under subjection, my Lord," quoth Elfric, "I will say that I think that we can do better than shut ourselves up in the house to wait for their coming. I heard their plan of approach, and it is this: They are all to remain concealed where they are until it be dark. Then Ivo Taille-Bois is to march through the wood, and surround the house with one hundred men, while that bull-headed Torauld, who seemeth not to relish the fighting with soldiers so much as he doth the fighting with unarmed monks, is to lodge himself with the other hundred men on the skirts of the wood, so as to prevent the people of the township from coming to the manor-house."

"Art thou sure," said Hereward, "that thou knowest Norman French enough to make out all this sense from their words?"

"Quite certain, my Lord. I was close to them, and they talked loud, as is their wont. Nay, they talked even louder than common, being angered, and Ivo-Taille saying that as it was church business the churchman ought to go foremost; and Torauld saying that Ivo did not enough respect the lives and limbs of Norman prelates. Set me down this Torauld for a rank coward! They told me at Peterborough that he was as big as a bull and for that much so he is; but from my hiding-place in the rushes I could see that he quaked and turned pale at the thought of leading the attack."

"Thou wast ever a good scout," said the Lord of Brunn, "but a wary commander never trusts to one report. We have lads here that know the paths and the bye-paths. We will have these Normans watched as it grows dark."

In the meantime all the good people of the township were forewarned, and called to the manor-house. The aged, with the women and children, were to stay within those strong walls; but all the rest were armed, and kept in readiness to sally forth. Of the sixty merry men that had stolen the march upon Torauld and got to Peterborough before him, some had been left at Crowland and some at Spalding, and some had taken up their long stilts and had walked across the bogs to see their kindred and friends in Hollande. Only one score and ten of these tried soldiers remained; the good men of the township of Brunn that put on harness and were ready to fight, made more than another score; and besides these there was about half a score of hardy hinds who had followed the Ladie Alftrude from her home.

As it grew dark the scouts reported that the Normans were in motion, and that they were moving in two separate bodies, even as Elfric reported they would do. Then the Lord of Brunn went himself to watch their movements. He made out, more by his ears than by his eyes, that one body was coming straight on for the wood and the house, and that the other body was turning round the wood by a path which would bring them to a little bridge near the edge of the wood, this bridge being between the township and the manor-house. By his own prudent order lights had been left burning in one or two of the better sort of houses, and the whole town thus looked as it usually did at that hour; while bright lights beamed from every window of the manor-house, to make Ivo Taille-Bois believe that the Lord of Brunn was feasting and carousing and wholly off his guard.

"Thus far, well!" thought Hereward, as he ran back to the house. "It will take these heavy Normans a good length of time to cross the stream and get into the wood; and while Ivo is coming into the wood on the one side, I will go out of it on the other side, and catch this bully monk and his people as in a trap. And Taille-Bois shall rue the day that he turned his face towards Brunn."

Leaving half a score of his best men in the house, and commanding all that were in the house to be silent and without fear, the Lord of Brunn sallied forth with all the rest of his merry men: and as soon as he and they were beyond the moat, the little garrison drew up the drawbridge and made fast the gate. When he counted his troop, he found it to be not more than fifty strong; but every man of them was vigorous and well equipped; and there was truth in the Saxon song which said that every true Saxon in arms was equal to three Frenchmen, and that the Lord of Brunn never turned his back even upon six Frenchmen. Warned by Elfric, that best of all scouts, when Ivo was crossing the stream, and calculating his only time to a nicety, Hereward marched through a corner of the wood and took post on some broken ground near the end of the little bridge. His people were all as silent as the grave, and so they continued; nor could they be seen any more than they could be heard, for they lay in the hollows of the ground with their faces prone to the earth, and their bows and weapons under them: and the night was now rather dark, and the trees which grew close behind the broken ground cast a deep shadow over it. The Saxons had not been long in this their ambuscade when they heard a loud shouting of "A Taille-Bois! A Taille-Bois!" which came from the side of the manor-house; and the next instant they heard another loud shouting in their front of "Torauld! Torauld!"

"So so!" said Hereward, "the twain have timed their marches well! The monk will be here anon; but let every Saxon among us remain on his face until he cross the narrow bridge, and then up and fall on!"

And as the Lord of Brunn said, so was it done. Eager to get possession of the bridge, the monk from Fescamp avoided the little township, and came straight to the stream which flowed between it and the manor-house, and crossed over the bridge with all his people: and no sooner were they all over than the Saxons started up like armed men springing from the bowels of the earth, and shouting "Hereward for England!" they fell upon their amazed and confounded enemy, who could neither discover their strength nor form themselves into any order of battle. Instantly some of the Normans screamed that these were the devils of Crowland risen again; and so, screaming, they made a rush back to the bridge.
Now the bridge was very narrow, and walled on either side with a parapet wall of brickwork; and when the

whole of Torauld's force began to follow the first fuyards, with a mad rushing and confusion, they got jammed together upon that narrow bridge, or falling one over the other they obstructed the passage. Torauld, that big monk, could not get upon the bridge at all, or near to it. And as he stood crowded and squeezed by his disordered men, and heard the Saxon battle-axe ringing upon their mailed armor and plated shields, he set up his big voice and cried "Quarter! Quarter! Mercy, O Lord of Brunn!"
"Dost thou surrender, Torauld of Fescamp?" shouted Hereward.
"Aye, and at thy discretion," said the terrible abbat, no longer terrible.
"Normans, do ye all surrender upon quarter?" shouted Hereward, who had already slain three of them with his own hand.

The Normans, not even excepting those on the bridge, or even those five or six that had gotten beyond the bridge, all declared that they surrendered at discretion.
"Then," quoth the Lord of Brunn, "hand me your swords, and come hither and lay down all your arms!"

And, in that grim darkness, Torauld, and the several leaders of the band, stretched out their hands and delivered up their swords to Hereward; and Hereward, as he got them, handed them to his sword-bearer, and Elfric made a bundle of them all under his left arm, singing, as he had wont to do in the choir at Spalding, but with a louder note, "*Infixæ sunt gentes!*—The heathen are sunk down in the pit that they made: in the net which they hid is their own foot taken!" And all the Norman men-at-arms, seeing but dimly what they were doing, and taking the trees on the skirts of the wood for Saxon warriors, piled their arms in a trice, and allowed themselves to be bound with their own girdles and baldrics.

When Hereward's people proceeded to bind Torauld, that tamed monster made a miserable lamentation, for he thought that the Saxons would bind him first, and then slay him; and none knew better than himself the intolerable wrongs he had done since his first coming to the kingdom, and the outrages he had been guilty of in the monasteries and churches of England. But Elfric bade him bellow not so miserably, and told him how that it was the custom of the Lord of Brunn not to slay his prisoners, but only to send them to a place of safe keeping, such as the Camp of Refuge, or the strong vault under Ely Abbey. And when the Normans were all bound, Hereward made his sword-bearer count them all; and Elfric, groping among them as the shepherd does among his sheep when the night is dark, found and reported that there were four score and ten of them. The rest had been slain, or had rushed into the stream to get drowned.

All this work by the bridge had not been done without much noise. In making their sudden onslaught, and in raising their shout for Hereward, the Saxons had made the welkin ring; and the cries and screams of the discomfited Normans were distinctly heard across the wood and at the manor-house. The Saxons within that house heard both cries, and well understood what they meant: Ivo Taille-Bois and his men also heard them and understood them; and so, cursing Torauld the monk for a fool, Ivo halted his men under cover of the trees; and then, after listening for a brief space of time, and after hearing plainer than before the Norman cry of misericord instead of attempting to surround the house, Ivo began to retrace his steps through the wood.

And although the night was brightening up elsewhere, it continued so dark in that wood, and his people ran in so great hurry, that at almost every step some of them missed the narrow path, or fell over the roots of the trees. And as Ivo thus retreated, his ear was assailed by the taunting shouts of the Saxons in the manor-house, and by the triumphant shouts of those who had sallied forth with Hereward to smite Torauld in the dark.

But louder and louder still were the shouts in the good house of Brunn when its young Lord returned unhurt (and not a man of his was hurt) with the captives he had made, and notably with the once terrible Torauld.

"Thou seest," said Hereward, "that thy friend Ivo hath not stayed to keep his appointed meeting with thee at my humble house! But stay thou here awhile, oh monk of Fescamp! And I will even go try whether I can overtake Ivo, and bring him back to meet thee! He hath the start, but is not so good a fenner as I am. So, come, my merry men all, one horn of wine apiece, and then for a chase through the wood and across the stream! And we catch not the great wood-cutter, we may perchance cut off part of his tail. But first lock me up these prisoners in the turret. Our women and old men will suffice to take care of them while we follow the chase."

The Ladie Alftrude, and sundry other persons, thought and said that Lord Hereward had done enough for this one night; but the Lord of Brunn thought he had never done enough when there was more to do, and before Ivo Taille-Bois could get clear out of the wood, Hereward was upon his track, with fifty of his merry men. Some of the Normans, missing the ford across the stream, were captured on the bank; but the rest got safely over, and ran for their lives across the plain, whereon they never could have run at all if the summer had been less hot and dry. They were closely followed by the Saxons, who took a good many more of them, and killed others: but Ivo was too far ahead to be caught; and it was all in vain that Hereward shouted and called upon him to stop and measure swords with him on dry ground, and on a fair field. So the Lord of Brunn gave up the pursuit, and returned to his manor-house, taking with him a good score more prisoners. And if the louts who had been sent to keep guard at Edenham had not gone to Corby wake, and had not drunk themselves drunk there, Ivo Taille-Bois would have been captured or killed, with every man that followed him, before he could have got out upon the road which leads from the fen country to Stamford. The rest of that night was given to festivity and joy. On the morrow morning Hereward brought his Norman captives forth from the turret into the great hall, and made inquest into their names and qualities.

There were several knights of name among them; several that had high rank and good lands in Normandie before ever they came to plunder England. Now these proud foreign knights condescended to address the Lord of Brunn as one of the military confraternity, and they spoke with him about ransom as knight speaks to knight. Hereward, knowing well how the Abbat of Ely had been constrained to lay hands on that which had been offered on the shrine of the saints, and to deal with unbelieving and usurious Jews, and how sorely money was needed throughout the Camp of Refuge, did not gainsay these overtures about ransoms; but he fixed the total ransom at so high a price, that Torauld and the Norman knights all vowed that they could never pay or get their friends to pay it.

The Lord of Brunn, who believed them not, told them that they must pay the three thousand marks he had named, or live and die in the fastnesses of the fen country. Torauld who loved money more than he loved his own soul, and who never doubted but that Hereward had all the treasures he had taken from Peterborough, and meant to keep them for his own use and profit, offered, as lawful superior of that house, and abbat appointed by King William, to give the Lord of Brunn a title to all those things as the price of the ransom for himself and the Norman nobles. But here at the Lord of Brunn was greatly incensed, and said, "Robber that thou art, dost thou take me for a sacrilegious robber?

The treasure of Peterborough is not here, but at Ely, in the safe keeping of the good Lord Abbat Thurstan, to be kept or even used for the good of England, and to be restored to Peterborough with bot, and with other treasure, at the proper season. But thou, oh Torauld of Fescamp, thou hast no right to it, or control over it; and if thou hadst it, it is not my father's son that would barter with thee for the goods of the church and the spoils of the altar! Torauld of Fescamp, and thou Piron of Montpinchon, and thou Olivier Nonant, and thou Pierre of Pommereuil, and the rest of ye, I tell ye one and all, and I swear it by the blessed rood, that I will never liberate ye, or any of ye, until the three thousand marks, as ransom, be paid into my hands, or into the hands of the Lord Abbat of Ely! So, look well to it. Three thousand marks, or a lifelong home and a grave in the safest and dreariest part of the fens."

One and all, they again protested, and even vowed that so large a sum could never be raised for their liberation; and that they would not so much as name the sum to their friends and families.

"Well," said the Lord of Brunn, "then to-morrow we will clap ye all on ship-board and send ye across the salt sea Wash for Ely and the Camp of Refuge."

And on the morrow, by times, all the Norman captives, gentle or simple, knights or men-at-arms, were marched off to the Welland and put on board ship and under hatches: nor ever did they get free from their Saxon prison in the fens until twelve good months after their capture, when they got the money, and paid down the three thousand marks, together with some small pecunia for their meat and drink, and the trouble they had given during their captivity. And long did Torauld bemoan the day when he accepted the office of abbat of Peterborough, and went to take vengeance on that house on account of Lord Hereward's knighthood. He came forth from the fens an altered and subdued man; and although he tyrannically ruled a religious house for many years after these his misadventures, he was never more known to tweak his monks by the nose with his steel gloves on, or to beat them with the flat of his sword, or to call out "Come hither, my men-at-arms." In truth, although he plucked up spirit enough to rob and revile monks, he never put on armor or carried a sword again.

Thus had the good Lord of Brunn triumphed on the land which he inherited from his father and recovered with his own sword; thus within the good manor of Brunn had he foiled the stratagems of his enemies, and beaten them and humbled them, and made them the captives of his sword: but he could not long remain to enjoy his triumph there; his sword and his counsel were wanted in other parts; and deeming that the unwonted dryness of the season might perchance enable Ivo Taille-Bois or some other Norman lord to make another attempt upon Brunn, he took his ladie with him whither he went. A small but trusty garrison was left in the old manor-house, together with sundry matrons and maids, but Mildred went with her ladie, as did Elfric with his lord.

As they came to the Welland, on their way to Ely, there came unto Lord Hereward some brave men from the world beyond the fens, to tell him that a great body of Saxon serfs had gathered together at the edge of Sherwood forest and on the banks of the Trent, and that all these men were ready to join him and become his servants and soldiers. Hereward gave the messengers the encouragement they seemed to merit, and sent his sword-bearer back with them to see what manner of men the band was made of, and to bring them across the fens if he should find them worth their bread and meat.

Now the men that had collected were hardy and fit for war, and many of them, being natives to the forests and trained to hunting, were keen bowmen. The Lord of Brunn, who knew the worth of the English bow, much wanted good bowmen; and thus Elfric would gladly have brought away all these foresters with him. But when the marching time came, sundry of these churls said that they were well where they were in Sherwood:—and for that matter so they were, for the Normans could not easily get at them, and they were lords of the forest and of all the game in it, and they robbed all that came near to the forest.

But all the churls were not so churlish, nor so fond of living without law and order, nor so careless as to what became of their countrymen; and many were the good bowmen that said they would go to the Saxon camp. Some of these upland churls, however, who had not led so free a life as the fenners, and had not had such good Lords as the Abbat of Ely and the Lord of Brunn, began to say to the men of the hills that were following Elfric, that they thought they were engaging in an idle chase and a very useless struggle, inasmuch as they would still be all serfs and bondmen whether the Normans or the Saxons ruled the land.

But Elfric, hearing this, bade them all remember that it was one thing to obey a Lord that spoke their own tongue, and another to obey a stranger Lord who spoke it not and despised it; that the good Saxon Lords were ever merciful and kind, not putting more labor on the serf than the serf could bear, and feeding and entertaining him well when sickness or when old age allowed him not to work at all; and that the good old Saxon laws and customs did not leave the eyes, limbs, life, and conscience of the serfs in the hands of their lords and masters, nor allow Christian bondmen to be treated as though they were beasts of the field; in which fashion the Normans were now treating them.

Quoth a grey-beard in the crowd, "There is some truth in what the young man saith. That was not a bad law which said, 'Let the churl keep the fasts of the church as well as the Lord, and let the master that feeds his serfs on fast-days with meat, denying them bread, be put in the pillory.'"

"Aye," said another elder, smoothing his beard, "but that was a still better law which said, 'Let not the serf be made to work on the feast-days of the church, nor to do any manner of work on the Sabbath: Let all have rest on the seventh day, which is the day of the Lord God!'"

Here one who had been a mass-priest in the upland country, but who had fled from the intolerable persecutions of the Normans and was now armed against that people, spoke as one that had tasted books, and said, "Many were our good old Saxon laws for keeping holy the Sabbath-day, and making the seventh day a day of rest for all that live in the land, whether rich or poor, master or slave.

The fourth commandment, which the Normans set at nought in as far as the poor English serf is concerned in it, was a most binding law with all good Saxons, and was enforced by many royal laws and civil enactments, and with the imposing of penalties upon all such as broke the commandment. The laws and ordinances of King Edward the Elder said—'If anyone engage in Sunday marketing, let him forfeit the goods and pay a fine of thirty shillings. If a freeman work, let him forfeit his freedom, or redeem it by paying wite; if a Lord oblige his churl to work, let him pay wite.' And, after this, King Athelstane said in his dooms 'that there should be no marketing and no labor on Sundays, and that if anyone did market on Sundays he should forfeit the goods and pay thirty shillings.'

And, after this, King Ethelred said in his dooms, 'Let Sunday's festival be rightly kept by all, as is becoming, and let marketing's and folkmotes be carefully abstained from on that holy day; let hunting's and worldly works be strictly abstained from on that day.'

And by the laws of King Edgar no man was to work from noontide of the Saturday till the dawn of Monday; and soul scot was to be paid for every Christian man to the priest, in order that the priest might pray for him and instruct him. And the canons of Ælfric, inhibiting the breach of the sanctity of the Lord's day, say, 'The mass-priests shall on Sundays explain to the people the sense of the Gospels in English, and explain to them in English the pater-noster and the creed, to the end that all the people may know the faith and cultivate their Christianity.' And in this very canon the pious Ælfric saith, 'Let the priest and teacher beware of that which the prophet said; *Canes muti non possunt latrare*, dumb dogs cannot bark!' But what are these Norman teachers and priests from beyond the sea but dumb dogs to the Saxon people, seeing they know no English and will not learn it?"

"Yes," said the ancient who had first spoken, "until these Normans came among us the bondman had one day in seven to himself, and on every other festival of the church he was allowed to forget his bonds, and to take rest and enjoyment, and to think of his soul; but now we be treated as if we had no souls."

"And," said another of the serfs, "in former days the laws protected the money and goods of a bondman, if so be he could obtain any, for the Saxon law said that the master must not take from his slave that which the slave had gained by his industry. But now the serf cannot so much as call his life his property."

"Nor can any other true Saxon call anything his own, unless he stand up and fight for it, and prove strong enough to keep it," said Elfric, who was well pleased to see and hear that his discourse on the difference between the old bondage and the present was not thrown away upon the upland serfs.

Quoth the priest who had before spoken, "Our old Saxon laws were chary of blood, and held in tender respect the life of all men, whether they belonged to the nobility or were in a state of villainage. Few crimes were punished with death or even with mutilation. The commandment that man shall do no murder was not only read in churches, but was recommended and enforced in the laws and dooms of many Saxon kings. 'If anyone be slain,' said the old law, 'let him be paid for according to his birth.' If a thane slew a churl, he had to pay for it...."

"Aye," said one of the serfs, "but the value of the life of a churl was not more than the price of a few bullocks; whereas hides of land or the worth of hundreds of bullocks was to be paid by him that slew a thane."

"Tush!" quoth Elfric, "thou canst not expect that the life of a churl can ever be priced so high as that of a noble, or that the same doom shall await the man that kills a Lord and the man that kills a peasant!"

The priest and all the bystanders said that such an expectation would be too unreasonable, and that such a thing could never come to pass in this world: and so the discontented churl merely muttered that he thought, since it was allowed the churl had an immortal soul, even as the thane, that the life of a churl was worth more than a few bullocks; and then said no more about it, bethinking himself that even that price was better than no price at all, and that no Normans that he knew of had ever yet been made to make bot for maiming or killing a Saxon serf.

Some few of these men returned into Sherwood forest, to live at large there, but the major part of them tied on their buskins, fastened their sheep-skin jackets, put their bows and quivers to their backs, and marched off merrily with the sword-bearer to join Lord Hereward at Ely or in the Camp. And after this, and at various times, many upland churls, discontented with their lot, came from the northern side of the Trent and from other parts of the country to join the Saxon army in the fens. It must not be thought that the Lord of Brunn was unmindful of the old laws, which ordained that no Lord or free man should harbor or entertain the churl that had fled from his rightful owner; but Hereward felt that no Norman could have the right of property over Saxon serfs; and therefore he harbored and entertained such as came freely to him.

If the case had been otherwise, he would, like the just Lord that he was, have put collars and chains upon the serfs and have sent them back to their masters.

CHAPTER XVIII.

THE DANES AND THEIR KING'S SON

Svend Estrithson sat upon the throne of Denmark, and was a powerful king and a great warrior, having fought many battles by sea against his neighbor the King of Norway. When his brother Osbiorn Jarl abandoned the Saxons and returned from England into Denmark, Svend Estrithson was exceedingly wroth at him, and his anger was the greater because the Jarl had not only lost the treasure which William the Norman had given him as the price of his treasons to the English people, but had lost likewise nearly the whole of the Danish fleet; for a great storm arose at sea and swallowed up most of the two hundred and forty returning ships. Osbiorn Jarl escaped drowning; but when he presented himself before the face of his brother the king, Svend loaded him with reproaches, deprived him of his lands and honours, and drove him into a disgraceful banishment. Even thus was bad faith punished, and vengeance taken upon the Danes for that they had both plundered and betrayed the Saxon people, who were fighting for their liberties against the Normans.

Svend Estrithson, being of the line of the great King Canute, raised some claim to the throne of England, and had ever considered his right better and more legal than that of William of Normandie. Before the arrival at his court of the earnest invitation of the monks of Ely and the great Saxon lords in the Camp of Refuge, he had resolved in his own mind to try his fortune once more on our side the sea, hoping that if he should do no more he should at least be enabled to make up for the loss of his great fleet, a loss which pressed heavily upon his heart, and destroyed his peace by day and his rest by night. He had summoned his jarls and chiefs, the descendants of the sea-kings or great pirates of old, and had taken counsel of the old sea-rovers and warriors who had been in England with the great Canute, or who had served under Canute's sons, King Harold Harefoot and King Hardicanute.

Now these jarls and chiefs, together with many of their followers, were well acquainted with all the eastern side of England from the Scottish border to the end of Cornwall; and they knew every bay, harbor, and creek on the coast, and all the deep inlets of the sea and the rivers which gave access to the interior of the country, for they had warred or plundered in them all, aforetime. Being called upon by King Svend to give their advice, these chiefs and nobles all said that another expedition ought to be attempted without loss of time; and it was agreed at a great meeting of the Viborgting, which corresponds with the Witangemot of old England, that another great fleet should be got ready, and that the king or his eldest son should take the command of it.

Some doubts, however, occurred as to the present strength of the Normans and the present condition of the English; and, although they meant to betray them or conquer them themselves, the Danes proposed to begin merely as allies of the English, and felt little good could be done unless the English on the eastern coast were unsubdued by the Normans, and ready to receive the Danes with open arms.

At this juncture a ship arrived from Lynn with the envoy from the Camp of Refuge on board. As soon as the Englishman had presented the letters and the gold and silver he brought to Svend Estrithson, the king called together his great council. The envoy from the Camp of Refuge was allowed to speak at great length before the council, and the shipmen of Lynn were more privately examined touching the present situation of affairs in the fen country. All doubts were removed, and the fleet was forthwith ordered to get ready for the voyage to England. Already many thousands of long and yellow-haired warriors had been collected for the enterprise, and now many thousands more flocked towards the fleet from all parts of Jutland, Zealand, and Holstein, and from Stralsund and the Isle of Rugen, and the other isles that stand near the entrance of the Baltic Sea; for whenever an expedition to the rich and fertile country of the Anglo-Saxons was on foot, the hearts of the Danes rejoiced in the prospect of good booty, even as the hearts of the coast-dwelling people rejoice when they hear that a rich wreck or a large fat whale hath been stranded near to their doors.

King Svend Estrithson, of a certainty, would have gone himself into England with the fleet, but his royal shield fell to the ground and broke as he was lifting it down from the wall, and a hare crossed his path as he was walking in his garden, and the priest his chaplain sneezed three times while he was saying mass before him, and he was greatly enamored of the Princess Gyda, and in consequence of all these evil omens the king resolved to stay at home, and to send his eldest son Knut into England. Taking with him the royal standard of the black raven, and many jarls of high renown into his own ship, Knut began his voyage forthwith, being followed by two hundred and fifty keels, large and small.

The royal ship was rich and splendid; it had thirty benches of rowers; its prow was adorned with a dragon's head, the eyes of which were of precious stones and the tongue of red gold; and the sides and the stern of the ship glowed with burnished gold; the whole body of the ship glittered in the sun like some great and marvelous fish or some swimming dragon; and, in sooth, the whole ship was dragon-shaped. The masts and the cordage and the sails were surpassing rich and gay; the masts were covered with ivory and pearl, the cords seemed to be covered with white silk, and the sails were of many and bright colors.

There were cloths of gold spread all about, and the flag that waved at the mainmast-head was all of silk and gold; and the windlass and the rudder were repainted with blue and gold. And on board this right royal ship every warrior wore bright steel-chain armor, and carried a shield and battle-axe inlaid with gold and jewels, and each of value enough to purchase a hide of land. A few other ships there were in this great fleet only a little less splendid than that of Knut. The rest were of a coarser make and with no adornments about them except the figure-head at the prow and the banner at the mast-head; and they varied in size and burthen from the great ship which could carry two hundred fighting men, down to the little bark which carried but ten.

To speak the truth, many of the fleet were little better than fishing barks. The summer wind blew fresh and fair for England, the waves seethed before their prows, and on the morning of that glad evening at Brunn when Lord Hereward captured Torauld of Fescamp and put Ivo Taille-Bois to flight and shame, nearly the whole of the great fleet came to anchor off the Wash, and not far from the chapel of our Ladie. Knut, the king's son, being uncertain and suspicious, like one that had treacherous plans in his own mind, dispatched one of his smallest and poorest keels with a crafty and keen-sighted chief up the Wash and up the Ouse, to confer with Abbat Thurstan and the Saxon chiefs at Ely, to spy into the condition of the Camp of Refuge, and to invite the Lord Abbat and some of the great chiefs to come down to Lynn, in order to hold there a solemn conference with his jarls and chiefs. The messenger-bark proceeded on her voyage prosperously, and landed the cunning Dane at Ely. Good Abbat Thurstan wondered and grieved that the prince had not come himself; yet he bade his envoy welcome, and feasted him in his hall. But still more did Thurstan wonder and grieve when he was told that Knut meant not to come to Ely, but was calling for a congress at Lynn.

"There may be danger," said the Lord Abbat to the cunning old envoy, "if I quit this house, and the great thanes leave the Camp of Refuge, though only for a short season; but there can be no peril in thy prince's coming hither, and assuredly it is only here that we can entertain him as the son of a great king ought to be entertained."

The old Dane said that the prince his master had schemes of operation which would not allow him to send his ships up the Ouse for this present; that he would come hereafter, when good progress should have been made in the war against the Normans; and that in the meanwhile it were best for my Lord Abbat, and some other of the prelates, and some of the great lay lords, to go down to Lynn and hold a conference, and make a combined plan of operations with the prince and the jarls.

Much did the Saxon lords wish to make out what was the nature of the plan the prince had already adopted; but the astutious old envoy would tell them nothing, and protested that he knew nothing about it. The Saxons plied him hard with wine; but the more he drank the more close the old Dane became. And although he would tell nothing himself, he wanted to know everything from the English: as, what was the strength of their army in the Camp of Refuge—what their means of subsistence—what the names of all their chiefs—what their correspondence and alliance with other Saxon chiefs in other parts of England—what the strength of the Normans in various parts of England, and which the provinces and the chiefs that had entirely submitted to them, with many other particulars. It was too confiding, and indeed very unwise so to do; but the Saxons, albeit often betrayed before now, were not much given to suspicion, and so they satisfied him according to the best of their knowledge on all these points, and conducted him into their camp that he might see with his own eyes how matters stood there, and afforded him all possible opportunities of judging for himself as to the means they had in hand, and the chances they had of successfully terminating a struggle which had already lasted for years.

The crafty old man thought the nakedness of the land much greater than it really was, and he afterwards made a report conformably to Knut his master and prince. Yet, on the morrow morning, when he was about to take his departure from the ever hospitable house of Ely, he took the Lord Abbat aside, and with bland looks and most gentle voice asked him whether he had not in the abbey some small matter to send as a present and welcoming gift to the royal Dane. Now good Thurstan, who was never of those that had expected a vast and unmingled good from the coming of the Danes, told him how he had broken open the shrine-boxes and stripped the shrines, and contaminated the house with dealing with usurers, in order to get what had been sent into Denmark as a present for the king.

"But," said the greedy Dane, "have there been no pilgrims to thy shrine since then?"

"Nay," said the Lord Abbat, "some few there have been that have left their little offerings; and, doubtless, many more will come ere many days be past, for in this blessed month occur the festivals of our saints, to wit, that of Saint Sexburga, queen and second abbess of this house, and that of her kinswoman and successor, Saint Withburga, virgin and abbess. On such seasons the donations of the faithful were wont to be most liberal; but alas! Few are the Saxons now that have anything left to give to Saxon saints! And the matter we have in our coffers at this present is too small for a gift to a prince, and is, moreover, much needed by this impoverished brotherhood."

To this the cunning, clutching old Dane said that a small matter was better than no money at all; that it had been the custom in all times to propitiate kings and princes with free gifts; that the Lord Abbat had better send such gold and silver as he had; and that the great Knut might come up to Ely after the festival of the two saints, when the shrine-boxes would be fuller, and so give the monks of Ely occasion to make a more suitable offering.

At these words Lord Thurstan grew red in the face, and stared at the Dane with a half incredulous look; and then he said, "Wouldst thou skin us alive? Wouldst take the last silver penny? Wouldst see the shrines of four among the greatest of our saints left in dirt and darkness? Dane, can it be that thou art herein doing the bidding of a royal and a Christian prince? Hast thou thy master's orders to ask that which thou art asking?"

Not a whit discountenanced, the old Dane said that men who lived with princes learned to know their wishes, and hastened to execute them, without waiting for express commands; and that he must repeat that he thought the best thing the Abbat of Ely could do, would be to send Prince Knut all the money he had in the house.

"By the rood," quoth Thurstan, still more angered, "these Danes be as rapacious as the Normans! By Saint Sexburga and Saint Witburga, and by every other good saint in the caldarium, I will not consent to this! I will not rob the shrines to get a mere beggar's alms. I cannot do the thing thou askest of mine own authority. Such matters must be discussed in full chapter, and settled by the votes of the officials and cloister-monks of the house. But I will not do even so much as to name the matter!"

"Then," said the phlegmatic old Dane, "I will speak to the prior, or to the chamberlain, or to some other official; and as time presses, my Lord Abbat, thou wilt hold me excused if I go and do it at once!"

And thus saying, he left good Thurstan, and went to some of the monks who had been standing near enough to overhear every word that had been said since the Lord Abbat waxed warm. The envious prior was there, and being ever ready to give pain to his superior, he proposed that the chapter should be summoned on the instant. This being agreed to by the major part, the monks withdrew towards the chapter-house, the cunning and cool old Dane saying to some of them as they went thither, that he much feared that if any distaste or disappointment were given to Knut, he would take his fleet back to Denmark and do nothing for the English. Short, therefore, was the chapter, and decisive the vote, notwithstanding the opposition of Thurstan and a few others: the shrine-boxes were again emptied, and the truly beggar-like amount of silver and gold was put into a silken purse to be carried to Lynn.

So incensed was the bounteous Lord Abbat, who ever had a large heart and a scorn for mean and covetous things, that he almost vowed not to go back with the old Dane to salute his royal master, and be present at the delivery of such a gift; but he bethought him that if he went not the prior must go, and that if the prior went some evil might come of it. And so the right noble Abbat of Ely went down to Lynn, together with the exiled abbats of other houses and sundry lords from the Camp of Refuge, much wishing that the Lord of Brunn were with him to aid him in the conference.

As Thurstan landed at Lynn, where he expected to see the royal ship and a good part of its attendant fleet, he was mortified to find that there were no ships there except a few Lynn barques; and, upon going into the town, he was yet more disappointed and distressed by hearing, from some good Saxons who had come in from the hamlets on the coast, that the Danish fleet had sailed away to the northward, leaving only a few of the smaller barks at the anchorage near the Wash. Sharply did he question the old Dane as to these movements. The Dane said that it was possible the prince had run a little along the north coast to pick up news, and that it was quite certain he would soon be back.

More than this he would not say, except that patience was a virtue. Some of our Saxons went almost mad with impatience; but on the next day they received intelligence that the fleet had returned to the anchorage off the chapel of our Ladie, and on the day next after that, Knut, with six of his largest ships, sailed up the Wash. In his run to the northward, if he had not picked up much news, he had picked up every English ship or barque that he found afloat, and he had plundered every defenseless village or township that lay near to that coast. He now cast his anchor a long way before he came to Lynn, and instead of proceeding to that good town to meet the English prelates and nobles, he sent up a messenger to summon them on board his own ship. At this the Abbat of Ely was much vexed and startled; and he said to himself, "Who shall tell me that this is not a plot, and that the Danes will not seize us and carry us off, or even deliver us up to the Normans?" but nearly all those who had accompanied him from Ely despaired of the salvation of England without Danish assistance, and were eager to go on shipboard and meet the prince in the way it pleased him to prescribe, and Thurstan grew ashamed of his fears and suspicions. Other good men, however, had their suspicions as well as the Lord Abbat; and when he embarked in the small Danish craft which had been left waiting for the envoy at Lynn, many trusty Saxons of the township and vicinage would absolutely go with him, and every bark or boat that could swim was crowded by the bold Lynn mariners, and rowed down to the Wash.

Knut, the son of the king of Denmark, standing on his proud gilded ship, received the English prelates and chiefs with great stateliness, yet not without courtesy; and when the silken purse and the scrapings of the shrine-treasures had been presented to him (Thurstan blushing the while), he sat down with his jarls on one side of a long table, and the Englishmen sat down on the opposite side; and then the conference began. Unhappily for the English landsmen a summer storm began to blow at the same time, causing the royal ship to roll, and thus making them feel the terrible sickness of the sea. At this Thurstan almost wished that he had let the prior come, instead of coming himself. Knut, the prince, spoke first in a very few words, and then his jarls further propounded and explained his plan of the war.

The Danes indeed had nearly all the talking to themselves, for not many of them understood what the English said, or had patience to hear it interpreted; the qualms and sickness of the English almost took away their power of speech, and, moreover, they very soon discovered that nothing they could say had any effect in altering the opinions and decisions of the predetermined Danes. It was grievous; they said that the English, who had been so rich, should now have so little money to share with their friends and deliverers! They hoped that the good prelates and lords would be able to hold out in the Isle of Ely and throughout the fen country; and as they had held out so long, no doubt they could hold out longer.

In the meanwhile they, their good allies the Danes, would divide their fleet, and scour all the coast, and sail up all the great rivers, for this would distract the attention of the Normans, would alarm them at one and the same time in many different and distant places, and infallibly compel them to recall their forces from Cam-bridge and Stamford, and to give up all premeditated attacks on the fen country.

"Aye," said a sea-rover, whose yellow hair had grown as white as snow with excess of age, and whose sunken eye glistened at the memory of past adventures of that sort, "Aye, Saxons! We will sweep all this eastern coast from north to south and from south to north, as with a besom! We will sail or row our barks up every river that flows into the sea on this side of your island, and that hath keels on its waters or towns on its banks. Tweed, Tyne, and Humber, Trent, Orwell, Stour, and Thamesis, with all the rivers that run between them or into them, shall hear our war-cry as of yore!"

"But, alas!" said one of the Saxon lords, "who will suffer in this kind of war but the Saxons? The Normans have very few ships. The ships on the coast and on the rivers, and the townships and hamlets, are all English still, and cannot be seized or destroyed without ruin to us and the cause which the king of Denmark hath engaged to support."

The old sea-rover was silent, and the other Danes pretended not to understand what the Saxon lord said. Abbat Thurstan told the prince that of a surety the Saxons in the Camp of Refuge could continue to defend themselves; but that they could do still better if the Danes would spare them some arms and other warlike harness, and remain for a while in the Wash and in the rivers which empty themselves into it, in order to co-operate with the Saxons. Knut, who well knew that there was nothing to be picked up in those waters, shook his head, and said that his own plan was the best, and could not be altered; and that, touching the matter of arms and harness, he had none to spare, but that he would send over to the Netherlanders' country and buy, if the Saxons would give him the money. Here the abbat and the Saxon lords were silent. But when Knut spoke of the great losses which the Danes had suffered in the foundering of their return fleet the year before, Thurstan reddened and said, "The Jarl Osbiorn acted a traitorous part, and hath been treated as a traitor by his brother and king. That loss was the direct judgment of Heaven! The fleet was loaded with the spoils of England and with the money taken from the Norman for betraying the English! Prince and jarls all! If ye be come to do as Osbiorn did last year, I say look to your fleet, and look to the health of your own souls!"

Hereupon Knut and his great chiefs began to cross themselves, and to make many promises and protestations; and then the prince called for wine and pledged the Lord Abbat of Ely and the other English lords, lay and ecclesiastic, severally: and when they had all drunk wine, he broke up the conference and dismissed them in a very unhappy state both of mind and of stomach, for the storm had increased, and the wine was sour and bad. The royal Dane hauled in his anchors and set sail to get out of the Wash and from among the dangerous sandbanks. As soon as the Saxon lords got ashore at Lynn, and free from their exceeding great sickness, Thurstan said that he greatly feared a woeful error had been committed in inviting the Danes back again, and that a short time would show that the Lord of Brunn had been quite right in recommending the Saxons to trust to their own arms and efforts for their independence; but those lords who had voted for the invitation said that it was clear the Danes would have come back whether they had been invited or not, and that it was equally clear that England could not be saved without the aid of some foreign nation. These lords also thought that a crowned king like Svend Estrithson would not break his royal word, and that the prince his son would not act like Osbiorn, albeit he might, in the ancient manner of the Danes, be too eager to scour the seas and rivers and capture whatever he might find, whether it belonged to friend or foe, to Saxon or to Norman. Yet, truth to say, these lords were far from feeling assured, and save one or two, that were afterwards proved to be false traitors in their hearts, they all returned to Ely sadder men than they were when they left it to go to meet Knut.

That which the white-headed sea-rover had said, and a great deal more than he uttered, speedily came to pass: north and south the English coast was plundered; and, ascending the many rivers in their lighter vessels and in their boats, the Danes went far into the interior of the country, pillaging, burning, and destroying, even as their forefathers had done in the heathenish times. Up the broad Humber they went until they got into the Yorkshire Ouse, and they would have gone on to the city of York, but that it was strongly garrisoned by Normans, and the whole country a desert—a desert which Osbiorn and his evil company had made in the preceding year. On the river Yare they went as high as the good city of Norwich, but they ventured not to attack the Normans in that place. The Waveney, too, and the Ald they visited, nor left the poor Saxons there so much as a fishing-boat. Up the river Deeben as far as the wood bridge, where a pleasant town hath since risen; and between the pleasant, green-wooded banks of the Orwell, they sailed many a league. After ravaging the banks of the Stour, Knut collected all his ships together and then spread his sails on the smooth Medway and the broad Thamesis, going up the Thamesis almost to London; and then mooring his ships, and making a great show as though he intended to land an army and lay siege to the Tower of London, which the Normans were then busily enlarging and strengthening.

Not all the doings of the Danes, and the robberies and cruelties they committed upon poor defenseless Saxons, could be known in the Camp of Refuge; yet enough was known by the report of the country people to grieve every English heart in the camp, and to confirm the worst suspicions which Abbat Thurstan had conceived. On the other hand, it was made apparent that the Normans were greatly distracted by this new invasion, and that, while their vicomtes and knights and men-at-arms were marching in almost every other direction, none of them came near to the last asylum of Saxon liberty. In truth, the posts which had previously been drawn round the fen country were so far weakened that the Lord Hereward, who had again taken a direct and entire command in the Camp of Refuge, made several good sallies from the fens and brought back not a few Norman prisoners, together with good store of provision.

Matters were in this good train in the camp when intelligence was brought that Knut, with the whole of his mighty fleet, had returned to the Wash. The Danish faction, or all those Saxon lords who counted more upon Danish assistance than upon their own valor and the valor of their countrymen, were greatly rejoiced at these tidings, and would not allow any man to doubt that Knut, having made good seizing's and spoils, was now come to co-operate with the English warriors and their great captain the Lord of Brunn; and these unwise lords, being partly guided or misguided by traitors, outvoted the Lord Abbat, and sent down a deputation to Lynn to salute and welcome the royal Dane, and to invite him and escort him to Ely. And this time Knut was nothing loth to come: and he came up the river with a part of his fleet of ships and with many of his jarls and most famed warriors. Crowned kings had visited the great house of Ely before now, and kings of the Danish as well as of the Saxon line, but to none of them had there been given a more splendid feast than was now given to Knut, who as yet was but a jarl and a king's son. The Saxon dames of high name and beauty came in from the Camp of Refuge, or from houses in the township of Ely, or in circumjacent hamlets, to welcome the princely stranger and adorn the festival; and fairest among these fair was Alftrude, the young wife of the Lord of Brunn. The Lord Hereward himself was there, but much less cheerful and festive than was his wont; for on his last sally from the fens he had heard more than he knew before of the evil doings of the Dane; and, moreover, he had ever suspected their good faith.

When the feasting was over, the cunning old Dane, that had come up to Ely before as envoy from the prince, began to relate what great mischief Knut had done to Duke William, and what great service he had rendered to the House of Ely and the Camp of Refuge, and the whole fen country, by the diversion he had made with his ships; and before any of the Saxon lords could reply or make any observation upon these his words, the astute Dane asked whether the festivals of Saint Sexburga and Saint Withburga had been well attended by pilgrims, and whether the shrine-boxes had had a good replenishing? The chamberlain, who ought not to have spoken before his superior the Lord Abbat, said that the festivals had been thronged, and that, considering the troublesome times, the donations of the pilgrims had been liberal.

"That is well," said the old fox, "for our ships have had much wear and tear, and stand in need of repairs; and the prince wants some gold and silver to pay his seamen and his fighting men, who are growing weary and dissatisfied for want of pay."

Here the Lord Abbat looked rather grim, and said, "Of a truth I thought that thy people had made great booty! By Saint Etheldreda, the founder of this house—the house was never so poor as it now is, or had such urgent need of money as it now hath! By my soul it is but a small matter that is in our shrine-boxes, and all of it, and more than all, is due unto the Jews!"

"It is sinful and heathenish to pay unto Jews the gold and silver which Christian pilgrims have deposited on the shrines of their saints," said one of the Danish jarls.

And here at the Lord Abbat Thurstan blushed and held down his head, much grieving that, though against his vote and will, the house had been driven to traffic with Israelites and money-changers; yet still remembering that this evil thing had been begun in order to get money to send to the insatiate Danes. All this while Prince Knut kept his state, and said not a word. But the cunning old man went on to say, that hitherto the profits of the expedition had not been half enough to pay King Svend Estrithson the price of half the ships he had lost last year; and that, although the amount of gold and silver in the shrine-boxes might be but small, there was a rumor that there was other good treasure in the house.

Here it was that the Lord of Brunn grew red, for he was the first to understand that the greedy Dane meant to speak of the chalices and pateras, the crown of gold, the gold and silver tables, and the other things of great price that he had brought away with him from Peterborough in order that they might be saved from Torauld of Fescamp. Again speaking, when he ought not to have spoken—before Abbat Thurstan could speak or collect his thoughts—the chamberlain said, "Verily, oh Dane! I have under my charge some strong boxes which the Lord of

Brunn sent hither from Peterborough; and, albeit, I know not with precision what these strong boxes contain..."

Here Abbat Thurstan stopped the talkative chamberlain and said, "Let the strong boxes contain what they will, the contents are none of ours! They be here as a sacred deposit, to be returned to the good monks of Peterborough when they can get back to their house and their church, and live without dread of Saxon traitors and Norman plunderers!"

But many of the Danes, believing the Peterborough treasure to be far greater than it was, said that it would be no such sin to employ it for secular purposes, or to give it for the support of friends and allies who had quitted their homes and their countries, and had crossed the stormy ocean to aid the English; for that, when the Danes and the English between them should have driven the Normans out of the land, there would be no lack of gold and silver wherewith to replace the sacred vessels, and to give back to Peterborough Abbey far more than had been taken from it. Some of them declared, and severally promised and swore by their own saints, that if Knut, their leader, and the son of their king, was but gratified in this particular, he would land all his best warriors and join Hereward the Saxon, and so go in search of Duke William and bring the Normans to battle: and if Knut did not swear by his saints, or say much by word of mouth, he nodded his head and seemed to consent—the christened infidel, and unprince-like prince that he was.

It may be judged whether Lord Hereward was not eager for such an increase of strength as might enable him to carry the war into the heart of England or under the walls of the city of London! It may be judged whether he did not burn for the opportunity of fighting a great and decisive battle: but Hereward had a reverence for the property of the church, and a great misgiving of the Danes; and he whispered to his best friend, the Lord Abbat, "If we put this guilt upon our souls, and give these insatiate Danes all that they ask, they will do not for us that which they promise, but will sail away in their ships with the plunder they have made as soon as the storms of winter approach."

This too was the doubt if not the entire belief of Thurstan. But the chamberlain and the prior called out aloud for a chapter; and those who were of a party with the prior and chamberlain labored might and main to convince the whole brotherhood that the Danes ought to be gratified, and that they could be gratified without sin. Nay, some of them whispered to the more timid part of the community, that if the Peterborough treasure, as well as the shrine-money, were not quietly given to Knut, he would take it by force, as the house and the avenues to it were filled with his armed men, and as his barks were lying close under the abbey walls. The call for a chapter now became so loud and general that the Lord Abbat could not resist it; and so, leaving his guests in the hall, Thurstan went to the chapter-house, and, being followed by all who were competent to vote, the doors were closed, and the brotherhood deliberated.

That deliberation was long, and would have been longer but for the impatience of the Danes, who vociferated in the hall, and even went the length of running to the door of the chapter-house and striking upon it, with loud and most unmannerly shoutings. At last it was resolved by the majority, and sorely against the will of the Lord Abbat, that the Danes should have the shrine-money, with other Ely treasure, and all the Peterborough treasure, with the exception of the relics, for which it was thought they would care but little, inasmuch as they were not relics of Danish saints.

Thurstan was so grieved at this resolution that he would not report it in the hall; but the prior gladly charged himself with the office, and then he and the chamberlain and the sacrist conveyed the cunning old Dane, and the prince, his master, into the treasury of the house, and there counted and delivered over to them all the gold and silver, and all the gilded crosses and silver vessels, and all the silks and hangings, with everything else which had been brought from Peterborough, except the relics. But even these last were taken out of the reliquaries which held them, as the said reliquaries were made of gold and of silver, or of crystal and amber curiously wrought, and so Knut would carry them away with him.

Let Peterborough weep for its own, and Ely weep for that which was its own! King Canute, who had so loved to keep the festival of the Purification in great solemnity at Ely Abbey, had once brought his wife unto the abbey, and Emma, the queen, had given many rich gifts to the church. A piece of purple cloth, wrought with gold and set with jewels, such as there was none like it in the kingdom, she offered to St. Etheldreda; and to the other saints there, she offered to each of them a covering of silk, embroidered and set with jewels, but of less value than the former.

Also did Emma, the queen of King Canute, give, as a covering for the high altar, a large pall of a green color, adorned with plates of gold, to be used on the grand festivals; and to be placed over this she gave a great piece of fine linen of a deep red color; and this linen covered the whole of the altar, and reached from the corners quite down to the ground, and it had a gold fringe more than a foot in breadth, and making a rich and glorious show. Prince Knut knew of these precious gifts of Queen Emma, for the fame of them had gone into foreign lands, and therefore his cunning old man asked for them and got them, to the great displeasure of the saints.

As the Danes were carrying all this treasure down to their ships, the cunning old man renewed his assurances that the prince, being thus gratified, would soon do great things for the Saxon cause. Hereward asked the old man in his plain direct way, when Knut would land his warriors? The cunning man replied that it was not for him to fix the day and hour, but that his lordship would soon hear news of the fleet. The Lord of Brunn then turned aside and said to the Lord Abbat—"By Saint Ovin and his cross, I believe the first news will be that the fleet has started back to Denmark! Let us yet stop this treasure and send them away empty-handed, at least from Ely! I care nought for their serried ranks, and ponderous battle-axes. We have a good force, my Lord Abbat, in the township, and, were that not more than enough; a few blasts of the Saxon horn would bring us warriors from the Camp!"

"My son," said Thurstan, "I fear their battle-axes no more than thou dost; but I cannot dare act in violation of the decisions of the chapter. Alas! There are jealousies and animosities enough already. As sure as the sun shines in the heavens, that dark browed, envious prior is in a plot against me! Could he find the opportunity, he would deprive me of my authority by a vote of the house in chapter. I dare not resist the will of the majority: the gold and the treasure must even go, since traitors and fools, but more fools than traitors, have so willed it."

"Then," quoth the Lord of Brunn, "Let us only hope and pray that this Knut may have more good faith and honor than we give him credit for."

"I will speak to him again, ere he departs," said the Abbat. And Thurstan spoke earnestly to Knut, and Knut nodded his head, and uttered many Ahs! And Ohs! but said nothing farther. It was thought by some that this taciturnity did not proceed from choice but from necessity, as the son of the Danish King had swallowed a prodigious quantity of wine, and could hardly stand on his legs without support. And in the drinking of wine and strong drinks, if other nations marveled at the Saxons, the Saxons themselves marveled at the Danes. So great was the quantity consumed on this day that the wine-cellars at Ely, which had not been replenished since Lord Hereward's first return from foreign parts, were left almost dry. And thus, having drunk nearly all the wine and taken off all the treasure of the house, the Danes and their prince got back to their ships. Knut stood up on the deck of the royal galley, just under the royal standard of Denmark, and made some gestures, as though he would make a speech. Such of the monks of Ely, and such of the Saxon lay lords as had given him their attendance to the water-side, stood a-tip-toe on the river-bank, and strained their eyes to see, and opened wide their ears to hear; but nothing came from Knut but an Ah! and an Oh! and a loud hickup; and the galley being unmoored and the rowers on their banks, Knut waved his hand, and the vessel glided down the river towards Lynn.

That very night the town of Lynn, which had received the Danish fleet in all friendship and with much hospitality, was plundered and set fire to; and before the next night the whole fleet had quitted the Wash and the English coast, and was in full sail for Denmark, loaded with the plunder of England and with the money which had been again paid by the Normans as the price of Danish treachery.

Even while he was lying in the river Thamesis with his great fleet, and seemed to threaten the Tower of London, Knut received on board envoys and rich presents from Duke William, and was easily made to sign a treaty of

CONQUEST OF THE ISLE OF ELY

amity and alliance with the Normans, even as his uncle Osbiorn had done the year before. And did the traitorous Danes enjoy the spoil they had gotten? Not so. When they got into the middle of the sea there arose a violent storm and dispersed the ships wherein were lodged the spoils made at Ely and at other places, and some of these ships went to Norway, some to Ireland, and some to the bottom of the sea; and all of the spoils of Ely and Peterborough that reached Denmark consisted of a table and a few reliquaries and crucifixes; and these things, being deposited in the church of a town belonging to King Svend, were consumed by fire, for the careless and drunken shipmen set fire to the town and church by night, and so caused the loss of much more treasure than that which the shipmen had brought with them from England.

The amount of the total treasure paid to Knut by Duke William was never known with any certainty in England, out of the very vitals of which it was torn; but it is known in another place, where all these acts of treachery are recorded, and heavily will it press upon the soul of Knut, and upon the selfish soul of his father, Svend Estrithson, who ratified the foul bargain he had made. And, even in this world, hath not the avenging hand of Heaven smitten them twain? Hath not the excommunication of the holy church fallen twice upon Svend? Hath not unnatural warfare raged long between the sons of Svend, and hath not Knut been murdered in his prime—aye, murdered, in a church, to which he fled for sanctuary? He had offended the saints by his broken faith, and by plundering the shrines in England; and therefore no shrine or altar could save him from the treachery and malice of his own subjects.

All the evils done to England by Knut and his Danes are not yet told, but they will plainly appear hereafter.

CHAPTER XIX.

THE NORMAN WITCH

So the Danes and their ships were gone with all that they could carry with them; and the Saxons of Ely and in the Camp of Refuge, after being robbed as well as betrayed, were left to their own devices. Much was Duke William heartened by the departure of Knut, and the treaty he had made with him; and, seeing no enemy in any other part of England, he gave his whole mind to the war in the Fen-country. More knights and adventurers had come over from France and from sundry other countries to aid the Conqueror in his enterprises, and to seek provision and fortune in unhappy England. Choosing some of the best of these new comers, and joining them to troops that had been tried in the hard warfare of the Fen-country, the Son of Robert the Devil by the harlot of Falaise sent strong garrisons to Grantham and Stamford, and Peterborough, and Cam-Bridge; and, carrying with him his chancellor and nearly the whole of his court, he quitted London and went himself to Cam-Bridge to direct the war in person. As he and his mighty great host were marching through the country towards the river Cam, and as the poor Saxon people counted the number of the lances, they said, "Miserere Domine! The conquest of our country is complete, and not even Hereward the Brave will be able longer to defend the Camp of Refuge!"

When Duke William arrived in the camp at Cam-Bridge, and examined the Fen-country which lay before him, he severely censured the folly and rashness of Eustache of Ambleville; and also chiding the impatient and self-confident knights that were now with him and eager to fall on, he swore his terrible oath, by the splendor of God's face, that he would not allow of any fighting until the ancient causeway should be repaired and fortified with towers, and another and a broader causeway carried across the marshes into the very heart of the fens, and opposite to the point where on the Saxons had constructed the main defense of their Camp of Refuge. Timber and stones and baked bricks were brought from all parts of the country, and every Saxon serf that could be caught was impressed, and was forced to labor almost unto death upon works intended for the destruction of his countrymen. Skillful artisans and men experienced in the making of roads and the building of bridges were brought to Cam-Bridge from the city of London, from the city of Caen in Normandie, and from other places beyond the seas; and the task which William had in hand was made the easier by the long-continued, unwonted dryness of the season.

But the Lord of Brunn, although he prayed heartily for rain, did in no wise lose heart; and in proportion as his difficulties increased, his wit and invention increased also. The working parties on the roads were constantly covered and protected by great bodies of troops put under the command of vigilant officers; but this did not prevent Hereward from stealing through the tall, concealing rushes of the fens, and the forests of willows and alders, and falling upon the workmen and destroying their works. On several occasions he cut the Norman guard to pieces before they could form in order of battle; and several times he destroyed in a single night the labor of many days, levelling the Norman towers with the ground, breaking up their bridges, and carrying off their timber and their tools and other good spoil. It always happened that when his enemies were surest he would not come, he came; and when they expected him at one given point, he was sure to make an attack upon another and distant point. At times his ambuscades, surprises, and onslaughts were so numerous and rapid that he seemed to have the faculty of being in many places at one and the same time. Many a Norman knight was surprised at his post, or even carried off from the midst of a camp, and dragged through the rushes and forests at the dead of night, an astounded and helpless captive. Many a time a great body of Norman troops would take to flight and leave all their baggage behind them, upon merely hearing the shout of "Hereward for England!" or those other shouts, "The Lord of Brunn is coming! Fly, ye Norman thieves! Out! out!" Such were Lord Hereward's successes, and such the Norman awe of his unforeseen stratagems and unaccountable surprises, that the Normans entirely believed Hereward to be in league with the devil, and to be aided by witches and necromancers and fiends worse than the blubber devils of Crowland.

Now it was true that, for many of his stratagems and devices, and for many of the sleights and tricks with which he appalled the Normans, Hereward was indebted to the science and travail of that thin, dark man of Salerno and Norman-hater, Girolamo; and, by means of deserters from the camp, and by means of ransomed Normans that had been allowed to quit the camp, the Salernitan, if he had not been made well known to the Normans, had been much talked about, and had become the object of so much dread that no knight or man-at-arms ever named his name without crossing himself. Nor were the Normans long before they agreed, one and all, that the dark and silent Salernitan was Hereward's chief magician, the devil-dealing necromancer to whom he stood indebted for all his successes.

Loudly did they raise their voices against this supposed wickedness; and yet, when they found that their misfortunes and losses went on increasing, they came to the resolution to meet what was no witchcraft at all with real witchcraft, and they told Duke William in Cam-Bridge Castle that he must send over into Normandie for the most famed witch of that land, where there was no lack either of witches or of warlocks; and the son of Robert the Devil, whose father, as his name imports, had been liege man to Lucifer, sent over to Normandie accordingly to seek for the most dreaded of Norman witches.

Now, whether it was this wickedness that did it, or whether it was that the moist air of the fens and the autumnal season did not suit Duke William, certain at least it is that he fell sick of a fever and ague, and thereupon took a hurried departure from Cam-Bridge and travelled towards London, having first sent to call from Stamford town Ivo Taille-Bois to take the command of the great army. Now, when Ivo came to Cam-Bridge, and when Duke William was away in London, matters went far worse with the Normans than before, for the Viscomte was not a great captain, as the Duke assuredly was. Moreover, many of the troops took the ague, and others were so unmanned by their fears that they could never be made to stand their ground; and, in fine, all vowed that they would not venture among the woods and bulrushes, nor attempt any feat of arms whatever until the great witch should arrive from Normandy to countervail the black arts of the Salernitan and the other wizards and witches they falsely believed to be employed by the pious Lord of Brunn.

At last a terrible Norman witch arrived at Cam-Bridge, and she was received in the entrenched camp and in the castle with transports of exceeding great joy. Loathsome and wicked at the same time were it to describe the person and features, the attire and demeanor, the spells and incantations of this frightful and detestable portentous.

Her years far exceeded the ordinary length of human life, and they had all been spent in sin and in the practice of infernal arts: in sin and actual devilry had she been conceived and born, for her mortal father was none other than that arch-heresiarch and enemy to the saints, Leutarde of Vertus, in the bishopric of Chalons, who went about with a sledge-hammer breaking the images of God's saints, and preaching that God's prophets had not always prophesied the truth, and that God-living servants and ministers of the altar had no right to their tithes!

Since the day when her sire, pursued by his bishop, cast himself head foremost into a deep well and was drowned (for the devils, in their compact with him, had only agreed that he should never be burned), this foul Strega, his only daughter, had wandered over the face of the wide earth doing mischief, and dwelling most in those forsaken, accursed parts of the earth where witchcraft does most flourish. It was said that she had been as far north as that dread isle which is covered with snow, and which yet is forever vomiting smoke and flames; even to that northern isle which pious men believe to be one of the entrances into hell, and which has been notoriously inhabited at all times by devils and devil-worshippers; that she had lived among the Laps, who call up demons by beat of drum; and that she had dwelt in the Orcades, where the devil's dam and her handmaidens use to raise great storms, and to sell wind foul or fair.

Of a surety was there no witch of all that congregated round the witch-tree of Beneventum more known than this! It was known, too, how she came by that broken leg which made her limp in her gait. Once in flying through the air to the hellish Sabbath at Beneventum she came too near to the cross of Saint Peter's Church at Rome, and so fell to the earth.

Ivo Taille-Bois, profane man as he was, would have turned with horror from the witch, but in his sinful ignorance he believed that the devil's arts might be employed against the devil, and he saw that all the soldiery, nay, and all the chivalry put under his command, believed that without witchcraft they could never cope with the Lord of Brunn, nor make any way in the Fen-country. As for the witch herself, she promised the men immediate and most marvelous victories. Therefore it was agreed that she should go forth with the troops and the working parties and penetrate into the fens, and that she should take her station on a high wooden tower, and thence give her directions as well to the working men as to the fighting men.

Now Lord Hereward and Girolamo of Salerno, being advised of the arrival of the hag and of the plans of the Normans, took counsel together, and trusted, with the aid of the saints, to break the spell and sortilege, and consume the witch while in the very act of her witchcraft. Calling in his merry men from all their outposts, and posting them behind a river, Lord Hereward allowed the Normans to advance a good way into the fens, and he offered them no molestation while they were building a lofty wooden tower in the midst of an open plain.

But when the tower was finished and the witch was at her incantations, and when the Norman band was gathered round the foot of the tower in that open plain, Hereward and Girolamo, aided only by Elfric and a few other alert Saxons, came round unseen to the edge of the plain and set fire to the dense reeds and rushes that grew upon it. It is the custom of the fenners to burn their reeds and stubble in the month of November of every year in order to fertilize the soil with the ashes thereof; and at this season one sees all this Moorish country in a flame, to his great wonder and surprise, if he be a stranger in these parts. It was now the burning-time, and owing to the exceeding dryness of the summer and of the autumn likewise, the reeds and junci in this plain were all as dry as matches: add to this that the Saleritan had brought with him and had sprinkled over the plain some of his marvelous compounds which made a raging and inextinguishable fire, and that the wind was blowing keenly from the north-east right across the plain and towards the tall wooden tower, and then it may be, to some degree, imagined, how rapidly and awfully the flames, once lit, rolled over that broad open field, crackling, and hissing, and then roaring in the wind, while columns of thick, pungent, suffocating smoke rolled after them, darkening the sun and sky and making visible the horrible red glare.

At the first glimpse of the mighty blaze the hag stopped her incantation and let the hell-broth she was brewing drop from her skinny hands with a hideous yell; and the men-at-arms and the laborers that were gathered at the foot of the tower cast a look of dread and horror to windward and screamed like the witch, and then took to their heels and ran across the plain in the desperate hope of keeping before the winds and the flames, and paying no heed to the witch, who had no means of descending from her tower.

"Ha! ha! Thou hag! where is thy witch-tree of Beneventum now, which no mortal axe can cut down or lop, and no earthly fire consume? Ha! witch! where be the broad double channels and the rapid and cool streams of the river Calor? If they flowed by thee close as they used to do when thou wast perched on that witch-tree, high as is thy tower, wouldst not leap headlong into the deep water? Ha! Accursed daughter of Leutard Iconoclastes, wouldst call upon the saints whose blessed effigies were broken by thy fathers sledge hammer? What! Dost scream and raise thy skinny hands to Heaven? 'Tis vain, 'tis vain! the saints in Heaven will not hear thee, so down with thy hands towards earth and the fiery plain, and invoke the fiends to whom thou hast sold thy soul. So, so! The fire catches and thy tower of wood crackles in the flames, and the flames mount upward and embrace thee round about and lick thee with their blistering tongues! Ha! Shriek and writhe! These flames give only a mild foretaste of thine eternal doom. These flames are but fed with dry rushes and fen-grass, and the wood of the oak and pine; but the unquenchable flames of the nethermost pit are fed with brimstone and naphtha. See! The tower falls and she is consumed, flesh and bones, in the hissing fire!—and so perish all witches!"

Thus spoke Girolamo of Salerno, like the true believer that he was, as the Norman witch was burning. But the hag did not perish alone; the crackling fire, carried onward by the strong wind, overtaking and consuming nearly all the Normans that had advanced with her into the plains to set up her accursed tower. Ivo Taille-Bois, with the rest of the Norman host, had stopped at the ford where the witch had crossed before she came into the plain; but when he saw the fire kindled and roll across the fen almost as rapidly as the waters of a mighty cataract, and saw the smoke arise and shut out the sight of the blessed sun, Ivo turned and fled, and every man with him fled in wild dismay, nor stopped until they came to the castle by Cam-Bridge. And the ford where the hag crossed over into the plain is called unto this day Witchford.

And when the fire which Girolamo had lit had burned itself out, and the smoke had cleared away, the fierce wind fell and there came on a terrible storm of thunder and lightning; and when this was over the long delayed rains began to fall in torrents, filling the rivers and brooks and marsh pools, and making the whole country once more impassable; and these rains, intermitting only for brief hours, continued to fall for seven days and seven nights; and that part of the causeway which had been built by Duke William's orders was undermined and washed away, so that no trace remained of it. And then, while the Normans remained penned up in the castle and in the entrenched camp, the Lord of Brunn and his Saxons launched their light boats in the rivers and meres, and destroyed all the works which had been built to defend the whole road. Thus in the next year the Conqueror had everything to begin anew. In the meanwhile Ivo Taille-Bois gave up the command in despair, and went away to Stamford, where he had left his wife, the Ladie Lucia. During the winter this Vicomte of Spalding made an essay to recover possession of the Ladie Lucia's manor-house and estates at Spalding; but as the Saxons had still a little fleet of barks and the entire command of the Welland river, Ivo failed entirely, and was not even able to do so much as disturb the tranquility of the good Saxon monks of Crowland.

And while the Norman vicomte was thus unsuccessful, other and great successes attended the Saxon lord. With one numerous band collected near his house at Brunn, the Lord Hereward found his way across the country as far as Newark, where he defeated a great body of Normans, and found good spoil; and after this, with another band, drawn mostly from the impenetrable bogs of Hollande, he ascended the Witham as far as Boston and there surprised and captured three Norman knights, and some three-score Norman men-at-arms.

And it so chanced that among these three knights was that unlucky wooer Geoffroy, the brother of Ivo, who had found in some upland part of England a Saxon wife and heiress, but one neither so handsome nor so rich as the Ladie Alftrude, for it was a widow quite old enough to be Sir Geoffroy's mother, and her whole estate was not much larger than one of the Ladie Alftrude's farms. Having no money to pay for his ransom, and his brother having none to give or lend him, Geoffroy was sent into the fens and kept there as a close prisoner. And before the Lord of Brunn had done, he made other members of that family know what it was to live among the bulrushes.

But now, having done all these things, and performed many other exploits, Hereward, at the approach of spring, brought his fair young spouse from Ely to his house at Brunn, and a very few days after her arrival the lady gave birth to an heir to the united honours of Brunn and Ey. And hereupon followed high rejoicings, and a christening, and such an hospitable feast as only true Saxon lords knew how to give. The good-hearted Lord Abbat of Crowland baptized the child, and sundry of his monks, and the good prior of Spalding among them, were bidden to the feast. "Elfric, my trusty sword-bearer," said the Lord of Brunn when the feast was over, "Elfric, I say, methinks I have given proof, that a man may love and fight, and be a husband and a soldier, at one and the same time, and that if we are to put off thy espousal day with maid Mildred until this war be over, thou wilt run a chance of never being married at all!"

"Good, my Lord," said Elfric, "This is what I have been thinking for more than these nine months past."

"Then be shrew me," said the Lord of Brunn, "thou and Mildred shall be made one before the world be a moon older!"

The Lord of Brunn meant what he said; but Heaven ordered it otherwise.

CHAPTER XX.

THE NORMAN DUKE TRIES AGAIN

William of Normandie sate in his gorgeous hall in the royal citadel of Winchester: the proud crown of England was on his head, and the jeweled scepter in his hand, and knights, lords, and prelates stood in his presence to do his every bidding, and to tell him that he was the greatest of conquerors and sovereign princes; yet a cloud was on his broad brow, and his face was sad and thoughtful.

"I am no king of England," said he, "so long as this Hereward the Saxon holds out against me or lives! This scepter is a child's plaything unless I can drive the Saxons out of the Camp of Refuge!"
"The robbers and outlaws shall be driven out," said Hugo of Grantmesnil.
"Hugo," said the duke, "it is five years since thou first toldest me that, and the camp seems stronger now than ever it was."
"If it were not for the drowning waters, and the sinking bogs, and all the abominations of those fens and forests, which are fit only for Saxon hogs to wallow in, the deed were easy to do," said Peter of Blainville.
"Be it easy or be it hard," quoth Duke William, "the deed must be done, or we must all prepare to go back into Normandie, and give up all that we have gotten! It bots us little to have bought off the greedy Dane; for Philip of France, whom some do call my suzerain lord, is one that will prefer conquest to money; and Philip is not only threatening my dominions in Normandie, but is also leaguing with mine enemies in this island; he is

corresponding with the King of the Scots, and with Edgar Etheling the Saxon, and guest and brother-in-law to the Scottish king; and if this rebellion in the Fen-country be not soon suppressed, we may soon count upon seeing a French army on the coast, and a Scottish army marching through the north; and then the wild men will rush from the mountains of Wales and invade us in the west, as they have done aforetime; and thereupon will ensue a universal rising of the Saxon people, who are nowhere half subdued. By the splendor! While these things last I am no king!"

One of the Norman prelates lifted up his voice and asked, whether the offer of a free pardon, and the promise of a large sum of money, would not make Hereward the Saxon abandon the Saxon cause, and desert from the Camp of Refuge?

"By Notre Dame of Bayeux!" said Bishop Odo, the warlike and always fighting brother of Duke William, "by Notre Dame, and by my own sword and soul, this young man Hereward is not like other men! He hath been offered a free pardon, with possession of his lands, whether his by marriage or by inheritance, and he hath been promised as much gold and silver as would pay for a king's ransom; and yet he hath rejected all this with scorn, and hath vowed, by his uncouth Saxon saints, that so long as a hundred men can be kept together in the Fen-country, he will never submit, or cease his warfare against the Normans!"

"But that devil from beyond the Alps," said the Norman prelate who had spoken before, "that rebel to the house of Guiscard, that necromancer, Girolamo of Salerno, is he not to be bought?"

"It hath been tried," said Bishop Odo, "but to no effect. That Italian devil is more at thirst for Norman blood than is the Saxon devil. Before he quitted his home and fled beyond seas to seek out new enemies to our race, he gained a name which still makes the bravest of our Normans in Italy say a Libera nos when they utter it! We will burn him alive when we catch him, but until that hour comes there is nothing to hope and much to fear from him, for he hath given up his life and soul to vengeance, and he hath more skill in the art of war, and is more versed in the diabolical arts of magic, than any other man upon earth."

"But what of the Saxon Abbat of Ely?" said the prelate who had before spoken about the efficacy of bribes, "what of this Thurstan?"

"There is not a stubborn Saxon out of hell," replied Odo, Bishop of Bayeux; "he hath been tried long since. Thou mightest as well attempt to bribe the raging sea! Thou mightest grill him on a gridiron like Saint Lawrence, or tear him into small pieces with iron pincers like Saint Agatha, and he would only curse us and our conquest, and pray for the usurper Harold, whom the fools firmly believe to be alive!"

"But," said the other prelate, "among the other clownish monks of Ely, may there not be found a———"

"Peace!" said Duke William, "that hath been thought of already, and perhaps something may come of it—that is, if ye be but silent and discreet. Ye are all too loud-tongued, and overmuch given to talking; and these walls, though raised by Norman hands, may yet have Saxon ears! Retire to the innermost council chamber."

And William rose and withdrew to the innermost room, and those who had the right followed, and the chamberlains closed the door and kept guard on the outside, and the heavy door-curtains were drawn within so that none might approach the door, and not even the chamberlains hear what passed inside. That secret council lasted till a late hour of the evening. The words which were said be not known, but the things determined upon were made known but too soon. It was the eve of Saint Mark the Evangelist, and, before the feast of Saint Bede the Venerable, Duke William was again at Cam-Bridge, and with a far greater army and train than he had sent thither the preceding year; and at the same time a great fleet of ships and barks began to be prepared in the London river. No more witches were sent for, but William called over many more experienced warriors from France, and ordered barks to be equipped in the rivers and ports of Normandie. The traitorous Dane had told him that he must leave his war horses in their stalls, and think of ships and boats, if he would drive the amphibious Saxons out of the Fen-country.

While the banner of William floated over the Julius Tower, or Keep, on the tall mound by Cam-Bridge, country hinds and laborers of all sorts, and horses and draught oxen, and mules and asses too numerous to count, were collected within the fortified camp; and again timber and stones and burned bricks were brought from all parts of the land, and in greater abundance than before. For several weeks nothing was heard but the sawing of wood and the hewing and chipping of stone, and a loud and incessant hammering. A stranger to the history and present woes of England might have thought that the Normans were going to build a Tower of Babel, or that, penitent for the mischief they had done, they were going to rebuild the town at Cam-Bridge, in order to bring back the affrighted muses, and the houseless professors of learning, and the pining English students, to sumptuous inns and halls.

In truth, there seemed work and stuff enough to furnish out a great city altogether new. But, upon a near view, a knowing eye would have seen that all this toil was for the making of engines of war, of towers to place along the

CONQUEST OF THE ISLE OF ELY

where his Norman witch had crossed over. But the ford was now guarded by a double castle, or double fort; the one on this side of the stream, and the other on that; and the farther bank and the plain beyond it seemed, as the duke approached a little nearer, to be covered with a Saxon army, and with trophies taken from the Normans.

Onward, however, he went until he saw the banner of his half-brother Count Robert held out over the wooden walls of the Saxons; but then he understood full well what had befallen his people at Wisbech; and so, like the persevering and prudent commander that he was, he ordered an immediate retreat. But it passed his skill and his might to conduct this retreat in a safe and orderly manner; the Normans got confused, and Hereward, crossing at the ford, charged through thick and thin, through bog and dry ground, and along the temporary causeway which had been made: the bridges of wood broke down under excess of weight; Duke William himself fell into deep water and was nearly drowned, and many of his people were wholly drowned or smothered, while many more were slain by the sword or taken prisoners. And still the bold Saxons, as they followed, shouted, "Hereward for England! Stop, thou Bastard William! Thou art running as fast as thy brother Robert ran from Castle Hereward!"

After this misadventure Duke William judged more favorably of the conduct of his many commanders who had failed in the same enterprise; and seeing all the difficulties of the war, and the inexhaustible resources of that cunning captain, the Lord of Brunn, he called a council in the castle at Cam-Bridge, and there determined to try no more battles and assaults, but to rely solely upon a close blockade of the Isle of Ely. Forthwith orders were sent to all the commanders of posts round the Fen-country (the dull-witted Count Robert was recalled from

Wisbech, and an abler captain sent to that vicinage) to strengthen themselves in their several positions by building towers and walls, and digging trenches, and by increasing the numbers of their men-at-arms; but at the same time they were strictly commanded to make no movement beyond the limits of their defensive works, however great the temptation to attack the Saxons might be. The great fleet so long collecting in the river Thamesis, and which was in good part composed of English vessels which the Danes had captured and then sold to Duke William, was sent round the coast well filled with fighting men, and piloted by some of those Danish mariners and sea rovers who knew so well all the bays and rivers on this eastern coast; and by the end of the month of July, or a little before the Feast of Saint Ethelwold, every station on the coast, from the mouth of the Orwell to the broader mouth of the river Humber, was watched and guarded, and every estuary, river, or creek that gave egress from the Fen-country was blocked up by ships and barks, in such sort that the Saxons in the Camp of Refuge could no longer have any communication with the sea, or with the countries beyond the sea, from whence they had been wont to draw arms and munitions of war, and corn, wines, and oil, and other supplies.

By the same means all aid and friendly intercourse were completely cut off; the good Saxons dwelling in a sort of independence on the northern shores of England, and the good Englishmen that had fled into Scotland, could no longer send their barks up the Wash and the Ouse with provisions and comfort for the house of Ely and the Camp; and thus the whole Isle of Ely was cut off, by land and by water, from all the rest of the world, and was girded by a mighty chain, the links of which seemed every day to grow stronger.

Many were the bold essays which the Lord of Brunn made to break up this blockade. Twice, descending the Ouse, or the Welland, with the barks he had stationed at Ely, and near to Spalding, he defeated and drove away the enemy's ships, and burned some of them with that unquenchable fire which the Salernitan knew how to make; but after these actions the Normans and their shipmen became more watchful and cautious, keeping outside of the mouths of the rivers, and continuing to increase their force; for other ships and barques, both great and small, came over from Normandie, and others were hired for this service among the sea-dwelling Netherlanders, who seemed evermore disposed to serve whatever faction could pay them best.

And alas! The Normans had now their hands in the great and ever-filling treasury of broad England, and the true sons of England, whether at Ely or in the Camp, had no longer any gold or silver! or any means of sending forth that which can bring back money or the money's worth. Horned cattle had they still in some abundance, nor was there, as yet, any scarcity in sheep, or in wool, or in hides; but of corn to make the bread, which is the staff of life, and of wine, which maketh glad the heart of man, was there little or none left in this part of the land; forasmuch as that the Fen-country did not grow much corn at any season, and the last season had been one of dearth, and only a few butts of wine had been brought over since the departure of the Danes, owing to the lack of money above mentioned.

Those sea-rovers, having drunk almost the last drop of wine as well as carried off the last treasures of the house, had greatly disheartened and troubled many of the monks of Ely, and murmurs, and censures, and base thoughts now began to rise among several of the cloister-monks who, down to this evil time, had been the steadiest friends of the Lord Abbat, Thurstan. Truly, truly, their trial was hard, and difficult for true Saxon stomachs to bear! The octaves of Saint John had come and passed without anything that could be called a feast: on the day of Saint Joseph of Arimathea they had no wine to drink, and on the day of that high Saxon saint, Osevald, king and martyr, they had no bread to eat with their roast meats. These were sad things to a brotherhood that had been wont to fare so well, and whose feasts, it hath been said by our old poet (a monk of the house), were as superior to the feasts of all the other monasteries of England as day is superior to night:—

Prævisis aliis, Eliensia festa videre
Est, quasi prævisâ nocte, videre diem.

Yet the bountiful Abbat Thurstan, who had given the best feasts of all that the house had ever known, and who loved as much as any man to see the drinking-horn go round, kept up his good spirit without wine—it was sustained by his generous love of country and liberty!—and he reasoned well with those he heard murmur, and yet held out to them the prospect of better times when corn should come in from the upland country in abundance, and good wine from beyond-sea.

If want began to be felt among the monks of Ely, it is not to be believed but that it was felt still more sharply among the Saxon fighting men collected in the Camp of Refuge. But the stomachs of these warriors were not so dainty as the stomachs of the monks, and the commonalty of them, being accustomed to fare hard before now, made no complaint. Alas, no! It was not through the malcontent of these rude men, nor through these lay stomachs, but through the malice and gluttony of cloister-monks, that the sanctuary was violated.

The Lord of Brunn having emptied his own granaries and cellars for the behoove of the house at Ely, made sundry very desperate forays, breaking through the Norman chain of posts, and going far in the upland country in search of supplies, and risking his noble life, more than once, for nought but a sack of wheat, or a cask of ale, or a firkin of mead. While the blockade was as yet young, a few devout pilgrims, who would not be shut out from the shrines of the Saxon saints at Ely, nor fail to offer up their little annual offerings, and a few sturdy friends who knew the straits to which the monks were about to be reduced, eluded the vigilance of the Normans, and found their way, through those mazes of waters and labyrinths of woods, to the abbey, and carried with them some small supplies: but as time went on and the force of the Normans increased as well by land as by water, these hazardous journeys were stopped, and divers of the poor Saxons were caught, and were then pitilessly hanged as rebels and traitors; and then a law was banded that every man, woman, or child, that attempted to go through the Fen-country, either to Ely Abbey or the Camp of Refuge, would be hanged or crucified.

But, alack! real traitors to their country were afterwards allowed to pass the Norman posts, and go on to Ely Abbey, and it was through their agency and the representations of some of the Normans that were taken prisoners in war and carried to the monastery, that the envious prior, and the chamberlain, and the cellarer, and the rest of that foul faction were emboldened to raise their voice publicly against the good Abbat, and to lay snares in the path of the Lord of Brunn.

Now the same troubles arose out of the same causes in Crowland Abbey, where sundry of the cloister monks began to say that since they could get no bread and wine it were best to make terms with the Norman Abbat of Peterborough (that Torauld of Fescamp who had been released upon ransom, and was again making himself terrible), give up the cause of Lord Hereward, who had restored them to their house, and had given up wealth and honours abroad to come and serve his country, and submit like peaceable subjects to King William, whose power was too great to be any longer disputed. But here, at Crowland, these things were for a long time said in great secrecy, and whispered in the dormitories by night. It was the same in the succursal cell at Spalding; and the coming danger was the greater from the secrecy and mystery of the traitorous part of these communities.

Father Adhelm, the good prior of Spalding, knew of no danger, and could believe in no treachery until the Philistines were upon him; and it was mainly owing to this his security, and to his representations of the safety of that corner of the fens, that the Lord of Brunn sent his wife and infant son, with maid Mildred and other women, to dwell in the strong manor-house at Spalding, which belonged to the Ladie Lucia, wife of Ivo Taille-Bois, and cousin to the Ladie Alftrude.

The Camp of Refuge and the town of Ely had not, for some time past, been fitting abiding-places for ladies and delicate children; but now the Normans were closing in their line of blockade on that side, and, although they meant it not, they seemed to be on the eve of making a desperate assault on the Camp, having, with incredible labor, laid down under the eyes and with the direction of Duke William, another causeway, which was far broader and more solid than any of the others, and which ran across the fens towards the waters of Ely for the distance of two well-measured miles. It was Elfric that commanded the party which gave convoy to the Ladie Alftrude; and well we wot he wished the journey had been a longer one: yet when his duty was done, and the whole party safely lodged in the battlemented and moated house at Spalding, he quitted maid Mildred, though with something of a heavy heart, and hastened back to join his toil-oppressed master. And careworn and toil-oppressed indeed was now that joyous and frank-hearted Lord of Brunn, for he had to think of everything, and to provide for everything; and save in Girolamo the Salernitan, and Elfric his armor-bearer, he had but few ready-witted men to aid him in his increasing difficulties. Nevertheless, the defenses at the Witchford were strengthened, numerous trenches and canals were dug to render the Witch plain impassable, even if the river should be crossed, and bands of Saxons, armed with bows, bills, pole-axes, swords, and clubs, or long fen-poles, were kept on the alert by night as well as by day, to march to any point which the Normans might attack.

Now, we have said it, William the Norman was a great and cunning commander (ye might have searched through the world at that time, and have found none greater!), and being thus skilled, and having a fearless heart withal, and a sort of lion magnanimity, he was proper to judge of the skill of other captains, and not incapable of admiring and lauding that skill even in an enemy. And as from his causeway (even as from a ship in the midst of the waters) he watched the defenses which Hereward raised, and all the rapid and wise movements he made, he often exclaimed, "By the splendor! This Saxon is a right cunning captain! It was worth half a realm could I win him over to my service. But, O Hereward, since thou wilt not submit, thou must perish in thy pride through hunger, or in the meshes which I am spreading for thee."

CHAPTER XXI.

THE MONKS OF ELY COMPLAIN AND PLOT

As no corn came, and no wine could be had, the tribulations and murmurings in the monastery grew louder and louder. Certain of the monks had never looked with a friendly eye upon Girolamo the Salernitan, but now there was suddenly raised an almost universal clamor among them that that dark-visaged and thin-bodied alien was, and ever had been, a necromancer.

Unmindful of the many services he had done, and forgetting how many times they had, when the drinking-horns could be well filled, rejoiced and jubilated at his successes, and specialiter on that not far by-gone day when he had burned the Norman witch, in the midst of her incantations, with the reeds and grass of the fen, the monks now called him by the foulest and most horrible of all names, and some of them even called out for his death. These men said that if Girolamo were brought to the stake and burned as he had burned the Norman witch, the wrath of Heaven would be appeased, and matters would go much better with the house of St. Etheldreda, and with all the English people.

Albeit they all knew how innocently those devils had been made; and, albeit they had seen with their own eyes, that Girolamo was constant at prayers, mass, and confession, and that he never prepared his mixtures and compounds until after prayer and long fasting (to say nothing of his frequently partaking in the Sacrament of our Lord's Supper), they rumored, even like the Normans, that he had raised devils, and employed fen-fiends, and incubuses, and succubuses, and had lit hell-fires upon the pools and within the holy house at Crowland; that he was ever attended by a demon, called by him Chemeia; that he had been a Jew, and next a follower of Mahound; that he had sold his soul to the devil of devils at Jerusalem or Mecca: that he did not eat and drink like Saxons and Christians, only because he went to graves and charnel-houses at the dead of night, and feasted upon the bodies of the dead with his fiends and hell-hounds—with a great deal more too horrible and obscene to mention.

Now before a breath of this bad wind reached him, Girolamo had begun to grow a-weary of the Fen-country; and but for his deadly-hatred to the Norman race and his great love for the Lord of Brunn, he would have quitted it and England, long before this season, to wander again into some sunny climate. Often would he say to himself in his solitary musings,—"Oh flat, wet, and fenny land, shall mine eyes never more behold a mountain? Oh fogs, and vapors, and clouds forever dropping rain, shall I never see a bright blue sky again? Oh fireless, watery sun, scarcely brighter or warmer than the moon in my own land beyond the Alps and the Apennines, shall I never see thee again in thy glory? Am I to perish in these swamps—to be buried in a bog? Oh for one glimpse before I die of mine own blue mountains, and bright blue seas and skies!—one glance at thy bay, oh beautiful Salerno, and at the mountain of Saint Angelo and the hills of Amalfi, at the other mountains, and hills, and olive-groves, and gay vine-yards that gird thee in! There be no hills here but mud-banks; no trees but dull alders and willows. But courage, sinking heart, or sinking, shivering frame, for there is food here for my revenge; there be Normans here to circumvent and kill!"

So did the Salernitan commune with himself in his many lonely hours (many because he sought them and avoided the society of men) before the evil tongues were wagged against him. Upon his first hearing what the monks were then beginning to say of him, he only muttered to himself, "This is a dull-witted generation that I have fallen among! These Saxons go still on all-fours! They are but ultramontanes and barbarians, knowing nothing of the history of past ages, or of the force and effect of the natural sciences! Dolts are they all except the Lord Hereward, and his share of wit is so great that none is left for his countrymen. But Hereward is worthy of ancient Rome; and it is not the stupid sayings of his people that will make me quit his side and disappoint my vengeance. I have done these same Saxons some good service, and I will do them more before I die or go hence. They will think better of me when they know more of me, and of the natural means wherewith I work mine ends. Ha! ha! I needs must laugh when I hear that Girolamo of Salerno, the witch-seeker and the destroyer of witches, the sworn foe to all magic save the Magia Alba, which is no magic at all, but only science, should be named as a wizard and necromancer! Oh! ye good doctors, and teachers of Salerno who flourished and began to make a school for the study of Nature before the Normans came among us, think of this—think of your pupil, penitent, and devotee, being taken in these dark septentrional regions for a sorcerer! Ha! ha!"

But when Girolamo saw that the Saxon people were beginning to avoid him as one that had the pest, and that the monks of Ely were pointing at him with the finger, and that silent tongues and angry eyes, with crossings and spitting's on the ground and coarse objurgations, met him wherever he went, he grew incensed and spoke freely with the Lord of Brunn about it.

"Girolamo, my friend and best coadjutor," said the Lord of Brunn, "think nothing of it! This is but the talk of ignorance or malice. Beshrew mean I do not think that the Normans have gotten some traitor to raise this babel and thereby injure us. But the Lord Abbat Thurstan, who hath shrived and assoiled thee so often, will now answer for the purity of thy faith as for his own, and will silence these murmurers."

But it was not so: Hereward made too large an account not of the good will, but of the power of Thurstan, not knowing all that passed in the chapters of the house, nor so much as suspecting half of the cabals that were framing in secret meetings and in close discussions by night in the dormitories.

No sooner had the Lord Abbat begun to reprehend such as spoke evil of the Salernitan, than the factious and false parts of the monks declared among themselves that, Christian prelate as he was, he had linked himself with a sorcerer; and in charges they had already prepared, and with great privacy written down upon parchment, they inserted this—that Abbat Thurstan, unmindful of the duties of his holy office, and in contempt of the remonstrances of the prior, the chamber-lain, and others, the majority of the house Ely, had made himself the friend and defensor of the said Girolamo of Salerno, that dark mysterious man who had notoriously sold himself to the arch-fiend, who had gone into the depths and iniquities of necromancy beyond all precedent, and who had, by his truly diabolical art, raised devils, trafficked with witches, and brought hell-fires upon earth.

It was at this juncture of time that two pretended pilgrims and devotees of Saint Etheldreda arrived at the guest-house of Ely, giving out that they had with great risk and real danger found their way through the lines of the beleaguering Normans, but that, so entire was their devotion to the saint, no perils could prevent them from coming to the shrine.

It was not much noted at the time, but it was well remembered afterwards, and when it was all too late, that these two palmers spent much more of their time in walking and talking outside the abbey walls with the prior and the chamberlain, than in the praying inside the church and in the chapel of the saint: that they seemed to shun the Lord Abbat, and that they took their departure in a sudden manner, and without taking leave of the Abbat as good pilgrims were wont to do.

And almost immediately after the departure of the two false palmers, a proclamation was made by sound of trumpet and by Duke William's orders, that the Abbat of Ely, having leagued himself with a sorcerer (having long before leagued himself with traitors and rebels and robbers), had incurred the anathemas of the church, which would soon be pronounced upon him by bell, book, and candle, and with all the formalities in use. And after this had been proclaimed by sound of trumpet in the Camp, and at the cross of the town of Cam-Bridge, and at the crosses of Peterborough, Huntingdon, Stamford, and many other towns, the cloister-monks most adverse to the Lord Abbat began to throw off all secrecy and disguise, and to talk as loud as trumpets both in the streets of Ely and in the monastery, calling Girolamo a sorcerer and worse.

Upon this the dark Salernitan came up from the Camp to the monastery, and demanded to be heard in the church or in the hall, in the presence of the whole house.

Thurstan, with right good will, assented; and although some of the monks tried to oppose it, Girolamo was admitted to plead his own defense and justification in the great hall. It was the envious prior's doing, but the novices and all the younger monks were shut out, for the prior feared greatly the effect of the speech of the Salernitan, who by this time had made himself master of the Saxon tongue, while in the Latin tongue and in Latin quotations, Girolamo had few equals on this side the Alps.

He presented himself alone, having forcibly and successfully opposed the Lord Hereward, who would fain have accompanied him to the abbey. "If you should be with me," he had said to the Lord of Brunn, "they will impute it to me, in case of my effacing these vile stigmas, that I have been saved by your favor and interference, or by the respect and awe which is due to you, or by the dread they entertain of your arms; and should I fail in my defense, they might afterwards work you great mischief by representing you as mine advocate. No! good my Lord, alone will I stand upon my defense, and bring down confusion upon these calumniators!"

And thus it was all alone that the dark and thin and sad Salernitan entered the great hall, in the midst of a coughing and spitting, and an uplifting and a turning away of eyes, as if the monks felt sulphur in their gorges, and saw some fearful and supernatural object with their eyes. Nothing abashed, the Salernitan threw off the black mantle which he ordinarily wore, and stepping unto the midst of the hall—the monks being seated all round him—he made the blessed sign of the cross, threw up his hands for a moment as if in prayer, and then spoke.

And when he first began to speak, although he more immediately faced the abbat and his friendly honest countenance, his coal-black eyes, which seemed all of a blaze, rested and were fixed upon the envious false visage of the prior, who wriggled in his seat, and whose eyes were bent upon the ground, all unable to encounter the burning glances of that animated, irate Italian.

"My good Lord Abbat," said Girolamo, looking as we have said, not at Thurstan, but at the prior, "what is this horrid thing that I hear? What are these evil rumors which have been raised against me, while I have been adventuring my life for the service of this house and the good Saxon cause?"

"There hath been some idle talk about sortilege, and it grieves me to say that this idle talk hath of late become very loud in this house," responded Thurstan.

"And who be they who first raised this talk?" said Girolamo; "where are my accusers? Who are the members of this house that have not seen as well my devotion to Heaven as the earthly and natural and legitimate means by which I have worked out mine ends for the furtherance of the good cause? Where are they, that I may speak to them and tell them to their faces how much they have erred or how greatly they have lied? But they dare not look me in the face!"

And as he said these words he turned his burning eyes from the prior to the chamberlain, and then from the chamberlain to another cankerous monk, and to another, and another, and they all pulled their cowls over their brows and looked down upon the floor. But at last the chamberlain found voice and courage enough to raise his head a little; and he said, "Oh, stranger! Since thy first coming amongst us thou hast done things most strange—so strange that wise and good men have thought they have seen the finger of the devil in it."

Quoth the Salernitan, "It was to do strange things that I came hither, and it was because I could do them that the brave and pious Lord of Brunn brought me with him to bear part in a contest which was desperate before we came. But I tell thee, oh monk, that all of even the strangest things I have done have been done by legitimate and natural means, and by that science which I have acquired by long study and much fasting, and much travelling in far-off countries, where many things are known which are as yet unknown in these thy boreal regions.

To speak not of the marvels I have witnessed in the East, I tell thee, Saxon, that I have seen the doctors who teach, or who used to teach, in the schools of my native town before the Norman barbarians came among us, do things that would make thy dull eyes start out of their sockets, and the hair stand erect round thy tonsure; and yet these doctors and teachers were members of that Christian Church to which thou, and I, and all of us belong—were doctors in divinity, and priests, and confessors, and men of holy lives; and it never passed through their bright and pure minds that what the ignorant could not understand should be imputed to them or to their scholars as a crime. Saxon, I say, take the beam of ignorance out of thine eye, and then wilt thou see that man can do marvelous things without magic or the aid of the devil.

The real wizard or witch is the lowest and most benighted of mankind, and necromancy can be employed only for the working out of wicked and detestable ends. But what was and what is the end I have in view? Is it wicked to defend this house and the shrines of your national saints from violence and spoliation? Is it detestable in one who hath known in his own person and in his own country the woes of foreign conquest, to devote his sword and his life, his science, and all the little that is his, to the cause of a generous people struggling against fearful odds for their independence, and fighting for their own against these Norman invaders!"

"By Saint Etheldreda," said Abbat Thurstan, "these ends and objects cannot be sinful! and as sinful means can be employed only for sinful ends, so can righteous ends be served only by righteous means. Fire mingles with fire, and water with water: but fire and water will not mingle or co-exist." And divers of the cloister-monks, who had never been touched by the venom that was about to ruin the house of Ely and the whole country of England, took up and repeated the Abbat's words, speaking also of the facts in evidence, as that Girolamo the Salernitan had many times conferred great benefit on the Saxon cause, and the like.

And even some of the house who had turned too ready an ear to their own fears, or to the evil and crafty whisperings and suggestions of the prior and his faction, assented to Thurstan's proposition, and said that verily it appeared the Salernitan was free from the damnable guilt wherewith he was charged, and that if he had used any magic at all, it was only that Magia Alba, or White Magic, which proceeded from the study and ingenuity of man, and which might be used without sin.

Now as these things were said in the hall, the prior, fearing that his plot might be counter-plotted, and the meshes he had woven be torn to pieces, and blown to the winds, waxed very desperate; and, after whispering for a while in the ear of the chamberlain who sat by him, he threw his cowl back from his head, and standing up, spoke passionately. But while the prior spoke he never once looked at Girolamo, who remained standing in the middle of the great hall, firm and erect, and with his arms crossed over his breast.

No! Desperate as he was, the prior could not meet the fiery glances of that dark thin man; and so he either looked at the round and ruddy face of Thurstan, or in the faces of those monks of his own faction who had made up their minds to support him in all that he might say or do.

"It seemeth to me," said the prior, "that a wicked man may pretend to serve a good cause only for the sake of injuring it, and that a weak man may be brought to believe that good can come out of things that are evil, and that witchcraft and all manner of wickedness's may be employed against an enemy, albeit this is contrary to the doctrine of our Church, and is provocative of the wrath of Heaven. Now, from the first coming of this alien among us, things have gone worse and worse with us. Not but that there have been certain victories and other short glimpses of success, meant only to work upon our ungodly pride, and delude us and make our present misery the keener. When this alien first came, the Lord Abbat liked him not—I need not tell ye, my brethren, that the Lord Abbat said to many of us, that he liked not the looks of the stranger the Lord Hereward brought with him; or that I and the cellarius, and many more of us, thought from the beginning that the man was a Jew—an Israelite—yea, one of that accursed race that crucified our Lord!..."

"Liar or idiot," said the fiery man of Italy, "thou wilt be cursed for saying it!"

"That which I have said I have said," quoth the prior; "we took thee for a Jew, and the Lord Abbat confessed, then, that thou didst verily look like one, although he hath altered his tone since. And stranger, I now tell thee to thy face (but still the prior looked not in Girolamo's face) that I believe thou mayest well be that wandering Jew that cannot die until the day of Judgment come."

The Salernitan shrieked rather than said, "This is too horrible, too atrocious! Malignant monk, wouldst drive me mad, and make me slay thee here in the midst of thy brothers?"
"In this hallowed place I am safe from thy magic and incantations," said the prior.

Girolamo could not speak, for the words stuck in his throat, but he would, mayhap, have sprung upon the prior with his dagger, if the Lord Abbat had not instantly raised his hand and his voice, and said, "Peace! Stranger peace! Let the prior say all that he hath to say, and then thou shalt answer him. Nay, by Saint Etheldreda! by Saint Sexburga, and by every saint in our Calendarium, I will answer him too! For is he not bringing charges against me, and seeking to deprive me of that authority over this house which was given me by heaven, and by King Edward the Confessor, and by the unanimous vote of the brethren of Ely in chapter assembled?
Prior, I have long known what manner of man thou art, and how thou hast been pining and groaning and plotting for my seat and crozier; but thou art now bolder than thou wast wont to be. 'Tis well! Therefore speak out, and do ye, my children, give ear unto him. Then speak, prior! Go on, I say!" In saying these words, Lord Thurstan was well-nigh as much angered as Girolamo had been; but his anger was of a different kind, and instead of growing deadly pale and ashy like the Salernitan, his face became as red as fire; and instead of moving and clenching his right hand, as though he would clutch some knife or dagger, he merely struck with his doubled fist upon the table before him, giving the table mighty raps.
All this terrified the craven heart of the prior, who stood speechless and motionless, and who would have returned to his seat if the cellarer had not approached him and

comforted him, and if several cloister-monks of the faction had not muttered, "Go on to the end, oh, prior! thou hast made a good beginning."

And then the prior said, "I will go on if they will give me pledge not to interrupt me until I have done."

"I give the pledge," said the Abbat; and the Salernitan said, "The pledge is given."

Being thus heartened, the prior went on. Girolamo the Salernitan, he said, had been seen gnashing his teeth and shooting fire out of his eyes at the elevation of the Most Holy; had been heard muttering in an unknown tongue behind the high altar, and among the tombs and shrines of the saints; and also had he often been seen wandering by night, when honest Christians were in their beds, among the graves of the poor of Ely, and gazing at the moon and stars, and talking to some unseen demon. He had never been seen to eat and drink enough to support life; and therefore it was clear that he saved his stomach for midnight orgies in the church-yard with devils and witches.

It was not true that all the devils at Crowland were sham-devils, for some of the novices and lay-brothers of the house, and some of the clowns of Crowland town, who had been seduced, and made to disguise themselves in order to give a cover to what was doing, had since declared that, although all their company made only twelve in number, they had seen twice twelve when the infernal lights were lit in the dark cellars of the house where their pranks began; and it was a notable fact that one of the Crowland hinds, first cousin to Orson the smith, had been so terrified at this increase of number and at all that he had heard and seen on that fearful night, that he had gone distraught, and had never yet recovered it.

It was known unto all men how, not only on that night and in that place, but also on many other nights and in many other places, the alien had made smells that were not of earth, nor capable of being made by earthly materials, and had made fire burn upon water, mixing flame and flood! Now, the Lord Abbat himself had said that fire and water would not mingle! Nor would they but by magic. The convent would all remember this!

Not content with possessing the diabolical arts himself, Girolamo had imparted them to another: Elfric the sword-bearer, from whom better things might have been expected, considering his training in a godly house, had been seen mixing and using these hellish preparations which he could not have done if he had not first spat upon the cross and covenanted with witches and devils. Nay, so bold-faced had this young man been in his crime that he hath done this openly!

The stranger had been seen many times in battle, and in the thickest of the fight, yet, while the Saxons fell thick around him, and every man that was not killed was wounded, he got no hurt,—no not the smallest! When the arrows came near him they turned aside or fell at his feet without touching him. There was a Norman knight, lately a prisoner in the Saxon Camp, who declared that when he was striking at the thin stranger with the certainty of cleaving him with his battle-axe, the axe turned aside in his firm strong hands as though some invisible hand had caught hold of it.

Moreover, there was a Norman man-at-arms who had solemnly vowed that he had thrust his sword right through the thin body of the alien, had driven the hilt home on his left breast; and that when he withdrew his sword, instead of falling dead to the earth, the stranger stood erect, laughing scornfully at him, and losing no blood, and showing no sign of any wound. Now all these things fortified the belief that the stranger was the Jew that could not die! Seeing that a deep impression was made upon many of his hearers who had gone into the hall with the determination of believing that there had been no magic, and that nothing unlawful had been done by the defenders of the liberties of the Saxon people and the privileges of the Saxon church, the cunning prior turned his attack upon Thurstan.

It was notorious, he said, that Thurstan had been a profuse and wasteful abbat of that house, taking no thought of the morrow, but feasting rich and poor when the house was at the poorest; that he was a man that never kept any balance between what he got and what he gave; and that he had always turned the deaf side of his head to those discreet brothers the chamberlain, the sacrist, the cellarer and refectorarius, who had long since foretold the dearth and famine which the convent were now suffering. Here nearly every monk present laid his right hand upon his abdomen and uttered a groan. It was known unto all of them, said the prior that under the rule and government of Thurstan such things had been done in the house as had never been done under any preceding abbat.

The shrine-boxes had been emptied; the plates of silver and of gold, the gifts of pious kings and queens, had been taken from the shrines themselves; the treasure brought from the abbey of Peterborough had only been brought to be given up to the Danes and sent forever from England, together with the last piece of silver the pilgrims had left in the house of Ely! And then the Jews! the Jews! Had not dealings been opened with them? Had not a circumcised crew been brought into the patrimony of Saint Etheldreda, and lodged in the guest house of the abbey? Had not the abbat's seal been used in sealing securities that were now in the hands of the Israelites?

And was not all the money gotten from the Jews gone long ago, and was not the treasury empty, the granary empty, the cellar empty,—was there not an universal void and emptiness in all the abbey, and throughout the patrimony of St. Etheldreda? The monks groaned again. In concluding his long discourse the prior raised his unmanly voice as high as it could be raised without cracking, and said—"Upon all and several the indubitable facts I have recited, I accuse this Girolamo of Salerno of magic and necromancy; and I charge Thurstan, abbat of this house, and Elfric, whilom novice in the succursal cell of Spalding, of being defensors, fautors, and abettors of the necromancer. And what saith the sixteenth of the canons enacted under the pious King Edgar? And how doth it apply to our abbat? The canon saith this—'And we enjoin, that every priest zealously promote Christianity, and totally extinguish every heathenism; and for did necromancies and divinations and enchantments, and the practices which are carried on with various spells, and with frith-splots and with elders, and also with various other trees, and with stones, and with many various delusions, with which men do much of what they should not.' I have done."

For a while there was silence, the monks sitting and gazing at each other in astonishment and horror. At length, seeing that the abbat was almost choked, and could not speak at all, Girolamo said, "my lord, may I begin?"
Thurstan nodded a yea.
Hereupon the Salernitan went over the whole history of his past life, with all its sorrows, studies, and wanderings; and bade the monks reflect whether such a life was not fitted to make a man moody and sad and unlike other men. He acknowledged that, as compared with Saxons,

and more especially with the Saxon monks of Ely, he ate and drank very little; but this was because his appetite was not good, and his habit of life very different from theirs. He allowed that he was fond of wandering about in lonely places, more especially by moonlight, but this was because eating little he required the less sleep, and because the sadness of his heart was soothed by solitude and the quiet aspect of the moon and stars.

All this, and a great deal more, the Salernitan said in a passably composed and quiet voice; but when he came to deny and refute the charges which the prior had made, his voice pealed through that hall like thunder, and his eyes flashed like lightning. In concluding he said—"I was ever a faithful son of Mother Church. The blessed Pope at Rome—Pope Alexander it was—hath put his hand upon this unworthy head and given me his benediction. The pious abbat of the ancient Benedictine house of La Cava that stands in the chasm of the mountain between Salerno and the city of Neapolis held me at the baptismal font; cloister-monks were my early instructors, and learned doctors of the church were my teachers in youth and manhood.

I have been a witch-seeker and a witch-finder in mine own country. Ye have known me, here, burn, or help to burn, a witch almost under your own eyes. Jews have I ever abhorred, even as much as witches, necromancers, and devils! Saracens and Moors, and all that follow Mahound, have I ever hated as Jews, and as much as good Christians ought to hate them! Oh prior, that makest thyself my accuser, thou hast been a home-staying man, and hast not been called upon to testify to thy faith in the lands where heathens rule and reign, and Mahound is held to be the prophet of God, and superior to God's own Son. But I tell thee, prior, that I have testified to my faith in such places, and openly on the threshold of Mahound's temples, braving death and seeking a happy martyrdom which, alas! I could not find.

Saxons! In a town in Palestine wherein, save a guard of Saracens, there were none but Jews, I took the chief rabbi by the beard at the gate of his synagogue. Saxons! To show my faith I have eaten swine's flesh at Jerusalem, in the midst of Saracens and Jews. Saxons! In the Christian countries of Europe I never met an Israelite without kicking him and loading him with reproaches. Bethink ye then, after all this, whether I, Girolamo of Salerno, be a Jew, or Mahounder, or necromancer! If ye are weary of me let me be gone to the country from which I came. I brought little with me, and shall take still less away. If ye would repay with torture and death the good I have done ye, seize me now, throw me into your prison, load me with chains, put me to the rack, do with me what ye will, but call me not Jew and wizard!"

Sundry of the monks said that the words of the stranger sounded very like truth and honesty, and that of a surety the good Lord Hereward would not have brought a wizard with him into England, or have lived so long in friendship with a necromancer. Others of the cloister-monks, but they were few in number, said that Girolamo had disproved nothing, and that it could be but too well proved that woe and want had fallen upon the good house of Ely—that the treasury, granary, wine-cellar were all empty.

The Lord Abbat now spoke, but his anger had cooled, and his speech was neither loud nor long. He declared that every man, being in his senses and not moved by private malice, must be convinced that the Salernitan was a good believer and no wizard; and that, whatever he had done, however strange some things might appear, had been done by means not unlawful.

This being the case there could be no sin or blame in his having made himself the defensor of the stranger, and no sin in Elfric's having associated with him, and assisted in his works. "But," said the abbat, "though the prior hath not been bold enough to name that name, ye must all know and feel that, if this man were a necromancer, charges would lie far more against Hereward, our great captain, than against me or that poor young man, Elfric. Would ye accuse the Lord of Brunn of sorcery and witchcraft? I see ye dare not, nay, I see ye would not!"
As to the daring, Thurstan was right: but as to the will, he was wrong; for the prior and the chamberlain, and some others, would have accused Hereward if they had only had courage enough so to do.

The abbat next told the prior and all the members of the house that were present, that he had taken no important step without the advice and vote of the chapter; that of late, in many cases, the vote in chapter had been in direct opposition to his own wishes and declared feelings; and that whether it were the taking of the shrine-money, or the bargaining with the Israelites, or the calling back of the Danes (that source of so much woe), or the giving up of the Peterborough treasure, he had been out-voted by the majority, at the head of which had always stood the prior and the chamberlain.

If honest-hearted Thurstan had called for a vote of the brotherhood at this moment it would have gone for him, and the prior and his coadjutors would have been confounded; if he had ceased speaking altogether, and had dismissed the assembly, some mischief might have been avoided or delayed; but unluckily he went on to speak about the obligation the house lay under of feeding and supporting the Saxon lords and warriors in the Camp of Refuge, about his general administration of the revenues of the abbey, and about other matters which had nothing to do with the Salernitan or the foul charges brought against him; and, saying that these were things to be discussed in a chapter of the whole house, and that if it could be proved that in any of these things he had willfully done amiss or acted upon a selfish motive, he would readily resign mitre and crozier and return to the lowliest condition of a cloister-monk, he quitted the hall, beckoning Girolamo to follow him, and leaving the monks together to be wrought upon by the craft and malice and treachery of the prior and the chamberlain, who had sold their souls not to one devil but to two—the demon of lucre and the demon of ambition and pride. As soon as he was out of the hall, the prior put his evil face under the cowl of the chamberlain, and whispered, "Brother, 't was our good fortune that put the word in his mouth! We will soon call a chapter and depose him from his authority. Our task will then be easy; but as long as he is abbat many timid minds will fear him."

"But," whispered the chamberlain in return, "we must first of all shake the faith which too many here present have put in his words, and in the protestations of Girolamo."

"The logic of hunger will aid us," said the prior, "and so will the promptings of fear: there is not a measure of wheat in Ely, and the report hath been well spread that the Normans intend to begin their attack very soon, and to put every monk to the sword that shall not have previously submitted. To-morrow Hereward goes upon some desperate expedition to try to get us corn and wine: he cannot, and will not succeed; and, while he is absent, we can report of him and his expedition as we list."

"'Tis well imagined," said the chamberlain in another whisper; "but we must undo the effect of that devil

Girolamo's speech, and prepare the minds of the monks for the work we would have them do."

While the prior and the chamberlain were thus whispering together, divers of the old monks, who loved not their faction and who had grown weary of this long sitting, quitted the hall without leaving the mantle of their wisdom and experience behind them; and after their departure the prior and his faction so perplexed the dull wits of the honester part of the community, that they again began to believe that the Salernitan was a necromancer and the abbat his fautor, that there was no hope of getting corn or wine unless they submitted to Duke William, and that if they did not submit they would all be murdered by the Normans.
They also spoke, and at great length, of the privations they had undergone ever since the beginning of the war.

"Yea! how long and how manifold have been our sufferings," said the sub-sacrist. "When this accursed Camp first began to be formed, was not our house entirely filled with guests? Did they not seize upon our hall, nay, even upon our kitchen? And were not we of the convent obliged to take our meals in the dormitory, as well on flesh days as on fish-days? Were not all open spaces in the monastery crowded, so that the abbey looked more like a fair than a house of religion? Was not the grass-plot of the cloisters so trampled down by the feet of profane fighting-men that no vestige of green was to be seen upon it? And though most of these guests be now gone into the Camp, because there is little left here for them to devour, do not the cellars, the store-houses, the kitchen, and every part of the house speak of their having been here, and of the poverty and disorder in which they have left us?"

"Aye," said the refectorarius, "wonderful hath been the waste! The revenue of the abbat, the common property of the house, and the incomings allotted to the several officials to enable them to bear the charges and do the duties of their offices, have all been anticipated and consumed! And let our improvident Abbat tell me how I am to find that which I am bound to provide for the whole convent to wit, pots, noggins, cups, table-cloths, mats, basons, double-cloths, candlesticks, towels, plates, saltcellars, silver plates wherewith to mend the cups that be broken, and the like; besides furnishing three times in the year, to wit, at All Saints, Christmas, and Easter, five burthens of straw to put under the feet of the monks in the refectory, and five burthens of rushes and hay wherewith to strew the hall?"

"And I," quoth the cellarius, "how am I to be father unto the whole convent inasmuch as meat and drink be concerned, when I have not a penny left to spend in township or market? By the rules of the Order, Statutis Ordinis, when any monk at table asks me for bread or for beer, in reason, I am to give it him; but how am I to give without the wherewithal?"

"And I," said the chamberlain, "how am I to find, for both monks and novices, gowns and garters, half socks and whole socks, and bed and bedding, and linsey-woolsey for sheets and shirts, and knives, and razors, and combs, in order that the convent go clean and cleanly shaved? Aye, tell me how I am to change the straw of the beds, provide baths for the refreshment of the bodies of the monks, to find shoes for the horses and spurs for the monks when they are sent travelling, to keep and entertain two bathers and four tailors, when Abbat Thurstan hath taken mine all or hath forced me to give it to laymen and strangers and Norwich Jews? Let our universal poverty say whether this hath been a misgoverned house!

Brothers, judge for yourselves whether Thurstan, who hath brought down all this ruin upon us, ought to be allowed to rule over us!"

The crafty prior said in a quieter tone of voice, "For my part, I will not now dwell upon these temporal evils, albeit they are hard for men in the flesh to bear; but I would bid the convent take heed lest one and all they incur the sentence of excommunication by the pope himself. It is now quite clear that Pope Gregory wills that William the Norman shall be King of England, and that the English church, with all English houses of religion, shall submit to him, and take their instructions from Archbishop Lanfranc."

When the meeting in the hall broke up, the chamberlain said to the prior, "We shall yet have the pleasure of burning Girolamo as a necromancer!"

"And he be not the Jew that cannot die," quoth the prior.

When the Salernitan reached the Camp that evening he said to the Lord of Brunn, "Certes the monks of Ely will no longer say I am a wizard; but there be traitors among them, and much do I fear that their rebellious stomachs will make traitors of them all!"

"Against that must we provide," quoth the Lord Hereward; "to-morrow we must go get them corn and wine from the Normans. Our stratagem is well laid, but we must die rather than fail. So good night, Girolamo, and to our tents and sheepskins."

CHAPTER XXII.

HEREWARD BRINGS CORN AND WINE TO ELY

There was no cloister-monk of Ely that better knew the legends of the house than Elfric, for his father, Goodman Hugh, who had dwelt by saint Ovin's cross, and his father's father who had dwelt in the same place, had been great fenners and fowlers and gossips, and had hawked with the best of the abbats and monks, and had stored their memories with the history of the abbey and the saints of Ely, and had amused and sanctified the long winter-nights, when the fire of wood mixed with peat burned brightly on their hearth, by relating to little Elfric all the legends that they knew. Now there was one of these which had made a profound impression upon Elfric's mind, which, by nature, loved adventure and ingenious stratagem. It was a short tale, and simple withal, and easy to tell.

Saint Withburga, the fourth in order of the four great female saints that were and are the ornaments and shining lights of the great house, did not live and die as her sister Saint Etheldreda had done, at Ely, and as Lady Abbess. In her infancy she was sent to nurse at a village called Holkham, belonging to the king her father, Anna, king of the East Angles. In this place she lived many years, whence the village of Holkham was sometimes called Withburgstowe, and a church was built there in memory of her. On the death of the king her father, which befell in the year of grace six hundred and fifty-four, Withburga removed from Holkham to Dereham, another village in the country of East Anglia; and here, affecting a retired and religious life, she founded a monastery of nuns, over which she presided for many years. Peaceful and holy was her life, and blessed was her end. When she died, they buried her there, in the churchyard at Dereham. And lo! After many more years had passed, and the other tenants of this churchyard and even those that had been buried long after had moldered into dust, the grave of Withburga being opened, her body was found entire and without the slightest sign of corruption! Aye, there she lay in her shroud and coffin, with her hands crossed upon her breast, and with her little crucifix of silver lying upon her breast, even as she had lain on the bier on the day of her death so many, many years before.

The saintly incorruptible body was forthwith removed into the church, where it was preserved with great care and devotion by the good people of Dereham, and it continued there, not without manifold miracles, until the time of that pious monarch King Edgar, who restored the monastery at Ely, which the Danes had burned, and gave the house that precious charter which hath been named before as not being given privately and in a corner, but in the most public manner and under the canopy of Heaven.

Now, in restoring the abbey of Ely to its pristine splendor, and in augmenting the number of the brotherhood, it behooved the king to increase the lands and domains of the house; and, conformably, the pious Edgar (may all his sins be forgiven for the good he did the church!) conferred on the abbey of Ely the village of Dereham, with all its demesnes and appendages, and with the church wherein the body of the virgin Saint Withburga was preserved and venerated by the people of Dereham and by all the good Saxon people round about. Now the Lord Abbat on that day, having the grant of Dereham and all that appertained to it, could not feel otherwise than very desirous of getting possession of the body of the saint in order to translate it to Ely and there place it by the side of the body and shrine of the blessed Etheldreda.

The saintly virgin sisters had been separated in their lives and ought to be united in death; Ely Abbey could offer a more noble shrine than the small dependent church at Dereham; it was proper too, and likewise was it profitable, that the pilgrims and devotees to their four female saints of East Anglia should always come to Ely instead of going sundry times a-year to Dereham, as had been the custom, and that all the four shrines should be under one roof, and the contents of the shrine-boxes poured into one common treasury. All this had been laid before the king, and the pious Edgar, who never meant that others should keep what he had bestowed upon his beloved house of Ely, had given his royal license for the translation of the body of Saint Withburga to the abbey.

But the Lord Abbat, being a prudent and cautelous man, and taking counsel of his brother the bishop of Winchester and of other wise and peace loving men, came to this wise conclusion:—That, inasmuch as it was not likely that the people of Dereham and that vicinage would part with so valuable a treasure without resistance, if the intended translation should be made publicly known to them, it would be expedient and commendable, and accordant with the peaceable character of monks, to steal away the body privately, and to admit none but a few of the most active and prudent of the cloister-monks of Ely into the secret beforehand.

Accordingly no notice was given to the hinds and indwellers at Dereham, nor was there any mention made of the great matter outside of the Aula Magna of Ely Abbey; and on the day appointed the Lord Abbat and some of the most active and prudent of the monks, attended by the sturdiest loaf-eaters of the abbey all well-armed, and after hearing mass in the abbey church, set out on their journey to steal the body of the saint; and on their arrival at Dereham they were received with great respect by the inhabitants, who thought that they had come simply to take possession of the place in virtue of the king's charter and donation, and who suspected no further design.

The Lord Abbat, as lord and proprietor and chief, temporal as well as spiritual, held a court for the administration of justice in the manner usual with bishops and abbats, and according to the wise and good laws of our Saxon kings. And after this public court of justice, wherein such as had stolen their neighbors' goods were condemned to make bot, the bountiful Lord Abbat bade the good people of Dereham to a feast.

And while the good folk of Dereham were eating and drinking, and making merry, and were thinking of nought but the good meat and abundant drink before them, the sturdy loaf-eaters from Ely, unwatched and unnoticed, and working in great stillness, were making those preparations for the translation which they had been ordered to make. And, at the time pre-concerted and fixed, my Lord Abbat and his active and prudent monks took occasion to withdraw from the carousing company in the hall, and immediately repaired to the church under color of performing their regular devotions.

But they left the service of None's unsaid for that day, taking no heed of the canonical hours, but getting all things ready for the happy and peaceful translation. After a time the abbat and his prudent monks returned to the company and caused more drink to be brought into the hall, still farther to celebrate the happy day of his lordship's taking possession. The whole day having been spent in feasting and drinking, and dark night coming on apace, the company retired by degrees, every man to his own house or hut, his home or present resting place: and thereupon the monks went again to the church, opened the tomb (of which the fastenings had been forced), opened the coffin, and devoutly inspected the body of Saint Withburga, and having inspected and revered it they closed up the coffin again, and got everything in readiness for carrying it off. About the middle of the night, or between the third and fourth watch when the matutina or lauds are begun to be sung, the coffin in which the body of the saint was enclosed, was put upon the shoulders of the active and prudent monks, who forthwith conveyed it with great haste and without any noise-making to a wheeled car which had been provided for that purpose.

The coffin was put into the car, the servants of the abbat were placed as guards round about the car to defend it, the Lord Abbat and the monks followed the car in processional order, other well-armed loaf-eaters followed the abbat and the monks; and in this order they set forward for Brandon. The journey was long and anxious, but when they came to the village of Brandon and to the bank of the river which leads towards the house of Ely, they found ready and waiting for them the boats which the abbat had commanded, and immediately embarking with their precious treasure they hoisted sail and made ply their oars at the same time.

In the meanwhile the men of Dereham, having recovered from the deep sleep and the confusion of ideas which are brought on by much strong drink, had discovered that the monks of Ely had stolen the body of Saint Withburga. Hullulu! Never was such noise heard in so small a place before. Every man, woman, and child in Dereham was roused, and ran shrieking to the empty tomb in the church, and at the sound of the horn, all the people from all the hamlets and homesteads near unto the pleasant hill of Dereham came trooping in with bills and staves, not knowing what had happened, but fancying that the fiery Dane was come again. But when they saw or were told about the empty tomb, the people all shouted "Who hath done this deed? Who hath stolen the body of our saint?" Now no one could gainsay that the Abbat of Ely with his monks had done it. A serf who had gone early a-field to cut grass while the dew was on it, had met the car and the procession on the road between Dereham and Brandon; and what was of more significance, the presbyter or mass-priest of the church of Dereham, coming to the communion-table found upon it a piece of parchment whereon was written these words: "I, Abbat of Ely and Lord of Dereham, by and with the consent and approval of Edgar the King, have translated the body of Saint Withburga, to be hereafter kept in Ely Abbey with increased pomp, worship, and reverence; and this, oh presbyter of Dereham, is my receipt for the blessed body aforesaid."

Then, I wish, were heard words of much irreverence from the ignorant and rustical people of the place! Some of them stopped not in calling the right excellent abbat a thief, a midnight robber, a perturbator of the peace of saints, a violator of the tombs of the saints! Nor did they spare King Edgar more than the abbat, saying that although he might by his kingly power and without wrong grant to the house at Ely their lands and services, and even their church, he had no right to give away the body of their saint, and order it to be removed out of their church, wherein it had reposed for thrice one hundred years; and they all presently agreed to pursue the abbat and the monks, and endeavour to recover the prey. And so, arming themselves with whatsoever weapons they could most readily meet with, they all poured out of Dereham, and took the shortest way to Brandon.

They were brisk men these folk of the uplands, well exercised in the game of bowls, and in pitching the bar, and in running and leaping, and in wrestling on the church-green; they were light-footed men these men of Dereham; but although they ran their best it was all too late when they got to Brandon, for the monks had got a long way down the river with the saint's body.

Nevertheless the Dereham folk continued the chase; they divided themselves into two bands or parties, and while one party ran down one bank of the river, the other ran down on the opposite side. They even came abreast of the Lord Abbat's boats, and got near enough to see the pall which covered the coffin that contained the body of their saint; but the river being here broad and deep, and they being unprovided with boats (the prudent abbat had taken care for that), they could not get at the coffin or at the monks; and so, after spending some time on the banks shaking their bill-hooks and staves, and uttering threats and reproaches till they were tired, they gave up the pursuit as hopeless, and began to return home with sad and very angry hearts.

The Lord Abbat and the monks of Ely continued their voyage without molestation. They landed safely on the same day, about a mile from Ely Abbey, at the place called Tidbrithseie, but which men do now call Turbutsey. Here they were received with great joy and triumph by all sorts of people, who came down to the waterside, with the monks and mass-priests, to meet them, for all the in-dwellers of Ely town, and all the people that dwelt near it, were as glad to get the body of the saint as the people of Dereham were grieved to lose it. And at eventide, or about compline or second vespers, on this self-same day, the body and coffin of the saint, being put upon another car, was conveyed by land from Turbutsey to Ely, and into the abbey, with solemn procession and the singing of praises to God, and was then, with all due reverence and a Te Deum Laudamus in the choir, deposited in the abbey-church next to Saint Etheldreda, and near unto Saint Sexburga and Saint Ermenilda. Now this happy translation of Saint Withburga's body took place on the eighth of the month of July, in the year of our Lord nine hundred and seventy-four. And is not the day of this translation ever observed as a high festival by the monks of Ely?

Much did the Lord Abbat congratulate himself on his success; and well he might, for translations of the like kind, as well before his time and since, have often been attended with fighting and bloodshed, nay, with great battles between party and party, and the death of many baptized men! But through the good policy and great wisdom of this our Lord Abbat there was not a man that had either given or received so much as a blow from a staff or cudgel. Head-aches there had been at Dereham on first waking in the morning, but these had proceeded only from the over-free use of the abbat's strong drinks, and were cured by the fresh morning air and the good exercise the men got in running after their saint. *Decus et decor, divitiæ et miracula omnia—credit, grace,* and ornament, riches and many miracles, did the saint bring to the house of Ely!

And mark the goodness and bounty of the saint in making heavenly bot to the good folk of Dereham! There, in the churchyard, and out of the grave wherein Withburga had been first buried, sprang up a curing miraculous well to cure disorders of the spirit as well as of the flesh. And have its waters ever ceased to flow, and is it not called Saint Withburga's well? Albeit the vulgar do name it, now-a-days, the well of Saint Winifred.

Now it was in thinking upon this legend that Elfric, the sword-bearer of the Lord of Brunn, was brought to turn his thoughts upon the now well-peopled town and well-cultivated fields of the upland of Dereham; and thus thinking, and knowing the store of wine and corn that might be had in that vicinage, he had proposed to his lord to make a foray in that direction, and to proceed, in part, after the manner in which the Lord Abbat of the olden time had proceeded when he went to steal away the body of the saint. And Elfric had been thanked by the Lord Hereward for his suggestion, and had been called into council as well as Girolamo, and had given many hints as to the best means of carrying out the good plan of robbing the Saxons of Dereham (who had rather tamely submitted to the Normans), in order to feed the monks of Ely and the Saxons of the Camp of Refuge.

Because of the many waters and the streams that cut up the country into the form and appearance of some great echec board, Duke William had not been able to make his line of beleaguerment quite so perfect and strong on this side of the Fen-country as he had done on the other sides; but he had posted a good number of archers and spearmen on the uplands beyond the fens, and between Swaffham and Dereham, and upon these he relied for checking the incursions of the Saxons, and keeping them out of countries abounding with supplies.

Now Lord Hereward had caused to be collected a good number of skerries and other light and fast boats, even as the good abbat had done aforetime, and these boats had been sent up the river by night to the vicinage of Brandon, where, with the brave fellows on board of them, they lay concealed among the tall rushes. And while the Lord of Brunn, crossing the rivers and meres, collected a good force in front of Swaffham, which would not fail of drawing all the Norman troops towards that one point, his sword-bearer and the Salernitan were to make rapidly for Brandon with more men, and from Brandon to make for Dereham; so timing their movements, in small parties and along different paths, that they should all meet in the churchyard and by Saint Withburga's well at midnight of a moonless night, when the town would be buried in sleep.

On the day next after that on which the evil-minded prior of Ely had formally accused Girolamo of witchcraft, and had spoken so daringly against the Lord Abbat, Hereward marched from the Camp of Refuge with only a few men, his intention being to increase his strength on his march; and well did he know that at the sounding of his horn, and at the sight of his banner, the hardy fenners would follow him whithersoever he might choose to lead. The gleemen and minstrels who sang the songs which had been made in honor of him were the best and surest recruiters for the army of the Lord of Brunn.

They were ever going from township to township, with their voices and harps, or Saxon lyres. They were small townships these in the fenny countries, and rustical and wild. The fashion of house-building had little changed here since the days of the ancient Britons: the houses or huts were of a round shape, and not unlike the form of bee-hives; they had a door in front, and an opening at top to let out the smoke, but window to let in the light was there none; the walls were made of wattle and dab, the roofs of rushes and willow branches cut in the fens; but the better sort of the houses had stone foundations and rough stone pillars and traves for the door-way, the stone having been brought from the quarry belonging to Peterborough Abbey, or from some other distant quarry.

Yet these poor houses were not so comfortless within as might have been prejudged by those who only saw the outside; the hides of the cattle, the fleeces of the sheep, and the skins of the deer, and the abounding feathers of the fen-fowl were good materials for warm covering and warm clothing; neither turf nor wood for firing was ever lacking in those parts, and the brawny churls that came forth from the townships, blowing their blast-horns, or shouting for the Lord of Brunn, or brandishing their fen poles over their heads, did not look as if they were scant of meat, or fasted more frequently than mother church prescribed. At the same time Elfric and Girolamo, with their party, began their devious, roundabout march for Brandon, being instructed to keep as much out of sight even of the country people as was possible, and to shun any encounter with the Normans, even though tempted by ever so favorable an opportunity. Hereward had said to them, "Our present business is to get corn and wine for the abbey, and not to fight. Be cautious and true to time, and diverge not a hair's breadth from the plan which hath been laid down. Conjoint or combined operations fail oftener through vanity and conceit than through any other cause.

But ye be not men of that sort; ye will get your stores down to the boats at Brandon by daybreak to-morrow morning, or between lauds and prime, and I shall then have made my retreat, and be upon the bank of the river between Hockwold and Brandon, and ready to give ye the hand if it should be needful. Elfric, mind keep thy swinging hanger in its sheath, and think only of bread and wine!" And unto these, the parting words of their lord and captain, the sword-bearer and the Salernitan had both said, "Upon our souls be it!" And well did they redeem their solemn pledge. The wise monks who went to steal away the body of the saint were hardly so prudent and cautelous. Elfric even eschewed the marvelous temptation of falling upon a young Norman knight that was riding along the high-road between Brandon and Dereham, attended by only two men-at-arms and a horse-boy. By keeping under cover, and by creeping in little parties of twos or threes across the country where there was no cover to conceal them, the forayers all got safely into the churchyard and to St. Withburga's well at midnight. The Lord of Brunn, who had not sought concealment, but had taken the most direct and open road, and exposed his movement as much as he could do, had got behind Swaffham by the hour of sunset, and had made such a hubbub and kindled such a fire in the country between Swaffham and Castle Acre that all the Normans had marched off in that direction, even as had been anticipated.

Even the young knight and his attendants, whom Elfric had let pass on the road, had spurred away for Castle Acre, which, at one time, was reported to be on fire. In this sort there was not a Norman left in Dereham; and as for the Saxons of the town, after wondering for a season what was toward, they came to the conclusion that it was business which did not concern them, and so went quietly to their beds—the burgher and the freeman to his sheets of strong brown linen, and the hind and serf to his coverlet of sheep-skins or his bed of straw. The snoring from the little township was so loud that a good ear could hear it in the church-yard; the very dogs of the place seemed all asleep, and there was not a soul in Dereham awake and stirring except a grey-headed old Saxon, who came with horn lantern in one hand and a big wooden mallet in the other to strike upon the church bell which hung in a little round tower apart, but not far from the church. As the old man came tottering among the graves and hillocks of earth, behind which the foraying party was all concealed, Elfric whispered to Girolamo, "For this night the midnight hour must remain untold by church-bell in Dereham. We must make capture of this good grey-beard, and question him as to where lie the most stores, and where the best horses and asses."

And scarcely were the words said or whispered ere Girolamo had fast hold of the bell-knocker on the one side, and Elfric on the other. The patriarch of Dereham was sore affrighted, and would have screamed out if Elfric had not thrust his cap, feather and all, into his open mouth. Gaffer continued to think that he was clutched by goblins or by devils; as the dim and yellow light from the horn lantern fell upon the sharp dark face of the Salernitan, the old fellow, fortified in his belief, shook and trembled like leaves of the witch-elm, or more tremulous aspen, and nearly swooned outright. Elfric took the cap out of his mouth, and let go the right arm of the old man, who thereupon took to crossing himself, and muttering some fragment of a Saxon prayer potent against evil spirits.

"Father," said Elfric, who was now holding the horn lantern, "Father, we be no evil spirits or goblins, but honest Saxons from the Camp of Refuge come to seek corn and wine for the good monks of Ely; so tell us where we can best provide ourselves, and find cattle to carry our store down to Brandon. Come, quick, good Gaffer, for the time presses!"

When the old man looked into the merry laughing face of the ruddy-cheeked, fair-haired sword-bearer, his dread evanished, for there was no believing such a face to belong to any body or thing that was evil. Gaffer, moreover, bethought himself that he had never yet heard of spirit, ghost, or goblin asking for bread and wine. In brief, the old hind was very soon comforted altogether, and having no corn or wine of his own, and no great love for those that had, he soon gave all the information that was demanded of him; and this being got, Elfric gave a low whistle, and the armed Saxons started up from their hiding places behind the grave mounds, and Saint Withburga's well, and other parts and corners of the churchyard, and ranged themselves in battle-array, and marched into the one long single street of the town. The houses of Dereham, in this dry and rich upland country, were better than the houses in the fens, but still most of them were small, and low, and poor, and rudely covered with thatch. Some larger and better houses there were, and of most of these the Norman chiefs and their soldiers had taken possession.

The presbyter or mass-priest and the borhman had, however, kept the good houses that were their own, and they had granaries with corn in them, and cellars holding both wine and ale, and barns and yards behind their houses, and stables, that were not empty; but these it was resolved not to touch, except, perhaps, for the purpose of borrowing a horse or two to carry the corn and the wine, that might be gotten elsewhere, down to the boats below Brandon. While Girolamo remained with one good party at the end of the street watching the road which leads into the town from Swaffham and Castle Acre, Elfric with another party of the merry men proceeded right merrily to levy the contribution. He began with the Norman houses.

Here the Saxon serfs, though somewhat alarmed when first roused from their deep sleep, not only threw open their doors with alacrity, but also led Elfric's people to the cellars and store-houses. Nay, upon a little talk with the fen-men, and after an agreement made between them that the doors should be broken as if violence had been used, and some resistance attempted, they threw open all parts of the houses, stables, and outhouses, and assisted their countrymen in packing up their booty, in harnessing the horses and asses, as well as in other necessary offices. Not a murmur was heard until they came to visit some of the houses of the freed-men of Dereham. These men, who had some small stores of their own, were more angered than comforted by being told that the corn was to make bread for the monks of Ely; for, strange and wicked as it may appear, it was nevertheless quite true, that in Dereham the translation of Saint Withburga's body had never been forgiven, but was still held as a piece of cheating and thievery, notwithstanding the heavenly bot or compensation of the miraculous well, and in spite of King Edgar's charter, and the subsequent approval of our lord the Pope, and maugre the fact obvious to all men that the saint was better lodged at Ely than ever she could have been in this little church. In truth, those freemen made an exceeding great clamor. "To the devil with the monks of Ely for us," said they. "In the bygone times they came to Dereham and treacherously stole away the body of our saint by night, and now they send armed men to break upon our sleep and carry off our grain!"

Elfric bade them remember and mind that the Lord Abbat of Ely was lord and proprietor of Dereham, and that they were or ought to be his liege men; and as they continued to complain, and to say that they wished the Normans would soon get back from Swaffham and Castle Acre, Elfric broke the pates of two or three of them with one of their own staves. But nowhere could these men do more than grumble; their numbers being but small, and the serfs being mostly on the other side: moreover, arms had they none, their friends the Normans having taken care of that. Having found cattle enough elsewhere, Elfric would not molest the mass-priest, who slept so soundly that he heard nothing of what was passing, and knew nothing of the matter until Elfric had gotten down to the little Ouse, or twenty good miles from Dereham.

It was midnight when the fen-men arrived at Dereham town, and before prime they were below Brandon, and loading their boats with the corn and wine which had previously loaded a score of good upland pack-horses, and more than a score of dapple asses. "This," said Elfric, "is not a bad lift for one night's work! I should like to see the face of the Normans when they return from Swaffham and Castle Acre into Dereham!"

Even Girolamo seemed merry, and almost smiled, as he counted the measures of corn and the measures of wine. But hark! a brazon trumpet is heard from the other side of Brandon; aye, the blast of a trumpet, and a Norman trumpet too; and before the Saxons had half-finished loading their boats, a great body of Norman cavalry came trotting down the road which ran along the bank of the river, being followed at no great distance by a great company of Norman bowmen. It was not from Dereham that these foes came—oh no! the Normans who had quitted that town on the preceding evening to look after Lord Hereward, had not yet returned, and some of them never would return—but it had so chanced that an armament on the march from Saint Edmundsbury and Thetford came this morning to Brandon and caught sight of the boats on the river, and of the armed Saxons on the bank.

Some of the midnight party thought that it would be best to get into the boats and abandon the half of the booty; but this was not to be thought of, inasmuch as not a drop of the wine which the monks of Ely so much wanted had been gotten into the boats. Girolamo and Elfric saw at a glance (and it was needful to have quick sight and instant decision, for the Normans were almost upon them), that the ground they stood upon, being a narrow road, with a deep river on one side, and a ditch and a low, broad, and marshy meadow on the other, was good defensive ground, for the horse could only charge upon the narrow road, and it would take the archers afoot some time to get across the ditch into the fields, if, indeed, the archers should decide upon adventuring on that swampy ground.

"We can make them dance the dance we have given them before," said the Salernitan. "Tie me those pack-horses and asses tight together between the Norman horse and us, pile up these barrels and bags; leap, twenty good bowmen, into those boats, and ascend the river a little, and string to ear and take these horsemen in flank as they come down the road, while we meet them in the teeth with pikes and javelins."

"And," quoth Elfric, looking at the sun, "if we but keep our ground, Lord Hereward will be on the opposite side of the river before ye can say a dozen credos—so blow! Saxons, blow your horns to help that blatant trumpet in telling the Lord of Brunn that fighting is toward, and keep ready a few of the boats to waft over Lord Hereward's force to this side of the river!"

The Saxons blew their horns as loud as they could blow them, meaning the blasts to be as much a note of defiance to the enemy as a signal to their friends; and the Norman trumpeter kept blowing his brazon and far-sounding trumpet, and the Norman cavaliers kept charging along the road, shouting and cursing and calling the Saxons thieves and cowards—which they had no right to do. As the enemy came near, the Saxons set up a shout, and the scared horses and asses tied together on the road, set up their heels with such a kicking and braying and neighing as were never seen and heard; and up started from the sedge by the river bank the score of good Saxon archers that had gone a little up the river in the boats, and whiz went their arrows into the bowels of the horses the Normans were riding, and every arrow that did not kill, disabled some horse or man, the archers in the sedges being too near their aim to throw away a single arrow.

The knight in command ordered the trumpeter to sound a retreat, but before the man could put the brass to his lips, a shaft went through his cheeks and spoiled his trumpeting for aye. But the Normans showed that they could run without sound of trumpet; and away galloped the valorous knight to bring up his bowmen. These Norman archers had no great appetite for the business, and albeit they were told there was a great treasure to be gotten, they stood at a distance, looking now down the road, and now down the river, and now across the ditch and the plashy meadows beyond it; and thus they stood at gaze until they heard a round of Saxon cheers, and the too well-known war-cry of "Hereward for England!" and until they saw a warlike band advancing towards Brandon by the opposite bank of the river. A cockle shell to a mitre—but they tarried not long then! Away went the Normans, horse and foot, as fast as they could go through Brandon town and back upon the high road by which they had marched from Thetford.

"Ha! ha!" cried the Lord of Brunn to his friends from across the river; "what new wasps' nest is this ye have been among?"

The sword-bearer replied that it was a Norman force which had been marching from the south-east.

"'Tis well," said Hereward; "and I see ye have made good booty, and so all is well on your side. On our side we have led the Normans from Dereham and thereabouts a very pretty dance. I drew a party of them after me into the fens and cut them off or captured them to a man. I count as my prisoners one rash young knight and fifteen men-at-arms."

"We have loaded and brought hither more than a score of asses and a full score of pack-horses. Shall we finish loading? All the wine is here, and a good deal of the corn, and—"

"But shall we not pursue?" cried Girolamo. "Those Normans that came on so boldly are now running like sheep. By moving across this marsh, as light fen-men move, we shall be sure to cut off a part of them."

"Since the corn and wine are now safe, be it as you please, Girolamo; but take Elfric with thee, and go not too far in pursuit."

A light skerry was drawn from the river and laid across the ditch in less than a credo; and then away went the Salernitan and the sword-bearer, and all the best archers and boldest men of their party, across the plashy fields; and soon they came up with the rear of the flying Normans, and engaged them in battle on the dry road between Brandon and Thetford, and slew many of them, and captured many more, together with all the baggage and stores of the armament.

The short but fierce battle was over, and Elfric was counting the prisoners, when one of them after surrendering his sword, and after begging for and receiving quarter, sneaked out of the throng and endeavored to escape by running into a thicket near the roadside. The Salernitan, who was resting himself after his exertion, and leaning on the cross of his well-used sword, now in its sheath, saw the intention of the man-at-arms, and rushed after him into the thicket. Now that caitiff, in giving up his sword, had not given up a concealed dagger, and when Girolamo touched him on the shoulder, merely with the point of his still-sheathed sword, he drew that dastardly and unknightly weapon from his breast, and plunged it into the left side of the Salernitan. Girolamo fell to the ground with the murderer's knife in his side; but in the next instant, the murderer was shot through the brain by a well-directed arrow, and as he fell, several Saxons fell with their swords upon him, and, in their fury at his treachery, they hacked his body to pieces. Yet these honest men, though they saw the blood was welling from his side, had much ado to believe that the dark stranger was really hurt with a mortal hurt, and could die like other men. It would be hard to say how long they might have stood looking upon him, stupidly, but not unkindly, if he had not said, "Saxons, raise my head, place me with my back to a tree, and go seek Elfric, and tell him I am hurt by one of his felon prisoners."

Elfric came running to the spot with rage, grief, and astonishment on his countenance. The sword-bearer was breathless and could not speak; the Salernitan was already half-suffocated with the blood that flowed inwardly, but it was he that spoke first and said, "Elfric! After twenty-five years of war and mortal hate between me and them, the Normans have killed me at last! Elfric, let me not die unavenged. Slay me every Norman prisoner thou hast taken on this foul day."

The sword-bearer, knowing that Lord Hereward allowed not of such massacres, and wishing not to irritate Girolamo by a refusal, did some violence to his conscience and sense of truth, first by nodding his head as if in assent, and next by saying that the prisoners should assuredly rue the atrocious deed which had been done. But these words were truer than Elfric had reason to think they would be; for while he was in the wood some of the fen-men, having no longer any commander with them to control their wrath, beat and wounded the prisoners, and dispatched some of them outright. When the Salernitan spoke again he said, "Elfric, leave not my body here to be tracked and outraged by the accursed Normans. Get it carried to Ely and see it interred like the body of a Christian man. And, Elfric, sprinkle a little holy water over my grave, and go there at times to say a De profundis for the peace of my soul!"

Here the sword-bearer said he hoped the hurt was not so bad but that some skillful leech might cure it.

"Alas, no! not all the leeches between this and Salerno could do me any good. Dear Salerno! Shining bay, bright sky, blue hills, I shall never see ye more! I lived but for the hope of that, and for vengeance upon the Normans! My life hath been a life of woe, but I have done them some harm, thank God for that! But it is over.... I grow faint. Oh, that some godly confessor were at hand to shrive me!"

"Shall I run into Brandon and seek a priest," said the sword-bearer; "or shall I send one of these our true men into the town?"

"No, Elfric, thou must not leave me in my last agony, and there is no time for sending and seeking. But, Elfric, undo my collar, and unbutton this hard mail-jacket, and bring out the silver crucifix, which I received from my mother, and which hath never been from my neck—no, not for a second of time—during these last forty years. Elfric, I have kissed that silver crucifix openly, and in despite of the accursed ravings of Jews and Saracens, upon the very spot where our Lord was crucified! Elfric, that little cross was round my neck, held by the same silver chain to which my mother hung it, when, sailing between Cyprus and Palestine with turbaned infidels, the bark went down in deep water, and every soul perished, save only I! Kind Saxon, it was my faith in that cross that saved my health and life in Alexandria, when pestilence raged throughout the land of Egypt, and depopulated Alexandria, and all the cities of Egypt! Let my dying lips close upon that cross:—and, good Elfric, as thou hopest thyself to die in peace, and to be admitted into the dominions of the saints, see that chain and cross buried with me,—round my neck and upon my breast, as they now are! And take and keep for thyself whatever else I possess, except this sword, which thou wilt give in my name to the Lord of Brunn. Dear boy! The Normans have not left me much to give thee... but I had broad and rich lands once, and horses of high breed and price, and rich furniture, and sparkling jewels brought from the Orient by the Amalfitans!"

While the dying Salernitan was thus speaking—his voice ever growing fainter and fainter—the sword-bearer gently and piously did all that he had been required to do, undoing the collar, and unbuttoning the coat of mail which the Salernitan wore under his loose mantle of woolen cloth, and bringing out from beneath the under-vest the silver crucifix, and placing it in the feeble right hand of the Salernitan, who then kissed it and said, "Mother dear, I shall soon be with thee! Oh, heavenly Mother, let my soul pass easily from this hapless body!"

Here Elfric, who had been well indoctrinated in the days of his youth by the best of the monks of Spalding, crossed himself and said, that it was God himself who had enjoined the forgiveness of our enemies, and that holy men had ever declared that the moribund died easiest when he forgave all the wrongs that had been done him, and died in peace with all mankind.

Girolamo had to gasp for breath before he could speak; but at length he said, "Saxon, I die in peace with all mankind, or with all that profess the Christian faith—save only the Normans. I forgive all men as I hope to be forgiven. *Fiat misericordia tua, Domine*; yea, I forgive all and die in peace with all, save only the detestable ungodly Normans, who have heaped upon me such wrong as cannot be forgiven, and who have belied the promises made at their baptism, and who be Christians but in name. Elfric, remember! They slew my kindred and all the friends of my youth, or they caused them to die in sickly

dungeons or in exile and beggary; they surprised and stole from me the young bride of my heart and gave her over to violence and infamy! Elfric, wouldst ever forgive them if they should thus seize and treat thy Mildred?"
Elfric shook his head as though he would say he never could; but albeit Elfric was not dying, he ought not to have done this. Girolamo's head was now falling on his breast, and he several times essayed to speak and could not. At last he said to Elfric, who was kneeling by his side, "Tell the Lord Hereward that I die his constant friend, and call upon him to avenge my death! Elfric, put thine ear closer to my mouth.... So... and Elfric, go tell the monks at Ely that I am not the Jew that cannot die!"

Here the sword-bearer, who was supporting the Salernitan with his right arm, felt a short and slight shivering, and raising his head so as to look in his face, he saw that the eyelids were dropping over the dark eyes,—and, in another brief instant, Girolamo was dead.

The Saxons cut down branches of trees, and with the branches and their fen poles, and some of the lances which had been taken from the Normans, they made a rude catafalque or bier, and placing the Salernitan upon it, with many a De profundis, and many expressions of wonderment that he should have died, they carried him from the thicket and over the Thetford road and across the plashy meadows.

The bier was followed by the surviving Norman prisoners, all expecting to be offered up as an holocaust, and crying Misericord and Nôtre Dame. The pursuit and the fight, the capture and the woe which had followed it, had altogether filled a very short space of time; and Hereward, who had crossed the river with all his forces, and having embarked in the boats all that remained to be embarked, was congratulating Elfric on his speed, when he saw that the body stretched upon the bier was no less a man than Girolamo of Salerno. At first the Lord of Brunn thought or hoped that Girolamo was only wounded; but when his sword-bearer told him that he was dead, he started as one that hears a great and unexpected calamity, and he put his hand to his brow and said, "Then, by all the saints of Ely, we have bought the corn and wine for the monks at too dear a price!"

Some short season Hereward passed in silent and sad reflections. Then approaching the bier whereon the body of Girolamo lay with the face turned to the skies, and the little silver cross lying on the breast, and the limbs decently composed, all through the pious care of Elfric, the Lord of Brunn muttered a De profundis and a Requiescat in pace, and then said, "Elfric, I never loved that man! Perhaps, at times, I almost feared him, with the reach of his skill and the depth and darkness of his passions. I never could hate the foul fiend himself so much as Girolamo hated these Normans! But, be it said, his wrongs and sufferings have far exceeded mine. England and I stand deeply indebted to him!"

"He bade me give thee this, his sword, and to tell thee that he died thy friend," said Elfric.

"There never yet was sword deeper in the gore of our foes," said Hereward; "I know he was my friend, and in many things my instructor, and I reproach my heart for that it never could love him, albeit it was ever grateful towards him! But, Elfric, we must down the river without delay, for the monks of Ely will be clamorous for their wine, and traitors may take advantage of mine absence from the camp. See to it, Elfric, for a heaviness is upon my heart such as I have never known before. I had bad dreams in my last sleep, visions of surprising's and burnings by the Normans, and now the great loss and bad omen of Girolamo's death bring those dreams back upon my mind with more force than they had before."

"I have had my dreams too of late," said the sword-bearer; "but dreams, good my lord, are to be read contrariwise. Let me give your lordship a slice of wheaten bread and a cup of wine."

Quoth the Lord of Brunn, "'Tis not badly thought, for I am fasting since last sunset, and the monks of Ely must hold us excused if we broach one cask. Elfric, I say again, we have paid all too dearly for this corn and wine."

The dangerous marsh around Ely!

CHAPTER XXIII.

A CHAPTER AND A GREAT TREASON

No sooner had the Lord of Brunn quitted the Camp of Refuge, the day before that on which the Salernitan was slain, than the prior and the chamberlain and their faction called upon the Lord Abbat to summon a chapter of the house, in order to deliberate upon the perilous state of affairs; and notably upon the emptiness of the granaries and wine-cellars of the convent, there being, they said, barely red wine enough in the house to suffice for the service of the mass through another week. Now, good Thurstan, nothing daunted by the malice and plots of the prior (of which he knew but a part), readily convoked the chapter, and gave to every official and every cloister-monk full liberty to speak and vote according to his conscience and the best of his knowledge.

But much was the Lord Abbat grieved when he saw that a good many of the monks did not rise and greet him as they ought to do, and turned their faces from him as he entered the chapter-house and gave them his *benedicite, and pax vobiscum*. And the abbat was still more grieved and astonished when he heard the prior taking up the foul accusation of Girolamo which had been disposed of the day before, and talking about witchcraft and necromancy, instead of propounding some scheme for the defense of the house and the Camp of Refuge against the Norman invaders.

Much did the good Thurstan suffer in patient silence; but when the atrabilious prior went on to repeat his accusations against Elfric, the whilom novice of Spalding, and against himself, the Lord Abbat of Ely, as defensors, fautors, and abettors of the necromancer, and said that it was now known unto the holy Father of the church at Rome, and throughout all Christendom, that last year an attempt had been made to compass the life of King William by witchcraft (the Norman duke having only had a taste of our fen-fever, as aforesaid!), Thurstan could remain silent no longer, and striking the table with his honest Saxon hand until his abbatial ring was broken on his finger (a sad omen of what was coming!), he raised his voice and made the hanging roof of the chapter-house re-echo, and the cowardly hearts of the wicked monks quiver and shake within them.

"There is a malice," cried Thurstan, "worse than maleficcium! There is a crime worse than witchcraft, and that is—ingratitude! Prior, when I was but a young cloister-monk, I found thee a sickly beggar in the fens, and brought thee into this house! It was I that raised thee to thy present eminence and illustration, and now thou wouldst sting me to the heart! Prior, I say, there is worse guilt even than ingratitude, and that is treason to one's country! Prior, I have long suspected thee of a traitorous correspondence with the Normans, or at least of a traitorous wish to benefit thine own worldly fortune by serving them by the damnable acts of betraying thy country and this house. I have been but a fool, a compassionating, weak-hearted fool not to have laid thee fast in a dungeon long ago. Remember! It is more than a year since I threatened thee within these walls. But I relied upon the Saxon honesty and the conscience and the solemn oaths of this brotherhood, and so thought that thou couldst do no mischief, and mightest soon repent of thy wickedness. And tell me, oh prior, and look me in the face, and throw back thy cowl that all may see thy face; tell me, have I not a hundred times taken pains to show thee what, even in this world and in mere temporalities, hath been the hard fate of the Saxon monks and clergy that betrayed their flocks and submitted to the Normans? Speak, prior; I wait for thine answer."

But the prior could not or would not then speak.

"Hola!" cried the abbat. "Is mine authority gone from me? Is the power I hold from Heaven, and from the sainted Confessor, *Rex venerandus*, and by the one-voiced vote of this house, already usurped? Is my call to be disobeyed? Shall this false monk insult me before the brotherhood by refusing to answer me? I appeal to all the monks in chapter assembled."

Several of the monks said that the prior was bound to answer the question which the abbat had put to him; but the chamberlain stood forward and said with an insolent tone, that in a chapter like the present every monk might speak or be silent as he thought best; that the question was irrelevant; and that, moreover, Brother Thurstan (mark ye, he called him frater, and not *dominus or abbat!*) had put the said question in a loud, angry, and unmannerly voice; and was, as he was but too apt to be, in a very fierce and ungodly passion of rage.

"Oh chamberlain!" cried the abbat, "thou art in the complot against me and thy country and the patrimony of Saint Etheldreda, and I have long thought it, and...." "And I," said the chamberlain, audaciously interrupting the Lord Abbat while he was speaking, "And I have long thought that thou hast been leading this house into perdition, and that thou art not fit to be the head of it."

A few of the cloister-monks started to their feet at these daring words, and recited the rules of the Order of Saint Benedict, and called upon the chamberlain and upon all present to remember their vows of obedience, and the respect due to every lord abbat that had been canonically elected and appointed; but alas! the number of these remonstrants was very small—much smaller than it would have been only the day before, for the faction had travailed hard during the night, and had powerfully worked upon the fears of the monks, more especially by telling them that neither bread nor wine could anywhere be had, and that a new legate was coming into England from the pope to excommunicate every Saxon priest and monk that did not submit to the Conqueror. Now when Thurstan saw how few there were in chapter that seemed to be steady to their duty, and true to their vows and to the rules of the order (promulgated by Saint Benedict and confirmed by so many pontiffs of Rome, and so many heads of the Benedictine Order, dwelling in the house on Mons Casinium, by the river Liris, where Saint Benedict himself dwelt, and fasted and prayed, when he was in the flesh), his heart, bold and stout as it was, sank within him, and he fell back in his carved seat and muttered to himself, "My pastoral crook is broken! My flock are turned into wolves!"

But, among the true-hearted Saxon monks, there was one that had the courage to defy the prior and his faction, and to stand forward and to speak roundly in defense of the oppressed Lord Abbat; and when he had spoken others found heart to do the same; and thereupon the weak and unsteady part of the chapter, who had no malice against Thurstan, and who had only taken counsel of their fears and craving stomachs, began to fall away from the line where the factious would have kept them, and even to reprove the chamberlain and the prior. This change of wind refreshed both the body and the soul of Thurstan, who knew as little of fear as any man that lived; and who had been borne down for a moment by the weight and agony of the thought that all his friends were either arrayed against him, or were too cowardly to defend him.

Speaking again as one having authority and the power to enforce it, he commanded the prior and chamberlain to sit silent in their seats. And the two rebel monks sate silent while Thurstan, in a very long and earnest discourse, but more free from the passion of wrath than it had been, went once more over the history of his life and doings, from the day of his election down to the present troublous day; and spoke hopefully of the return of King Harold, and confidently of the ability of the Saxons to defend the Fen-country if they only remained true to themselves and to the Lord Hereward, without plots or machinations or cowardly and treacherous compacts with the enemy.

The Lord Abbat's discourse lasted so long that it was now near the hour of dinner; and, as much speaking bringeth on hunger and thirst, he was led to think about food and drink, and these thoughts made him say, "My children, ye all know that the Lord of Brunn hath gone forth of the Camp, at the point of day, to procure for us corn and wine. He hath sworn to me to bring us both—and when did the Lord of Brunn break his oath or fail in an enterprise? I tell ye one and all that he hath vowed to bring us wine and bread or die!"

The door of the chapter-house was closed and made fast, in order that none should go out or come in so long as the chapter lasted; but while Thurstan was saying his last words, the sub-sacrist, who was sitting near a window which looked into the quadrangle or open square of the abbey, very secretly and adroitly made a sign to some that were standing below in the quadrangle; and scarcely had the Lord Abbat pronounced the word "die" when a loud wailing and shouting was heard from without, and then the words "He is dead! He is dead! The Lord Hereward is killed!"

At these sounds Thurstan turned as pale as a whitewashed wall, and others turned as pale as Thurstan; and the traitor-monks smote their breasts and made a show of being as much grieved and astounded as any of them.

"Ah woe!" said the abbat, "but this is fatal news! What fresh sorrow is this upon me! Hereward lost! He dead, whose arm and counsels formed our strength! Oh! That I had died yesterday, or an hour ago! But who brings the dire news? What and where is the intelligencer? Suspend this miserable chapter, and throw open the door that we may see and hear."

The sub-sacrist was the first that rushed to the door, and threw it wide open and called upon a crowd of men without to come in and speak to the Lord Abbat.

The crowd rushed in. It was made up of hinds and serfs from the township of Ely, and of the gaping novices and lay brothers and serving men of the abbey; but in the head of it was an old fenner, who dwelt on the Stoke river between Hilgay and Downham-market, and who was well known for his skill in fowling and decoying birds, and for no other good deed: his name was Roger Lighthand, and he was afterwards hanged for stealing. He had his tale by rote, and he told it well.

He was going that morning to look after some snares near Stoke-ferry, when, to his amazement, he saw a great band of Normans marching across the fens under the guidance of some of the fenners. He concealed himself and the Normans concealed themselves: and soon afterwards there came a band of Saxons headed by the Lord of Brunn, and these Saxons fell into the ambush which the Normans had laid for them; and the Lord of Brunn, after a desperate fight, was slain, and his head was cut off by the Normans and stuck upon a spear; and then the Normans marched away in the direction of Brandon, carrying with them as prisoners all the Saxons of Lord Hereward that they had not slain—all except one man, who had escaped out of the ambush and was here to speak for himself. And now another fenner opened his mouth to give forth the lies which had been put into it; and this man said that, early in the morning, the Lord of Brunn, with a very thin attendance, had come across the fens where he dwelt, with a great blowing of horns, and with sundry gleemen, who sang songs about the victories of Hereward the Saxon, and who drew all the fenners of those parts, and himself among the rest, to join the Lord of Brunn, in order to march with him to the upland country and get corn and wine for the good monks of Ely.

"When the Lord Hereward fell," said this false loon, "I was close to him, and I afterwards saw his head upon the Norman lance." "And I too," quoth Roger Lighthand, "from my hiding-place among the rushes, saw the bleeding head of the Lord of Brunn as plainly as I now see the face of the Lord Abbat!"

The traitorous monks made a loud lamentation and outcry, but Thurstan could neither cry nor speak, and he sat with his face buried in his hands; while the prior ordered the crowd to withdraw, and then barred the door after them. As he returned from the door to his seat, the prior said, "Brethren, our last hope is gone!" And every monk then present, save only three, repeated the words, "Our last hope is gone!"

"The great captain hath perished," said the chamberlain: "he will bring us no corn and wine! There is no help for us except only in tendering our submission to King William, and in showing him how to get through the fens and fall upon the rebel people in the Camp of Refuge, who have consumed our substance and brought us to these straits!" Many voices said in a breath that there was no other chance of escaping famine or slaughter.

This roused the Saxon-hearted Lord Abbat, who had almost begun to weep in tenderness for brave Hereward's death; and, striking the table until the hall rang again, he up and said, "Let me rather die the death of the wicked than have part in, or permit, so much base treachery! Let me die ten times over rather than be false to my country! Let me die a hundred deaths, or let me live in torture, rather than betray the noblest of the nobles of England that be in the Camp of Refuge; and the venerable archbishop and bishops, abbats and priors that have so long found a refuge in this house—a house ever famed for its hospitality. Let me, I say...."

Here the prior, with great boldness and insolence, interrupted the Lord Abbat, and said with a sneer, "The few servants of the church that now be in this house shall be looked to in our compact with the Normans; but for the fighting-lords that be in the Camp of Refuge, let them look to themselves! They have arms and may use them, or by laying down their arms they may hope to be admitted to quarter and to the King's peace; or... or they may save their lives by timeous flight... they may get them back into Scotland or to their own countries from which they came, for our great sorrow, to devour our substance and bring down destruction upon our house. We, the monks of Ely, owe them nothing!"

"Liar that thou art," said Thurstan, "we owe them years of liberty and the happy hope of being forever free of Norman bondage and oppression. If ye bring the spoilers among us, ye will soon find what we have owed to these valorous lords and knights! We owe to them and to their fathers much of the treasure which is gone and much of the land which remains to this monastery: we owe to them the love and good faith which all true Englishmen owe to one another; and in liberal minds this debt of affection only grows the stronger in adverse seasons.

We are pledged to these lords and knights by every pledge that can have weight and value between man and man!"

"All this," quoth the chamberlain, "may or may not be true; but we cannot bargain for the lives and properties of those that are in the Camp of Refuge: and we are fully resolved to save our own lives, with such property as yet remains to this, by thee misgoverned, monastery. Nevertheless we will entreat the King to be merciful unto the rebels."

"What rebels? What king!" roared the Lord Abbat again, smiting the table; "oh chamberlain! Oh prior! oh ye backsliding monks that sit there with your chins in your hands, not opening your lips for the defense of your superior, to whom ye have all vowed a constant obedience, it is ye that are the rebels and traitors! *Deo regnante et Rege expectante*, by the great God that reigns, and by King Harold that is expected, this Norman bastard is no king of ours! There is no king of England save only King Harold, who will yet come back to claim his own, and to give us our old free laws!"

"We tell thee again, oh Thurstan! That Harold lies buried in Waltham Abbey, and that there be those who have seen..."

"Brother," quoth the prior to the chamberlain, "brother, we but lose our time in this idle and angry talk with a man who was ever too prone to wrath, and too headstrong. The moments of time are precious! Let us put the question."

"Do it thyself, oh prior," said the chamberlain, who then sat down, looking very pale.

"It is a painful duty," said the prior, "but I will do it."

And having so said, the prior stood up, right before the Lord Abbat, though not without fear and trembling, and, after stammering for some time, he spoke in this strain, looking rather at the abbat's feet than in his face:—"Thurstan, it is better that one man should suffer a temporary evil than that many men should perish! It is better that thou shouldest cease to rule over this house than that the house, and all of us in it, should be destroyed! I, the prior, and next in authority unto thee, and with the consent and advice of all the chief obedientiarii of the convent, do invite and entreat thee voluntarily to suspend thyself from all the duties of thine office!"

"Chick of the fens, art so bold as this?" cried Thurstan, "hast thrown thy respect for the canons of the church and the rules of this order of St. Benedict into the same hell-pit where thou hast thrown the rest of thy conscience? Children! Brothers! Ye, the ancient members of the convent, what say ye this?"

Three monks who had grown grey in the house, without ever acquiring, or wishing to acquire, any of the posts of eminence, to wit, Father Kynric, Father Elsin, and Father Celred, raised their voices and said, that such things had not been heard of before; that the prior, unmindful of his vows, and of the deep debt of gratitude he owed unto the Lord Abbat, was seeking to thrust him from his seat, that he might sit upon it himself; and that if such things were allowed there would be an end to the glory of the house of Ely, an end to all subordination and obedience, an end to the rule under which the house had flourished ever since the days of King Edgar, *Rex piissimus*.

Thus spoke the three ancient men; but no other monks supported them, albeit a few of the younger members of the convent whispered in each other's ears that the prior was dealing too harsh a measure to the bountiful Lord Thurstan.

The prior, glad to address anybody rather than the Lord Abbat, turned round and spoke to Kynric, Elsin, and

Celred: "Brothers," said he, "ye are mistaken as to my meaning. I, the humblest born of this good community, wish not for higher promotion, and feel that I am all unworthy of that which I hold. I propose not a forcible deprivation, nor so much as a forcible suspension. I, in mine own name, and in the names of the sub-prior, the cellarer, the sacrist, the sub-sacrist, the chamberlain, the sub-chamberlain, the refectorarius, the precentor, and others the obedientiarii, or officials of this goodly and godly house of Ely, do only propound that Thurstan, our Lord Abbat, do, for a season and until these troubles be past, quietly and of his own free will, cease to exercise the functions of his office. Now, such a thing as this hath been heard of aforetime. Have we not a recent instance and precedent of it in our own house, in the case and conduct of Abbat Wilfric, the immediate predecessor of my Lord Thurstan? But let me tell that short tale, and let him whom it most concerneth take it for a warning and example.—

The Lord Abbat Wilfric was a high-born man, as high-born as my Lord Thurstan himself, for there was royal Danish and Saxon blood in his veins. Many were the hides of land, and many the gifts he gave to this community and church: my Lord Thurstan hath not given more! Many were the years that he lived in credit and reputation, and governed the abbey with an unblemished character. Our refectory was never better supplied than in the days of Abbat Wilfric; and, albeit there were wars and troubles, and rumors of many wars in his days, our cellars were never empty, nor was the house ever obliged to eat roast and baked meats without any wheaten bread. It was a happy time for him and for us! But, in an evil hour, Guthmund, the brother of my Lord Abbat Wilfric, came unto this house with a greedy hand and a woeful story about mundane loves and betrothals—a story unmeet for monastic ears to hear. Guthmund, had paid his court to the daughter of one of the greatest noblemen of East Anglia, and had gained her love. Now Guthmund, though of so noble a family, and related to princes, was not entitled to the privileges of prime nobility, neither took he rank with them, forasmuch as that he had not in actual possession a sufficient estate, to wit, forty hides of land.

This being the case, the father of the maiden forbade the troth-plight, and bade Guthmund fly his hawks in another direction, and come no more to the house. So Guthmund came with his piteous tale to his brother the Abbat Wilfric, who, thinking of temporalities when he ought to have been thinking of spiritualties, and preferring the good of a brother to the good of this house, did, without consulting with any of the convent, but in the utmost privacy, convey unto the said Guthmund sundry estates and parcels of land appurtenant to this monastery, to wit, Acholt, part of Mereham, Livermere, Nachentune, Bedenestede, and Gerboldesham, to the end that, being possessed of them, Guthmund might hold rank with the prime nobility and renew his love-suit with a certainty of success.

Wot ye well this pernicious brother of the abbat went away not with the sad face he had brought to the abbey, but with a very joyous countenance, for he took with him from our cartularies, the title-deeds of those broad lands which had been given to the abbey by sundry pious lords. Yes! Guthmund went his way, and was soon happy with his bride and the miserable pleasures of the flesh, and the pomp and vanities of the world. But the abbat, his brother, was never happy again, for his conscience reproached him, and the secret of the foul thing which he had done was soon discovered. The brotherhood assembled in chapter, even as it is now assembled, denounced the robbery, the spoliation, and sacrilege, and asked whether it were fit that such an abbat should continue to hold rule over the house? Wilfric, not hardened in sin, but full of remorse, felt that he could no longer be, or act as Lord Abbat, and therefore went he away voluntarily from the abbey, renouncing all authority. Yea, he went his way unto Acholt, where, from much sorrow and perturbation of mind, he soon fell sick and died: and, as he died very penitent, we brought back his body for sepulture in the abbey church; and then proposed that our brother Thurstan should be our Abbat and ruler."

"Saint Etheldreda give me patience!" said Thurstan, "Oh prior, what have I to do with this tale? Why revive the memory of the sins of a brother, and once superior and father, who died of grief for that which he had done, and which an excess of brotherly love had urged him to do? How doth this tale apply to me? What have I had to do in it or with it, save only to recover for this house the lands which my unhappy predecessor conveyed away? I have brought ye hides of land, but have given none to any of my kindred. That which hath been spent since the black day of Hastings, hath been spent for the defense of the patrimony of Saint Etheldreda, and for the service of the country. Have I not brought Guthmund to compound with me, and to agree to hold from, and under the abbey, and during his lifetime only, and with payment of dues and services to the abbey, all the lands which his brother, the Abbat Wilfric,—may his soul find pardon and rest!—alienated by that wicked conveyance? And hath not the same Guthmund given us the dues and services; and will not the lands of Acholt, Mereham, Livermere, Nachentune, Bedenestede, and Gerboldesham revert to the house so soon as he dies? Oh prior, that hast the venom of the serpent without the serpent's cunning, if ye bring in the son of the harlot of Falaise, and if some pauper of a

Norman knight get hold of these lands, the abbey will never get them back again!" And as Thurstan said, so it happened. The demesnes were given to one Hugo de Montfort, and the church was never able to recover possession of them.

"Brethren," said the prior, "I put it to ye, whether we be not now in greater tribulation and want than ever we were before? Abbat Wilfric gave away five manors and a part of a sixth; but the convent was still left rich."

"Aye! And the cellars full, and the granaries full," said the cellarius.

"And nothing was taken from our treasury or from the shrines of our saints," said the sub-sacrist.

"Nor was there any dealing and pledging with the accursed Israelites," said the chamberlain.

"Nor did we then bring upon ourselves the black guilt of robbing other religious houses to give the spoils to the half-converted, drunken Danes," said the sub-chamberlain.

"Slanderers and traitors all," shouted Thurstan, "ye all know how these things were brought about! There is not one of ye but had more to do in that of which ye now complain than I had! Ye forced me into those dealings with Jews and Danes."

"Thou wast abbat and ruler of the house, and as such thou art still answerable for all;" said the prior with a very insolent and diabolical sneer.

Thurstan could no longer control his mighty wrath, and springing upon the prior and seizing him by the neck he shouted, "Dog, I will answer upon thy throat! Nay, viper, that stingest thy benefactor, I will crush thee under my heel!"

And before the cellarer and chamberlain or any of that faction could come to the rescue, the puny prior, with a blackened face, was cast on his back upon the floor of the chapter-house, and the Lord Abbat had his foot upon him.

The prior moaned and then screamed and yelled like a whipped cur: the faction rose from their seats and came to his aid, but as they all knew and dreaded the stalwart strength that was in Thurstan's right arm, each of them wished some other monk to go foremost, and so the cellarer pushed forward the chamberlain, and the chamberlain pushed forward the sub-chamberlain, the sacrist, the sub-sacrist, and so with the rest; and maugre all this pushing, not one of them would venture to lay his hand upon the sleeve of the abbat's gown, or to get within reach of Thurstan's strong right arm.

But the Lord Abbat cooling in his wrath, and feeling scorn and contempt instead of anger, took his foot from the hollow breast of the recreant prior, and bade him rise and cease his yelling: and the prior rose and the abbat returned to his seat.

Now those of the faction who had not felt the tight grip of Thurstan's right hand, nor the weight of his foot, were greatly rejoiced at what had happened, as they thought it would give them a handle whereby to move a vote of the chapter for the forcible suspension of the Lord Abbat; and to this end they raised a loud clamor that Thurstan had acted uncanonically, tyrannically, and indecently, in beating a monk who was next in dignity to himself, and that by this one act he had merited suspension.

"Babblers and fools," cried Thurstan, growing wroth again; "Fools that ye are, though with more malice than folly, and with more treachery than ignorance, it is not unto me that ye can expound the canons of the church, or the rules of the order of Saint Benedict! Was I not bred up in this house from mine infancy? Was I not reputed sufficiently learned both in English and in Latin, many years before I became your abbat? Have I not read and gotten by heart the laws and institutes? Ye have a rule if ye would read it! and is it not this—that it is your duty to obey your Lord Abbat in all things, and that your abbat may impose upon each and all of ye such penance as he thinks fit, *secundum delictum*, even to the chastising of ye with his own hand? Chamberlain! I have seen Abbat Wilfric cudgel thee with his fen-pole until thy back was as black as thy heart now is. Sacrist! thou art old now, but thou wilt remember how Abbat Wilfric's predecessor knocked thee down in the refectory on the eve of Saint John, for being drunk before evening-song, and thine offence was small compared to that which this false prior hath given me before the whole house!"

The prior, who had now recovered his breath and removed himself to the farthest end of the hall, spoke and said—"But what say the canons of Ælfric?—'Let not a priest wear weapons nor work strife, nor let him swear oaths, but with gentleness and simplicity ever speak truly as a learned servant of God:'—and what sayeth Ælfric in his pastoral epistle?—'No priest shall be too proud nor too boastful. He shall not be violent and quarrelsome, nor stir up strife, but he shall pacify quarrels always if he can; and he may not who is God's soldier lawfully wear weapons, nor go into any battle:'—and what say the canons enacted under King Edgar, the great benefactor of this our house?—'Let each of God's servants be to other a support and a help both before God and before men: and we enjoin that each respect the other.'"

"Say on," cried the abbat; "thou sayest not all the canons of good King Edgar, for it ordains that all junior priests or monks shall respect and obey their elders and superiors. But I will not lose more time and temper in talking with thee and such as thou art; and since the major part of the convent have fallen off from their duty and the respect and obedience they owe me, I, Thurstan, by the grace of God Lord Abbat of Ely, entering my solemn protest against the wrong which hath been done me, and making my appeal to God against this injustice and rebellion, do here, for this time being, take off my mitre and dalmatic, and lay down my crosier, and take my departure for the Camp of Refuge, to take my chance with those whom ye are betraying."

And so saying, Thurstan laid mitre, dalmatic, and crosier upon the table, and then strode down the hall towards the door.

"Oh Thurstan," cried the chamberlain with a voice of great joy, "thou hast done wisely! But it would not be wisely done in us to let thee go forth of this house for this present! Sub-prior, cellarer, friends, all that would save the abbey and your own lives, look to the door! Prior, put it to the vote that the house in chapter assembled do accept the voluntary resignation of Thurstan, and that he, our whilom abbat, be closely confined within his own innermost chamber, until another chapter ordain otherwise, or until this exceeding great danger be past."

The door was more than secured; and save only the feeble voices of those three old and good monks, Fathers Kynric, Elsin, and Celred, not a voice was heard to speak against these wicked proposals, or in favor of the bountiful Lord Abbat, whose heart died within him at the sight of so much ingratitude, and who stood, as if rooted to the ground, at the end of the hall near the door, muttering to himself, "Hereward, my son, if thou hadst lived it ne'er had come to this! Oh noble lords and knights and warriors true in the Camp,—no longer a Camp of Refuge, but Castra Doloris, a Camp of Woe,—ye will be betrayed and butchered, and in ye will be betrayed and butchered the liberties of England and the last rights of the English church, before warning can be given ye!

Oh Stigand, my spiritual lord, and all ye Saxon bishops and abbats that came hither as to a sanctuary, ye have but thrown yourselves into the lion's den! Hereward, dear, brave Hereward, thou art happy, thou art happy in this, that thou hast at least died like a soldier! The rest of us will die like sheep in the shambles!"

While Thurstan, a sadder man than ever was Marius among the ruins of Carthage, was thus standing motionless, and communing with his own sad heart, the prior put to the vote the resolution which the chamberlain had moved; and the large majority of the house, some being deep in the plot, but more being carried by the dread of the Normans and the dread of famine, or being thrown into despair by the reported death of the Lord of Brunn, voted as the prior and chamberlain wished they would vote.

The prior would fain have cast Thurstan into that subterranean dungeon into which Thurstan had once threatened, but unluckily only threatened, to cast him; and he took much pains to show that it was needful to keep the deposed abbat in a place of great strength and security, to keep his imprisonment a secret, and to prevent all possibility of access to him or correspondence with him; but when he came to name the dark damp cold cells in the foundations of the abbey, wherein the rebellious son of an old East Anglian king had been immured, after having been deprived of his eyes, the monks testified compunction and disgust, and even sundry monks that had long been the most desperate of his faction spoke against the barbarity, and therefore the astute prior had not put it to the vote, and Thurstan was merely conveyed to the inner chamber of his own apartment; and this being done, and a strong guard being left in the abbat's apartment, the monks all went to their long delayed dinner, and as soon as the dinner was over, the prior, the cellarer, the chamberlain, the sacrist, and a large attendance of monks and lay brothers went forth to complete their treason, leaving behind them rigorous orders that all the gates of the abbey should be kept closed, and that none should be admitted therein until they returned from Cam-Bridge.

The way which the traitors took across the fens and broad waters of Ely was indirect and long, for they feared to be seen of any Saxon, and so shunned the good folk of the township of Ely, the faithful vassals and loaf-eaters of the abbey. Nevertheless they got to the causey which the Normans had made before compline, or second vespers, and finding fleet horses there waiting for them, they got to the castle at Cam-Bridge, and into the presence of Duke William and his fiercer half-brother, Odo, Bishop of Bayeux, two good hours before the beginning of lauds.

The false Saxons kneeled at the feet of the Normans, kissed their hands—mailed hands both, for the bishop, heedless of the canons of the church, wore armor and carried arms as frequently as his brother the duke, and, like the duke, intended to take the field against the last of the Saxons, and was only waiting for the summons and the sign which the monks of Ely were to give.

The compact had been propounded many nights before this; but now the duke, speaking as lawful sovereign of England, and the Bishop of Bayeux, speaking as one that had authority from the primate Lanfranc and from the Pope of Rome himself, laid their hands upon the relics of some Saxon saints which the traitor monks had brought with them, and solemnly promised and vowed that, in consideration of the said monks showing them a safe byway to the Camp of Refuge, and in consideration of their other services, they would do no harm, nor suffer any to be done either to Ely Abbey, or to any monk, novice, lay brother, or other servant soever of that house. Aye, they promised and vowed that the whole patrimony of Saint Etheldreda should remain and be confirmed to the Saxon brotherhood, and that not a hide of land should be taken from them, nor a single Norman knight, soldier, abbat, or monk be forced upon them, or enriched by their spoils. Aye, and they promised and vowed to enrich the shrines of the saints, and to restore to the abbey its pristine splendor and all its ancient possessions, not excepting those for which Guthmund, the brother of Abbat Wilfric, had compounded; and they opened unto the delighted eyes of the prior the sure and brilliant prospect of the mitre and crosier.

And upon this the false monks of Ely swore upon the same relics to do all and more than they had promised to do; and so kneeled again and kissed the mailed hands, and took their departure from that ill-omened castle on the hill that stood and stands near to Cam-Bridge; and riding along the causey as fast as the best English horses could carry them, and then stealing over the waters, across the fens, and through the woods of willows, like night thieves that blow no horn, because they will not that their going and coming be known to honest men, they got back to the abbey, and went to their several cells about the same hour of prime on which Elfric the sword-bearer, and Girolamo the Salernitan, got down as far as to Brandon with corn and wine for the house.

The order was again given that all the gates of the abbey should be kept closed; and during the whole of that day, or from the rising of the sun to the setting thereof, no living soul was allowed either to enter the house or to issue therefrom. So much did the traitors fear lest their treasons and the wrongs they had done unto the good

Lord Abbat should become known to the good folk of Ely town, and through them to the warriors in the Camp of Refuge. Some of the Saxon prelates had gone forth for the Camp several days before, and had not yet returned; but such as remained in the house (only a few sick and aged men) were told that the Lord Abbat was sick, and could not be spoken with, and that the doors and gates were kept closed in order that he might not be disturbed. Nor was this all false.

Thurstan's wrath, and then his grief and perturbations, had brought on a fever and ague and he was lying on his bed in a very helpless and very hopeless state, with none to help him or hear him, for the sub-prior had made fast the door of the inner chamber, and the door of the chamber which led into it; and the guard was stationed at a distance in the corridor.

CHAPTER XXIV.

THE DUNGEON

It was just before sunset of the disastrous day which saw the traitorous monks of Ely return from the castle at Cam-Bridge, that the Lord of Brunn and his trusty sword-bearer arrived at Turbutsey (where the monks of old had landed the body of Saint Withburga) with the corn and wine for the abbey; and also with the dead body of the Salernitan, which they hoped to inter in the abbey church-yard. Turbutsey had but few in-dwellers; and the poor hinds that were there had heard nothing of the foul report of Lord Hereward's death, which had wrought such mischief in the abbey.

Lord Hereward, eager to be at his proper post in the Camp of Refuge, took the direct road, or path, which led thereunto, carrying with him, for the comfort of secular stomachs, only a few flagons of wine and a few measures of wheat, and ordering Elfric to go up to the abbey with all the rest of the provision, as soon as it should be all landed from the boats and skerries.

But, before the landing was finished, there came down some gossips from the township of Ely, who reported with marvelous sad faces, that the gates of the abbey had been closed ever since the mid-day of yesterday; and that the whole house was as silent and sad as a pest-house, on account, no doubt, of the death of the good Lord of Brunn, the kind-hearted, open-handed lord, who had ever befriended the Saxon poor! Upon hearing them talk in this fashion, the sword bearer came up to the gossips, and told them that the Lord of Brunn was no more dead than he was.

"Verily," said the people, "the sad news came down to the township yesterday before the hour of noon; and ever since then the abbey gates and church gates have been closed, and the township hath been in tears."

Now, upon hearing this strange news, Elfric's quick fancy began to work, and apprehending some evil, albeit he knew not what, he resolved not to carry up the stores, but to go up alone by himself to see what strange thing had happened in the abbey, that should have caused the monks to bar their doors, and even the doors of the church, against the faithful. He thought not of the want of rest for one night, or of the toils he had borne on that night and during two whole days, for he had borne as much before without any great discomfort; but he looked at the stark body of the Salernitan, as it lay with the face covered in one of the boats, and then he thought of Girolamo's death-wound and dying moment, and of the ill-will which some of the convent had testified towards that stranger, and of the rumors he had heard of murmurings and caballing's against the good Lord Abbat, and he said to himself, "My heart is heavy, or heavier than it ever was before, and my mind is haunted by misgivings.

If the monks of Ely be traitors to their country, and rebels to their abbat, by all the blessed saints of the house of Ely they shall not taste of this bread, nor drink of this wine! And then this unburied, uncoffined, unanealed body, and the dying prayer of Girolamo for Christian burial, and a grave whither the Normans should come not!... I must see to that, and provide against chances."

And having thus said to himself, he said aloud to his troop of fenners: "Unload no more corn and wine, but stay ye here at Turbutsey until ye see me back again; but if I come not back by midnight, or if any evil report should reach ye before then, cross the river, and carry all the corn and the wine with ye deep into the fens; and carry also with ye this the dead body of Girolamo, unto whom I bound myself to see it interred in some safe and consecrate place; and go by the straightest path towards Spallding! Do all this if ye love me and reverence the Lord of Brunn; and in the meanwhile rejoice your hearts with some of the good drink: only be wise and moderate."

And the fenners said that they would do it all, and would be moderate: and thereupon, leaving behind him the Ely gossips, and the fenners, the corn, the wine, and the dead body of Girolamo, Elfric took the road to the abbey, and arrived ad *magnam portam*, at the main-gate, before it was quite dark. A few of the town folk had followed him to the gate, shouting with all their main that Elfric the lucky sword-bearer had come back, that the Lord of Brunn had come back, and that they had brought good store of corn, meal, and wine for my Lord Abbat Thurstan: for, upon reflection, Elfric had thought it wise to tell them this much.

But from within the abbey Elfric heard no sound, nor did he see the form or face of man, in the turret over the gate-way, or in the windows, or on the house-top. But there were those or the watch within who saw Elfric very clearly, and who heard the noise the town-folk were making: and anon the small wicket-gate was opened, and Elfric was bade enter; and the poor folk were commanded to go home, and cease making that outcry.

Once, if not twice, Elfric thought of withdrawing with the Ely folk, and then of racing back to Turbutsey; for he liked not the aspect of things: but it was needful that he should have a clear notion of what was toward in the abbey, and so blaming himself, if not for his suspicions, for his own personal apprehensions, he stepped through the wicket, taking care to shout, at the top of his voice, as he got under the echoing archway, "Good news! Brave news! The Lord Hereward is come back to the camp, and hath brought much corn and wine for this hallowed house! Lead me to Abbat Thurstan—I must speak with the Lord Abbat forthwith!

"Thou mayst speak with him in the bottomless pit," said the sub-prior. And as the sub-prior spoke, under the dark archway within the gate, a half-score from among the traitorous monks leaped upon the faithful sword-bearer, and put a gag into his mouth, so that he could cry out no more, and whirled him across the court-yards, and through the cloisters, and down the steep wet staircase, and into the cell or vault, or living grave, within and under the deep foundations of the abbey: and there, in the bowels of the earth, and in utter solitude and utter darkness, and with three several iron-bound doors closed upon him, they left him, making great haste to return to the refectory, and hoping that their plan had been so well managed that none but the desperate members of their own faction had either seen Elfric enter, or heard his shouts, or the shouts of the town-folk.

So soon as Elfric could get the gag out of his mouth, and recover from his first astonishment, he began to think; and he thought that this was but a bad return for his fighting and risking death for the sake of the stomachs and bowels of the monks of Ely; and he became convinced in his own mind that the traitorous monks must have made away with the noble Abbat Thurstan, and have consummated their treachery: and then he thought of his friends in the Camp of Refuge, and at Hadenham, and of the Lord Hereward and the Ladie Alftrude, and, most of all, of the maid Mildred! And then there came before him the ghastly face of the Salernitan, and rang in his ears, like a knell, the words which the dying Girolamo had used in the morning, when speaking of the hard doom of his beloved! And, next to this, he bethought himself of the fearful legend of the house of Ely, which related how the blinded prince, who had pinned so long in those dreary vaults, had ever since haunted them under the most frightful forms!

Yet when his lively fancy had brought all these things before him, and even when he had become convinced that he would be buried alive, or left to starve and gnaw the flesh from his own bones in that truly hellish pit, which he knew was as dark by day as by night, a sudden and sweet calm came over his distraught mind; and he kneeled on the cold slimy floor of the dungeon and raised to heaven his hands, which he could not see himself, but which were well seen by the saints above, unto whom thick darkness is as bright light; and when he had said a short prayer for himself and for his Mildred, for his generous lord and most bountiful ladie, he threw himself along the ground, and laying his left arm under his head for a pillow, he made himself up for sleep.

"Come what will," said he, "I have been true to my God, to my saints, to my country, to my church, to my lord and master, and to my love! This martyrdom will soon be over! Not these deep hollows of the earth, nor all the weight of all the walls and arched roofs and springing towers of Ely Abbey can crush or confine, or keep down, the immortal spirit of man! Mildred! My Lord Hereward! My noble lady and mistress! And thou, oh joyous and Saxon-hearted Lord Abbat Thurstan! if traitors have it their own way here, we meet in heaven, where there be no Normans and no Saxon traitors!"

And so saying, or thinking, and being worn out by excess of fatigue, or rather by the excessiveness of his late short moral anguish,—an agony sharper than that of the rack, upon which men are said to have fallen asleep,—

Elfric in a very few moments fell into the soundest of all sleeps. The toads, which fatten in darkness, among the noxious and colorless weeds which grow where light is not, and the earth-worms crawled over and over him, but without awakening him, or giving him any disturbance in his deep sleep. And as he slept, that black and horrent dungeon, in which his body lay, was changed, by the bright visions which blessed his sleep, into scenes as bright as the chapel of Saint Etheldreda in the abbey church, on the great day of the saint's festival, when a thousand waxen tapers are burning, and the whole air is loaded with incense and with music. It was the sunshine of a good conscience shining inwardly.

Now, while it fared thus with the captive below, much talk and discussion took place among divers of the honest monks above; for, notwithstanding the great care which had been taken to send away the Ely folk, and to seize and gag Elfric as soon as he came within the gate, the cry of the men of Ely, and the shout of the sword-bearer that Lord Hereward had come back, and had brought much corn and wine, were heard in almost every part of the house; and, upon hearing them, the monks that were not of the faction grievously lamented what had been done against the Lord Abbat, and in favor of the Normans, and very clearly perceived that a trick had been put upon them in the report of Lord Hereward's death.
"I tell ye now, as I told ye then," said Father Kynric, "that ye all make too much account of your meat and drink, and are all too impatient of temporary inconvenience. But what said the blessed Etheldreda? 'The fashion of this world passeth away; and that only is to be accounted life which is purchased by submitting to temporal inconveniences.'"

"And tell me," said that other good old Saxon monk, the Father Celred; "tell me, oh my brethren, tell me how Saint Etheldreda fared when she was in the flesh, and ruled this house as lady abbess?"

"Aye," said good Father Elsin, "Saint Etheldreda never wore linen, but only woolen; she never returned to her bed after matins, which were then begun immediately after midnight; and, except on the great festivals of the church, she ate only once a day, nor cared nor knew whether her bread was white or brown."

"Alack!" said Kenulph of Swaffham, a cloister-monk who had voted for the wicked prior solely because the cellars and the granaries were empty; "alack! Man's flesh is weak, and hunger is so strong! Saint Etheldreda was a woman, and a delicate princess; but, an she had been an upland man like me, and with such a sharp Saxon stomach as I have, she never could have lived upon one meal a day!"

"That is to say," quoth Father Cranewys, "if she had not been sustained by permanent and wondrous miracle, for ye wis, Brother Kenulph, that there be ladie saints in hagiology that have lived for octaves, and for whole moons together, upon nothing but the scent of a rose. I wonder, and would fain know, how much corn and wine the Lord of Brunn hath brought with him."

"Whatever he hath brought," quoth Father Kynric, "the Normans will get it all! the prior and the sub-prior, and all the rest of the officials speak in riddles, but none of us can be so dull as not to see that Duke William will be here to-night or to-morrow morning, and that the prior went to invite him hither. The mischief is now done, and the prior is too strong to be resisted; but if there were but three cloister-monks of my mind, I would break out of this house in spite of the sub-prior's calls, and locks, and bars! Yea, I would break out and release the brave boy Elfric, and away with him to the Camp of Refuge, to put my Lord Hereward and our other noble friends, and the whole Saxon host upon their guard. Everlasting infamy will rest upon the monks of Ely, if they be taken and massacred in their sleep."

"If," said the monk from Swaffham, "the supplies which the Lord Hereward hath brought be abundant, I would rather go and pass this autumn and coming winter in the fens, than stay here under the usurped rule of the prior, who beareth a mortal hatred against all of us that ever opposed him. Nay, I would rather continue to eat meat and fish without bread (provided only there was a little wine), than abide here to witness so foul treason as thou talkest of. But prithee, brother Kynric, how much corn and wine may a man reasonably expect to have been brought down, and where is it?"

Kynric responded, that he only knew that the Ely folk had cried, that there was good store of corn, meal, and wine, and that Elfric had shouted within the gate that there was much corn and wine.

Father Elsin said that he had heard the cellarer say to the sub-sacrist, that the good store of provision would be at Turbutsey, inasmuch as Hereward had promised to land it there; and that at a very early hour in the morning it should all be sent for and brought into the abbey.

"In that case," quoth the upland monk, "If a few of us could sally out before midnight, the corn and wine might be ours."

"Of a surety," said Father Kynric, "and we might carry it with us into the fens, which will not be conquered though the Camp of Refuge should fall; and we might share it with Lord Hereward and his true Saxons, and look to time and chance, and the bounty of the saints, for fresh supplies."

"Then by all the saints that lie entombed in Ely," said Kenulph of Swaffham, "I will break out and quit this dishonored and dishallowed community! The porter at the great gate came like me from Swaffham; Tom of Tottington, the lay-brother that waits upon the sub-prior, the holder of the keys, was brought into this house by me: there be other lay brothers and servientes that would do my will or thy will, oh Kynric, or thine, Elsin, or thine, Celred, sooner than the will of the prior, and the rather since they have heard of the corn and wine! Assuredly they will unbar doors and break out with us when they are told that the store is so near at hand as at Turbutsey!"

"And we could but carry off with us our true Lord Abbat Thurstan," said Father Kynric, "it were a glorious deed."

"But it cannot be," quoth Kenulph, "for the infirmarer told me anon that Thurstan is sick almost to death; and then he is watched and guarded by all the keenest of the faction, and the faction is too numerous and strong to allow us to proceed by force, or to attempt anything save by stratagem and in secrecy.

But, silence! We are watched, and that fox, the sub-sacrist, is getting within ear-shot. So let us separate, and let each of us, before going into the dormitory, and into his cell, speak with such of the house as he can with entire faith depend upon. I will go unto the gate-keeper."

It was the custom of the monks to walk and talk in the cloisters for a space between supper and bed time; and the above discourses were made in the quietest corner of the cloisters a very short time before the second watch of the night. Those who had made them separated, and very soon after they all withdrew to the dormitory; and the sub-prior, as was the bounden duty of his office, went through the dormitory and knocked at every cell-door, and called upon every monk by name, and heard and saw that each monk and each novice was in his cell for the night. And when the sub-prior had thus fulfilled what was in *statutis ordinis*, he went to his own chamber, which was in the turret over the great gateway; and being weary, he went straight to his bed, first putting under his pillow the key of the gate, and the keys of the foul dungeon into which Elfric had been whirled.

The prior, the chamberlain, the cellarer, and other chiefs of the faction, sate up awhile in secret conference in the prior's own private chamber; but then they too separated and went to their beds, comforting themselves with the prospect of the abundance which should henceforward reign in the house, and of the honours and advantages they should severally receive on the morrow from Duke William for their dark treason to their countrymen. Being all worn out with fatigue, they were soon fast asleep, each having proposed to himself to rise at a very early hour in the morning, in order to get in Lord Hereward's supplies, and to see to the proper decorating of the church for the reception of Duke William, and his brother the fighting bishop, and the rest of the Norman crew.

Above and below, the whole abbey of Ely was asleep when the good fathers Kynric, Elsin, Celred, Cranewys, and Kenulph, with two other cloister-monks who had determined to flee from the house, came one by one in perfect silence, and carrying their shoes and sandals in their hands, forth from the dormitory, and into the quadrangle of the abbey, and then under the low arched way, where the gatekeeper, that free layman from Swaffham, was standing ready to unbar the gate, and where the lay-brother that waited upon the sub-prior was waiting for his order to begin.

A word from Father Kenulph in his ear, and away went the sub-prior's man up into the chamber over the gateway. And before one might say three credos, the lay-brother was back again under the archway, with the four ponderous keys in his hand. Then they all went into the gatekeeper's room, where two cressets were burning brightly; and by that light the cloister monks saw that there was blood upon the heaviest of the keys.

"Tom of Tottington," said Kenulph, "what is this? What is it thou hast done?"

"Nothing;" said the serviens, "but only this: the sub-prior woke from his sleep as I drew the keys from under his pillow, and was going to cry out and alarm the house, and so I brained him. He was ever hard master unto me."

"Well!" quoth Kenulph, "'tis better that the sub-prior perish in his sins and unconfessed, than that we fail in our enterprise, and leave our friends in the Camp to be taken unawares. So, Tom of Tottington, hurry thee down to the prison and bring up Elfric."

The churl from Tottington grew quite pale, and said, "I dare not do it! I am no cloister-monk or mass-priest, and have no Latin whereby to lay spirits! I cannot adventure into the bowels of the earth to face the restless ghost of the blind prince.... I cannot go alone!"

"Well!" quoth Kenulph, who first crossed himself, "I will go with thee; so bear the keys, and I will carry the light, and say the prayer *Ab hoste maligno libera nos, Domine*, as we go."

The sword-bearer was still sleeping happily when the monk and the lay-brother came into the dark vault with the bright shining cresset; but as the light fell upon his eyelids he awoke, and saw Father Kenulph standing over him; and then he started up and said, "I have been dreaming a true dream; for when did Father Kenulph do aught but good to honest man and true Saxon! Ah! Tom of Tottington, art thou here too? Then shall I not be buried alive or starved to death!"

"Elfric," said Kenulph, "thou art safe and free, so rise and follow us. But tell me, good Elfric, what supply didst bring to Turbutsey?"

"We loaded with corn and with wine a score of upland pack-horses, and many more than a score of strong asses," said the sword-bearer.

"'Tis well," quoth Kenulph, licking his lips and rubbing his hands, "'tis better than well! So follow me, and when thou comest to the upper regions make no noise, for the Lord Abbat Thurstan is deposed from his authority and is sick unto death; the abbey is in the hands of the prior and his crew; and we and a few more honest members of the house are flying from it to get the stores at Turbutsey, and to give warning to the Lord of Brunn, that the false monks of Ely have sold and betrayed him."

"I thought as much as all this," quoth the sword-bearer; and without asking any questions, he followed the cloister-monk and the lay-brother to the gatekeeper's chamber, praising and blessing the saints for this his so speedy deliverance. As he entered the room, reverentially saluting the other cloister-monks, the porter gave him his sword, which had been snatched from him upon his being first seized under the gateway. Next the stout porter took down some swords and spears, and fen-poles, that hung in his room, and armed his friends and himself with them; and then, in less than a Credo, the whole party got out of the monastery through the wicket-gate, and, first closing and fastening the wicket on the outside, they all took the broad high road that leads to Turbutsey.

Six good cloister-monks, and ten good lay-brothers and servientes, were there in this company; but all the rest of the convent remained behind to await the slaughter of their countrymen in the Camp, to welcome the Normans to Ely, and to get from them—that which they deserved. Elfric and Tom of Tottington (an expert fenner, and much fitter to be a soldier than the waiting-man of a monk) presently quitted the road to take a rough path across the fens which led directly into the Camp: the rest hastened on to Turbutsey, and as they arrived there before the midnight, they were in good time to aid the true men Elfric had left there in getting the good stores across the river and well into the fens. Some of the party would have left the body of Girolamo behind at Turbutsey, or would have thrown it into the river; but the people said what Elfric had said to them concerning the dead body, and the fighting men who had fought the Normans near Brandon, and who had seen with their own eyes the Christian end the Salernitan had made, all declared that Girolamo must have Christian burial in some consecrated place where the Normans could not disturb his ashes.

The dungeon

CHAPTER XXV.

THE NORMANS IN THE CAMP

The Camp of Refuge, wherein the Saxons had so long withstood the violent threats of the Normans, was not in itself a very noticeable place. But for the army and the last hopes of England collected therein, the wayfarer might have passed it without any especial observation, there being several such places in the Fen country, partly surrounded by embankments of earth, and wholly girded in, and doubly or trebly girded by rivers, ditches, pools, and meres.

The embankments had been first made, in very remote ages, by those who first attempted to drain parts of the fen country; but tradition said that these peaceful works had been made to serve the purposes of defensive war, in those days when the Iceni stood against their Roman invaders, when the Britons stood against the first Saxons, and when the Saxons opposed the marauding Danes. The embankments which were made to keep out the water, and confine the rivers to their beds, were proper to keep out an enemy, even if he could reach them; and the fenners, who kept solely to the business of grazing, fishing, and fowling, knew best how to defend and how to stock such places.

In the upland countries men took shelter on the high hills; but here, when an enemy approached, men threw themselves within these flats and enclosures in the midst of the waters, taking with them their herds and flocks, and their hooks and nets for fishing, and their snares for fowling. At the first sound of this Norman invasion, and before any Saxon lord or knight fled for refuge into the

Isle of Ely, the people of the country drove their fattening beeves into the enclosed but wide space which afterwards came to be called the Camp, but which for a long season bore rather the appearance of a grazing-field than that of a place of arms; and even when the Saxon lords and knights came and gathered together their armed followers on that green grassy spot, the space was so wide that the cattle were left to remain where they were, and the many cowherds and shepherds were mixed with the Saxon soldiery, each by times doing the duty of the other; and now, when well-nigh everything else was consumed and gone, there remained within the broad limits of the Camp great droves of the finest and fattest cattle.

There was no moon, and the night was of the darkest, when Elfric approached the Camp, flying along the ground like a lapwing. As watches were set, and as the men were vigilant as became the soldiers of the Lord of Brunn, he was challenged sundry times before he reached his lord's tent. Hereward was asleep, but at the voice and tidings of his sword-bearer he was presently up and armed, and ready to go the round of the Camp.

"Elfric," said Hereward, "if the traitorous monks of Ely shall have called in their own people, who formed our outer guard, and have given the Normans the clue to the watery labyrinth which has been our strength and safety so long, we may still hold out against more than one assault behind the embankments of this Camp, provided only our people do not get panic-stricken by the suddenness of the attack, and in the darkness of this night. Would that it were morning! But come what may, there is one comfort: we shall have our harness on our backs before the fight begins!"

And having so said, the Lord of Brunn, followed by his sword-bearer, went from post to post to bid the men be on the alert, and from tent to tent, or from hut to hut, to rouse the sleeping chiefs to tell them that the monks of Ely were traitors to the good cause, and that the Normans were coming; and when this was done, Hereward, with an unperturbed spirit, and with all that knowledge of war which he had acquired beyond sea, and from the knowing Salernitan, and from all that quickness which nature had given him, laid down his plan for defending the interior of the Camp, and appointed every chief to the post he should hold, speaking cheerfully to them all, and telling them that five years had passed since the battle of Hastings, and that England was not conquered yet; and that if the Normans should be foiled in this attack, their loss would be terrible, their retreat across the fens almost impracticable.

By the time all this was said and done it was more than two hours after the midnight hour, and it had scarcely been done ere the war-cry of the Normans was heard close under the south-western face of the Camp. By using the name of the Abbat Thurstan, the false prior had made the people of the abbey abandon the fords in that direction; and by the same false prior's procurement, a traitorous fenner had guided the Normans through the labyrinth.

But there was more fatal mischief yet to proceed from the same dark cauldron and source of evil. Some other traitor, serving among the retainers of the abbey that had been left quartered in the Camp, because they could not be withdrawn without Lord Hereward's order set up the cry that the Saxons were all betrayed, and that the Normans had gotten into the Camp; and thereupon the poor bewildered wights, who knew but too well that the Norman war-cry could be heard where it was heard only through treachery, fell into disorder and dismay, and abandoning the post which they had been appointed to hold, and disregarding the voice of their commander, they fled across the Camp, shouting, "Treason! Treason! Fly, Saxons, fly!"

The Normans began to enter the Camp in overpowering numbers; and although the first glimmerings of day began to be seen from the east, it was still so dark that it was hard to distinguish between friend and foe. But Hereward soon found himself at the spot where the danger was greatest; and the foe, who had not yet recovered from the dread of his name, halted at the shouts of "Hereward for England!" and were soon driven out of the Camp, with a great slaughter. Whilst this was doing on the south-western side, another host of Normans, under the same traitorous guidance, got round towards the north face of the Camp, and after some hard fighting, got over the embankment, and into the Camp.

Leaving a brave old Saxon earl and his people to keep the ground he had recovered, Hereward rushed with Elfric and his own choice band to the northern side; and although the distance was considerable, his battle-axe was ringing among the Normans there before they had found time to form themselves in good fighting order.

But Odo, the fighting bishop, was among these Normans; and thus knights and men-at-arms fought most valiantly, and held the ground they had gained for a long time. Nevertheless, just as the rising sun was shining on the tower of Ely Abbey, Odo and his host, or such of his host as survived, retreated the way they had come; but while they were in the act of retreating, Duke William led in person an assault on another part of the Camp; and on the south-west side, the brave old Saxon earl being slain, his men gave way, and the Normans again rushed in on that side.

Also, and at nearly the same instant of time, Norman spears were discerned coming round upon the Camp from other quarters. As he paused to deliberate whither he should first direct his steps, and as he shook the blood from the blade and shaft of his battle-axe—a ponderous weapon which no other man then in England could wield—the Lord of Brunn, still looking serenely, bespoke his sword-bearer, "May God defend the house of Ely and the Lord Abbat; but the knavish monks have done the work of treachery very completely! They must have made known unto the Normans all the perilous passages of the fens. We are beset all about! But we must even drive the Normans back again. Numerous are they, yet their knights love not to fight on foot, and they can have brought few horses or none across the swamps. But Elfric, my man, thou art bleeding! Art much hurt?"

Now, although Elfric had got an ugly cut upon his brow, he smiled, and said, "'Tis nothing, good my Lord: 'tis only a scratch from the sharp end of Bishop Odo's pastoral crook. If he had not been so timeously succored, I would have cleft his shaven crown in spite of his steel cap, or have made him a prisoner!"

When this was said, and when the keen eye of Hereward had made survey of the whole field, he and his sword-bearer, and all his matchless band, who had been trained to war in a hundred fights and surprises, rushed towards the spot where floated the proud banner of Duke William. They were soon upon that prime of the Norman army; and then was seen how the Lord of Brunn and his Saxons true bore them in the brunt of war.

Thunder the battle-axes; gride the heavy swords! Broad shields are shivered, and the Norman left arms that bore them are lopped off like hazel twigs; helms are broken, and corselets reft in twain; and still this true Saxon band shouted, "Holy rood! Holy rood! Out! Out! Get ye out,

Normans! Hereward for England! Saxons, remember Hastings!" Stout young Raoul of Caen, the page that carried the arms and the shield (*arma ac scuta*) of the Duke, was slain by Hereward's sword-bearer; and where Raoul met his untimely death, other Normans perished or bled. Duke William shouted, "Notre Dame! Notre Dame! Dieu aide! Dieu aide!" but was forced to give ground, and the Duke retreated beyond the earth-raised mound or great embankment which girded the Camp on that side.

"The patrimony of Saint Etheldreda is not easy to conquer! We have beaten off the two brothers!" Thus spoke Elfric.

"So far is well," quoth Hereward! "But what is this I see and hear? What are those cravens doing in the center of the Camp? By the Lord of Hosts, some of them be throwing down their weapons, and crying for quarter! Wipe the blood from out thine eyes, Elfric; keep close to my side, and come on, brave men all!"

And away from the earth-raised mound, over which he had driven the Norman Duke, went the Lord of Brunn with his warrior band; and then was the fight renewed in the midst of the Camp, where some of the disheartened Saxons were using all the French they knew in crying, "Misericord! Misericord! Grace! Grace!"

"Fools!" shouted the Lord of Brunn, "these Normans will show ye no mercy! There is no grace for ye but in your own swords!" And then the Saxons took heart again, and rallying round Hereward, they soon charged the foe, and fought them hand to hand. In their turn the Normans began to yield, and to cry for quarter; but this band in the center was supported by another and another; and soon Duke William, and that ungodly bishop, his brother, came back into the interior of the Camp, with many knights and men-at-arms that had not yet tasted the sharpness of the Saxon steel, and that were all fresh for the combat.

CONQUEST OF THE ISLE OF ELY

Louder and louder waxed the war-cry on either side, and terrible and strange became the scene within the wide Camp; for the cattle, scared by the loud noise, and by the clash and the glittering of arms, were running wildly about the Camp in the midst of the combatants; and the fierce bulls of the fens, lashing themselves into furor, and turning up the soil with their horns, came careering down, and breaking through the serried lines of the invaders; and many a Norman was made to feel that his mail jacket was but a poor defense against the sharp horns of the bull that pastured on the patrimony of Saint Etheldreda. Also rose there to heaven a dreadful *rugitus*, or roaring, mixed with the loud bewailing and the shrieks of timid herdsmen, and of women and children; and the wives and children of the Saxons ran about the Camp, seeking for a place of safety, and finding none. The Saxon warriors were now falling fast, but the Normans fell also; and victory was still doubtful, when loud shouts were heard, and another forest of lances was seen coming down on the Camp from the south; and upon this, one entire body of the Saxon host threw down their arms, and surrendered themselves as prisoners.

Hereward, who was leaning upon his battle-axe, and wiping the sweat from his brow, said to his sword-bearer, "This is a sad sight!"

"A sad sight and a shameful," quoth Elfric; "but there are Saxons still that are not craven; Here our lines be all unbroken."

"And so will we yet fight on," quoth Hereward.

But the Lord of Brunn had scarcely said the words when a number of Saxon lords, old dwellers in the Camp of Refuge, and men that had fought at Hastings, and in many a battle since, gathered round Lord Hereward, and threw their swords and battle-axes and dinted shields upon the ground, and told him that the fight was lost, and that (*de communi concilio magnatum*), with the common advice and consent of the magnates, they had all determined to surrender upon quarter, and take the King's peace.

Quoth the Lord of Brunn, "Ye will not do the thing ye name! Or, if ye do it, bitterly will ye rue it! Your names are all down in a book of doom: the Normans will mutilate and butcher ye all! Better that ye die fighting! The battle is not lost; if ye will but think it is not. I was with King Harold at the battle by Stamford Bridge, and in a worse plight than now; and yet on that day we conquered. So, up hearts, my Saxon lords and thanes! Let us make one charge more for King Harold and the liberties of England! Nay, we will make a score good charges ere we die!"

But the Magnates would not be heartened, nor take up the shields and the arms they had thrown down; and when the reinforced battalia of the Norman center formed once more into line, and levelled their spears, and when the rest of that countless Norman host began to close round the Saxon army in the midst of the Camp, all the fighting men that obeyed these Saxon lords threw down their arms, and cried for quarter—for forgiveness and mercy!

Sad and sick was the heart of the Lord of Brunn; but this lasted but for a moment, and his eye was bright and his face joyous as he shouted to Elfric and the rest of his own devoted band, "Let the fools that court dishonor and mutilation, and an opprobrious grave, stay here and yield; but let those who would live in freedom or die with honor follow me! We will cut our way out of this foully betrayed Camp, and find another Camp of Refuge where there are no monks of Ely for neighbors!"

And at these good words three hundred stout Saxons and more formed themselves into a compact column, and the Lord of Brunn, with Elfric by his side, put himself in the head of the column, and the band shouted again,

"Hereward for England! Saxons, remember Hastings!" Then were heard the voices of command all along the different Norman lines, and from the right and from the left, from behind and from before, those lines began to move and to close, and to form living barriers and hedgerows of lances on every side: and next, near voices were heard offering fifty marks of gold to the man that should slay or seize the traitor Hereward.

But the Norman was not yet born that could withstand the battle-axe of the Lord of Brunn: and so the Norman lines yielded to his charge, and so he led his three hundred Saxons and more triumphantly out of the Camp and across the fens—yea, over rivers and streams and many waters, where Normans could not follow—until they came into a thick wood of willows, where they found the six good cloister-monks and the ten good lay-brothers who had fled with Elfric from Ely Abbey, and the party of true men from Turbutsey, who had carried with them the corn, meal, and wine, and likewise the body of Girolamo of Salerno.

Loudly was the Lord of Brunn greeted by every man that was in the wood. The first thing that was done after his coming was to bury the Salernitan. Near the edge of the wood, and by the side of a stream, the monks of Ely of the old time had built a small mass-house for the convenience of the souls of some of the fenners, who could not always quit their fishing and fowling and go so far as the abbey church; and on a green dry hillock, at the back of the mass-house, there was a small *cœmeterium* holding the wattled graves of not a few of the fenners.

"This ground," said Father Celred, "is consecrated ground; the Normans will not soon get hither, and we will leave no cross and make no sign to show the stranger's grave; and every man here is too true a man ever to betray the secret to the Normans."

"And when better days come, we will provide some suitable monument for the stranger who died in fighting for the Saxon. Girolamo, thou art happy in that thou hast not lived to see this foul morning! Father Celred, fathers all, I warrant ye he was a true son of the church, and died a good Christian. So withhold not to do the rites and give him Christian burial."

Thus spoke the Lord of Brunn as he gazed upon the awfully placid face of the Salernitan, whose body lay uncovered upon a rustic bier: and the good monks all said that they doubted not, and would never doubt, the word of Lord Hereward. And the Saxon hinds, under the direction of Elfric, rapidly scooped out a grave on the sunniest side of the green hillock, on the side which faced the south and was turned toward the sunny land in which the stranger was born; and when the grave was made, Hereward took his own good mantle from his shoulders and piously wrapped it round the dead body to serve it instead of shroud and coffin, which could not be had; and then Father Celred blessed the grave, and the lay-brothers laid the body reverentially in it; and then all the monks that had come from Ely said the service for the dead and chanted the *De Profundis*.

Next the earth was thrown in, and the green sods, which had been removed carefully and piecemeal, were laid upon the surface and joined together so as to unite and grow together in a few days, making the spot look like the rest of the sward: and thus, without mound or withy-bound hillock, without a stone or a cross, was left all that could die of Girolamo the Salernitan—far, far, far away from the land of his birth and of his love. Yet was his lowly grave not unhonored.

After these sad offices, Hereward and his party refreshed themselves with wine and bread, and renewed their march, going in the direction of the river Welland and the succursal cell at Spalding.

And, meanwhile, how fared it with the Saxon idiots in the Camp who had cast down their weapons, and trusted to Norman mercy and to Norman promises?—How fared it? In sooth it fared with them as the Lord of Brunn had foretold, and as it ever hath fared with men that surrendered when they ought to have fought on. The conquerors, in summing up the amount of the harm they did to the Camp of Refuge, counted not the lives of the churls and serfs—which went for nothing in their eyes—but they put down that they slew, after the fight was over, of Saxon nobles and knights and fighting-men of gentle blood, more than a thousand.

But happy those who were slain outright! A thousandfold worse the fate of those that were let live: their right hands and their right feet were cut off, their eyes were put out, and they were cast upon the wide world to starve, or were thrown into loathsome dungeons to rot, or transported beyond the seas to exhibit their misery to the scornful eyes of the people of Normandie and Anjou, to remain living monuments of Duke William's vengeance, and to be a terror to such as presumed to dispute his authority.

In this way some of the noblest of the land were sent into Normandie. Egelwin, the good Bishop of Durham, being found in the Camp, was sent a close prisoner to Abingdon, where he died shortly after of a broken heart. Never yet heard we of a fight more noble than that of the Camp of Refuge, while the Lord of Brunn was there and the Saxons in heart to fight; and never yet was there a sadder scene than that which followed upon his departure thence! Except cattle and sheep, and armor and arms, and human bodies to hack and destroy, the Normans found scarcely anything in the Camp, wherein they had expected to make great booty.

And how fared it with the guilty prior and the traitorous monks of Ely? Did they profit by their great treason? Were peace and joy their lot when the blood of their countrymen had been poured out like water? Did they and their house thrive after all that torture and horror in the Camp? Not so! not so!

Those who deal in treachery reap treachery for their reward; and all men hate and scorn even the traitors who have most served them. Before the butchery in the Camp was well over, a great band of Normans ran to the abbey and took forcible possession of it, and beat and reviled the monks because they did not bring forth the money and the bread and wine which they had not to give; and these rude soldiers lodged themselves in the house, and turned all the monks into the barns and outhouses—all but a few, who remonstrated and resisted, and who were therefore thrown into that noxious prison underground into which they had cast Elfric the night before.

And on the morrow of the fight in the Camp, the Norman Duke himself went up to the abbey with all his great chiefs, saying that he would pay his devotions at the shrine of St. Etheldreda, albeit she was but a Saxon saint. And William did go into the church, and kneel at the shrine of the saint. Yea, he did more than this, for he laid his offering upon the shrine. But what was the princely offering of this great prince who ruled on both sides of the sea?—It was just one single mark of gold, and that a mark which had been in the hands of the Jews and clipped! And when he had made this splendid donation, he called the monks together in the hall, and told them that they must pay unto him a thousand marks of gold as the price of his pardon for the long rebellion they had been in. And when the chapfallen chamberlain said, and said truly, that there was no money in the house, a sneering Norman knight told him that there were Jews at Norwich, and that the monks must get money by pledging their lands and by giving bonds to the Israelites.

The good Abbat Thurstan, being still sick in his bed, escaped the sight of much of this woe: but when the prior knelt at the foot of Duke William, and said that he trusted he would be merciful to the ruined house, and continue him as the head of it, and sanction his election by the brotherhood as lord abbat, the Duke swore his great oath, "By the splendor of God's face," that he was not so minded; and that Abbat Thurstan should be abbat still, inasmuch as he was a man of noble birth and of a noble heart. Sundry great Saxon lords, who had long since made their peace with the Norman, had spoken well for the high-born Thurstan; but that which decided the mind of Duke William was the reflection that, if so true and stout a man as Thurstan promised him his allegiance, he would prove true to his promise at whatsoever crisis; while no faith or trust could be put in the promises and vows of such a man as the prior.

And thus Thurstan was told on his sick-bed that his rule was restored, and that he should be allowed to appoint and have a new set of officials, instead of the prior, the chamberlain, the sacrist and sub-sacrist the cellarer, and all the rest that had been rebellious and traitorous unto him—provided only that he would promise to be at peace with the Normans.

And, after Thurstan had been most solemnly assured by some of the Saxon thanes who came to the abbey with the Conqueror, that King Harold, his benefactor, was assuredly dead, and lay buried in Waltham Abbey, and that good terms would be granted to his friend my Lord of Brunn if he would but cease the hopeless contest, Thurstan promised to live in peace and to think no more of resistance: and before Duke William departed from the house of Ely the lord abbat saluted him as King of England, and put his hand into his hand as a token and pledge that he was and would be true and liege man unto him. It cost his Saxon heart a pang which almost made it crack; but having thus pledged himself, nothing upon earth, being earthly, would ever make Thurstan untrue to the Norman.

In leaving the abbey, the Conqueror did not remove with him all the Normans. On the contrary, he called up still more knights and men-at-arms, and ordered them all to quarter themselves upon the monks, and be by them entertained with meat, drink, and pay, as well as lodging. The Norman knights and soldiers kept possession of the best parts of the house, respecting only the inner apartments of the restored abbat: the knights suspended their arms and shields in the great hall, where the arms of the Saxon thanes had lately hung, and in the refectory at every meal-time a hungry Norman soldier was seated by the side of every monk.

This was a strange and unseemly sight to see in the common hall of so noble and once so religious a house; but it was the will of the Conqueror that it should be so, and the monks had brought down all these mischiefs upon their own heads. From the lands and revenues especially appertaining to Thurstan as lord abbat, the Norman knights were not allowed to take much; but upon those appertaining to the monks in common, they fell without restriction and without remorse, seizing a manor here and a manor there, and getting them converted into heritable property, to their heirs forever, by grant and fief-charter from Duke William. And while so many broad hides were taken from them for good, the monks were compelled to pledge other lands, and the very revenues of the shrines, in order to pay the imposed fine of a thousand marks, and in order to find meat and drink, and whatsoever else was demanded by their rapacious guests.

Sad grew the monks of Ely, and every day thinner. The knights and men-at-arms ever helped themselves first, and very often left their unwilling hosts nothing to eat. The proverb about the glorious feast of the monks of Ely seemed to have become nothing but a proverb, or the mere legend of a state of happiness which had passed away never to return. Greater still had been the woes of the monks if the restored abbat had been prone to spite and vengeance, for the Normans were willing to put a rod of iron in his hands, and would have rejoiced to see him use it; but Thurstan had a forgiving heart, and when he had deprived the worst of the officials of their offices, and had gotten the prior and the chamberlain removed to other houses far away from the Isle of Ely, he took pity upon all the rest of the convent, and did what in him lay to comfort them in their afflictions, and to supply their wants from his own store.

Thus lived the monks, and thus the abbat, for about the space of three years: at the end of that time the good old Thurstan died, and was interred in the chancel among his mitred predecessors. And then still worse befell the monks; for Duke William, or his brother Odo, Bishop of Bayeux, brought over one of their most fighting and turbulent monks from Normandie, and made him lord abbat of Ely; and this new abbat did not cease from persecuting the Saxon monks until two-thirds of them were in their graves, and their places supplied by French monks. These were the things which befell the convent after their foul rebellion against Abbat Thurstan, and their fouler betrayal of the Camp of Refuge.

CHAPTER XXVI.

A FIRE AND A RESCUE

It was dark night before the Lord of Brunn and his party got near unto the river Welland and Spalding, and great had been their speed to get thither so soon. As they halted near the river-bank, under cover of some willows, they saw boats filled with Normans passing and repassing, and heard them hailing one another. In remarking upon this to his lord, the sword-bearer said, "Our barks on these waters have been overpowered! The Normans have been trying to encompass us by water as well as by land. No marvel were it to me to find them on every river between this and Trent or Humber; but it is not they that will stop good fen men like us."

"Yet we be come hither in good time, for they may be preparing to lay siege to my ladie in the moated manor house. I would wager my best trained hawk against a kestrel that Ivo Taille-Bois is come hitherward from Stamford to recover what he calls his own!" So said Lord Hereward.

Quoth Elfric: "An Ivo be here, we will beat him and catch him again! And when we catch him, we will not let him go, as we did, my lord, on the happy day of thy marriage."

While they were thus discoursing with low voices among the willow-trees, a great and bright light was suddenly seen in the direction of Spalding, from which they were still distant some three old English miles. A first they thought it was but a beacon-fire lighted by the Normans, or perhaps by the Saxons; but the light grew and spread very fast, and showed itself as a portentous blaze, and sparks were seen flying upwards into the murky night-air, and then a great body of smoke came rolling before the night-wind, which was blowing freshly down the river. Hereward uttered the name of his wife the Ladie Alftrude, Elfric uttered the name of Mildred, and both said a hurried prayer, for each believed that the Normans had set fire to the manor-house. In an instant the whole band was again in motion, rushing rapidly but silently along the willow-fringed bank of the Welland; but when they got nearer and came to a turn of the river, they made out that the fire was not on this, but on the other side of the river, and that, instead of the manor house, it must be either the succursal cell or the poor little township of Spalding that was in a blaze. And when they got nearer still, they saw that it was the little town; but they also saw that the cell was beleaguered, and that many armed men, carrying torches in their hands, were crossing the river and running towards the manor-house.

"Unto the blessed saints be the praise," said Lord Hereward, "but we be come just in time! My Saxons true, leave here among the willows the wine and stores, and let us forward to the rescue of the Ladie Alftrude and mine infant son. Be quiet till you reach the end of the causey, on which they are gathering their force, and then shout and fall on!"

Away went the Saxons among the willows and tall rushes, until they came close to the causey which led from the bank of the river to the moated manor-house, and which was hard and dry now, although in the winter season it was for the most part under water. The Normans, who were making an exceeding great noise themselves, heard not the little unavoidable noise made by Lord Hereward's people; and notwithstanding the light thrown up by the burning town, the Frenchmen saw not more of the Saxons than they heard of them, until they set up their shouts of "Hereward for England! The

Saxons to the rescue!" And scarcely had the first of these shouts ceased to be echoed ere Hereward and his true men were upon the causey and hewing down the astounded enemy, of whom not a few were without their arms, for they had been bringing across the river great beams and planks wherewith to cross the moat of the manor-house.

The Normans that were still on the opposite side of the river, beleaguering the succursal cell, came down to their boats and attempted to cross over to succor their countrymen on the causey; but Lord Hereward posted fifty good archers among the willows at the very edge of the water, and, taking good aim in the red fire-light, these good bowmen sent such fatal flights of arrows into the boats that the Normans put back in dismay: and the boats which had been going up and down the river, full of armed men, took all to flight upon hearing the shouts of "Hereward for England," and never stopped until they got out of the Welland into the broad Wash, where the Conqueror, by the advice of the false Danes, had collected a fleet of ships. At these good signs same of the town folk of Spalding, who had fled into the fens to escape the Norman fury, returned towards their burning town and threatened the rear of their foe; and some other of the town folk, who had thrown themselves into the Cell to assist the true monks who had driven out the false ones, now joined in shouting "Hereward for England;" and getting to the house-top, assailed their beleaguerers with arrows and javelins, and whatsoever else they could get to hurl at them.

Thus stood the Norman host, part on one side of the river and part on the other, and no communication between them. Yet when those on the causey were joined by a great band that had been up to the manor-house, they were far more numerous than the Saxon party. With the band that came down from the manor-house was Ivo Taille-Bois himself; and his people shouted as he came upon the ground where battle had been joined, "A Taille-Bois! a Taille-Bois!"

The Lord of Brunn, who had made a good free space with his own single battle-axe, now cried out in his loudest and cheeriest voice, "Welcome, oh Ivo Taille-Bois! I as good as told thee on my wedding-day at Ey that we should meet again! Ivo, all that I ask of thee now is that thou wilt not turn from me! Ivo Taille-Bois, this is a fair field! Here is good hard ground, and no fen-pool; so, Sir Ivo, stand forward, and let thee and me prove which is the better man and the better knight!"

But Ivo, remembering still the battle of Hastings and the weight of Lord Hereward's battle-axe—albeit it was but a stripling's arm then wielded it—would not stand forward; and he only cried from among his men-at-arms and the knights that were with him, "This is no fair field, and I have no horse, and a knight should engage in single combat only on horseback; and thou art no true knight, but only a priest-made knight, and a rebel and traitor!"

"For the last thou liest in thy throat," quoth the Lord of Brunn. "I am a free and true Saxon fighting for his country against invaders and robbers! Thou art but a beast to make thy valor depend upon a four-legged creature! But since thou wilt not stand forth and try thy strength and skill with me here in this good space between our two hosts, I will come and seek thee in the midst of thy people. So, Ivo, look to thyself!"

And having thus spoken, the Lord of Brunn waved his battle-axe over his head and sprang forward, and Elfric went close by his side, and the boldest of his Saxons followed him, shouting again "Hereward for England! Saxons to the rescue of the Ladie Alftrude!" And so loud were these shouts that they were heard afar off on either side of the river, and were given back not only by the true men in the succursal cell and by the returning townsfolk of Spalding, but also by the stanch little garrison which had been left with the Ladie Alftrude in the moated manor-house.

The torches which the Normans had been carrying were all extinguished and thrown away, and moon or star was none, but the ruddy flames from the burning town still gave light enough for the good aiming of sword, pike, and battle-axe. For a time the Normans stood their ground on the causey, and did manfully enough; but when Ivo Taille-Bois saw the carnage the Lord of Brunn was making, and saw that his battle-axe was opening a path through his dense phalanx to the spot where he stood, he bade his trumpet sound a retreat.

Ivo could not have done a worse thing, for so soon as his men began to retreat they got into a panic; and while some ran along the causey; others quitted that road and ran into the fens. Nay, Ivo himself was swept from the road, and compelled to run for it across a broad marsh where there was at this season little water, but much mud. Lord Hereward, who saw him go, said to his sword-bearer, "That big bully of Angevin is not worth my following: go, Elfric, and bring him hither; you will find him somewhere there among the bulrushes. He will surrender; so slay him not, but bring him here alive, and we will keep him and teach him to lead a fen life."

And while Elfric went in pursuit of Sir Ivo, other Saxons followed the Normans that were running along the causey and throwing away their arms to run the lighter, until they saw them a good way beyond the manor-house; and other Saxons going into the fens slew many of the unskilled Normans who had fled thitherward and stuck in the mud. On the opposite side of the river the Norman force which had been assaulting the cell was now in full flight for Stamford: in all its parts the army of the vicomte was discomfited and shamefully routed. Deep in the mud and among the bulrushes, and helpless as he was when with his brother Geoffroy he lay floundering in the fen pool near Ey, Elfric and the score of merry men he took with him found the great Ivo Taille-Bois with two Norman knights as helpless as himself: and upon being summoned by the sword-bearer and threatened by the Saxon soldiers, Ivo and the two knights crawled out of the mud upon their hands and knees, and gave themselves up as prisoners to Hereward the Knight and Lord of Brunn, for Ivo could call him knight now, aye, knight and lord!

When the great vicomte and so-called nephew of the Conqueror was brought into the presence of Hereward, that merry Saxon lord could not but laugh at the woeful figure he made: and he said, smiling all the while, "Oh, Sir Ivo, this is the second time we meet, and each time thou comest before me in very dirty plight! But, Ivo, the mud and slime of our fens are not so foul as the work thou hast each time had in hand! At Ey thou thoughtest to have surprised a defenseless maiden, and here hast thou been coming against a young matron, my right noble wife, and a poor defenseless little township and a handful of monks. Ivo, thou art a big man and hast a big voice, yet art thou but a braggart and coward! 'Tis well thou hast not had time to do mischief at the manor-house, for hadst thou done any, I would have hacked thee to pieces! As it stands thou art my prisoner, nor will I ever hear of ransom."

The Taille-Bois hung down his head, and said no word, except that he hoped the Lord of Brunn would yet remember that by marriage they were as good as cousins. The townsfolk of Spalding and the true and now relieved monks came across the river in the boats which the Normans had left behind them, and saluted and did honor to Hereward; nor did they forget Elfric, who had lived so long among them; and as they as yet knew nought of what had befallen the Saxons that morning in the Camp of Refuge, these poor men were all jubilant beyond measure. It was not an hour since Hereward first fell upon the Normans on the causey, and everything that he could do for this night was already done. He bade Elfric count the prisoners and the number of the slain. Without counting those who had perished in the fens, more than two score Normans lay stark dead on the causey. More were wounded, but not half a score of Saxons were slain. The exceeding great light which had come from the burning town was now dying away, for the flames had consumed everything that was consumable in Spalding. But many torches were soon lighted, and by their light the Lord of Brunn and his faithful sword-bearer marched hastily towards the manor-house, over which their hearts had long been hovering; and they were followed thitherward by Ivo Taille-Bois and the rest of the prisoners, and by a part of the Saxon force, the rest of those three hundred true men being left to guard the river and the succursal cell.

At the sound of his horn the drawbridge was lowered and the gates of the manor-house was thrown open to the Lord of Brunn; and then was there happy meeting in the hall with the Ladie Alftrude and the maid Mildred—so happy that Hereward and Elfric forgot for the time the shame and woe of that bloody morning, and the young dame and the maiden forgot their own late agony and danger: nor was it when the lady brought her first-born son, rosy from his sleep, and put him in the arms of his glad sire, and when maid Mildred hung upon the arm of the sword-bearer and called him her deliverer, and said that she would never more leave him, but go whithersoever he might go, that these sad things could be brought back to the mind, or that either Hereward or

Elfric could recollect that henceforward they and those who were dearest unto them must lead a wandering life in the wilds and the fens. Nay, when a cheerful fire was lit in the great hall, and the tables were well spread, and the drinking-horns well filled, every good Saxon present seemed to think that this joy must last.

Yet if, in the morning after this happy meeting, there came sad thoughts and many and much sadder recollecttions, there was no craven panic, nor so much as any visible perturbation or confusion. *Vir serenissimus*, a most serene and imperturbable man, was the Lord of Brunn: and to this high quality of his nature was mainly owing all that he had done and all that he lived to do afterwards. The Ladie Alftrude was worthy to mate with such a lord; and their serenity made serene and confident all those that were about them. And therefore was it that when the foul treason at Ely was made known to all of them, and when much more bad news was brought in, as that the Normans had stormed and taken the lady's manor-house at Ey and the lord's manor-house at Brunn, and had been admitted again into Crowland Abbey, these good Saxons lost not heart and abated not of hope, but vowed that they would fight to the last for Lord Hereward, and be true to him in every extremity.

All things were got ready for a retreat into the farthest parts of Lincolnshire, or into the impenetrable country upon the Wash, as expediency might dictate; for it was thought that the Normans, being so near, would not delay in bringing a great army against Spalding manor-house, and in making the most desperate efforts to seize the last great Saxon lord that was now in arms against them. But the autumn season was now at hand, and it was so ordained that the heavy rains set in earlier than usual and fell more heavily and lasted longer than common, in such sort that the fens were laid under water and the roads made impassable. And although many boats of all sorts and sizes were collected, they could not be used, for a fresh gathering on the Scottish border constrained Duke William to turn his attention thitherward and to dispatch to the river Tyne and to the river Tweed many of the warriors and shipmen that had been collected to complete the subjugation of the fen country.

When these Normans were gone, Lord Hereward drove their monks once more from Crowland Abbey, and got possession of his house at Brunn and of the stores which had been there deposited; and after making many good forays into the upland country, he brought his brave fenners back to Spalding, together with a good number of Norman prisoners, of whom some were of high degree. The poor unhoused townsfolk of Spalding found shelter for the winter in the large manor-house and in the succursal cell, or in Crowland Abbey, keeping themselves ready to move in the spring with the Lord of Brunn and his warlike band.

There was abundance of wine and corn, and meat and fish, and all good things in this new Camp of Refuge; and the winter passed merrily away, with all due observation made of saints' days and of all the feast days the Saxon church had appointed. But one feast there was which was more joyous than all the rest; and that was given by the Lord of Brunn, ever free of hand and large of soul, a short time before the quinzaine of the Nativity, when Elfric and Mildred were made man and wife.

Their hands were joined by the same Alefricus Diaconus who had been Lord Hereward's mass-priest at Brunn, and who had performed the marriage-rites for his lord and the Ladie Alftrude at Ey. But the true-hearted monks of Spalding, and the monks that had fled from Ely, took part in the ceremony in the chapel, as afterwards in the feast in the hall; for notwithstanding all the mischief that the monks of Ely had done him, Hereward was still *homo monachorum*, or a lover of monks—provided only they were true Saxon monks, and had no dealings with the Normans. But all true Saxons and bold fenners for many miles round feasted at Spalding on Elfric's wedding day; the freed-men being entertained according to their degree, and the churls and serfs according to their degrees. Alefric, the deacon, put these things into a book, but the pages are now missing.

Cambridge-shire / the Isle of Ely

CHAPTER XXVII.

HEREWARD STILL FIGHTS

At the return of spring, Duke William being at Warwick Castle, on the pleasant river Avon, gave forth his mandate for the collecting of a great army to proceed against the Lord of Brunn. Much had it vexed and grieved his proud soul that Hereward should have escaped from the Camp of Refuge in the Isle of Ely, and have made his name terrible in other parts: for, during the winter, Peterborough and Stamford—aye, Grantham and Newark—had heard the war-cry of the Lord of Brunn, and the Normans there had been plundered by his band; and further still, where Nottingham looks down upon Trent, Hereward had carried his successful foray.

"By the splendor," quoth Duke William, as he thought upon those things, "I would give back all the Saxon lives that were taken near Ely for the life of this one man, who hath more power of mischief in him than all the Saxons put together. Or I would give to him the broadest earldom in all England if he would but submit and be my liegeman! I need such a soldier, for the men that followed me from Normandie are become all rich in this fat land, and risk not themselves in battle as they used to do when their fortunes were to make by sword and lance. This shall be thought of again, albeit my half-brother Odo and all my Normans have vowed the death of that terrible Lord of Brunn, and think that every hide of land left to a Saxon is so much robbed from them."

During the spring months another mighty host was collected from out of the several shires of Huntingdon, Cam-Bridge, Leicester, Nottingham, Derby, Warwick, and others; and viscomtes and comtes, and knights of great fame and long experience in war, were placed in command, and were ordered to encompass the Lord of Brunn, and make an end of him or of his resistance. No stores were spared; nothing was spared that was thought likely to forward the one great object. Scarcely had William made a greater array of strength when he first landed at Pevensey, to march against King Harold at Hastings.

But Hereward, that cunning captain and excellent soldier, inclytus miles, was not idle during this season: he went hither and thither throughout the country on the Wash and the whole fen country, calling upon the fenners to be steady and true to him and their native land; and to get their bows and arrows ready, and to sharpen such swords and axes, or bill-hooks and spear-heads, as they might have; and to be ever in a state of readiness to fight, if fighting could stead them, or to retreat with their cattle into the inaccessible places and the labyrinths among the waters and the meres. And the wandering minstrels and gleemen, who had been driven hitherward from all other parts of England, with Elfric, who was as good a gleemen as any of the number, went from one township in the fens to another, singing the Saxon songs which did honor to the Lord of Brunn, and told how often he had prevailed in fight over the Norman invaders.

And at the sound of these songs the fenners gave up their peaceful occupations and prepared for war; while many hundreds went at once to join the standard of the Lord of Brunn. The men of Holland mounted themselves on their tall stilts, and came wading across marsh and mere unto the manor-house of Spalding; others came thither in their light skerries; others came on foot, with their fen-poles in their hands, leaping such waters and drains as could be leaped, and swimming across the rest like the water-fowls of the fens. Loud blew the Saxon horn everywhere: the monks of Ely could hear it in their cells by night, and their guests the Norman warriors, who ventured not to come forth beyond Hadenham or Turbutsey, could hear it in the hall or refectory by day.

The country seemed all alive and stirring, and full of strange sights: but the strangest sight of all was that of the men from the shores of the Wash marching in troops on their high stilts, carrying their bows and quivers and swords and pikes at their backs, and looking, at a distance, with their long wooden shanks and their bodies propped in the air, like troops of giant cranes or herons. And ever as they went, and whether they went upon stilts or upon their own feet, or in flitting skerries, or in heavier and slower boats, these brave fenners sung in chorus the good songs which they had learned from the gleemen.

In this wise the Lord of Brunn had a great force collected and in arms by the time of summer, when the waters had abated and the green fields were showing themselves, and the Normans were beginning to march, in the fantastic hope of encircling Hereward as hunters gird in a beast of prey. There were no traitors here, as at Ely, to show the short and safe ways across the fens; and Ivo Taille-Bois, the only Norman chief that could be said to know a little of the wild and difficult country, was a close prisoner in the house at Spalding, where he tried to beguile the tedium of his captivity by playing almost constantly at dice with the two Norman knights who had been captured with him in the marsh.

Add to all this that the Normans, who had not before tried what it was to make war in the fens, had a contempt of their enemy, and a measureless confidence in their own skill and prowess, and it will be understood that their discomfiture was unavoidable. They came down from the upland country in separate bodies, and towards points far apart; and before they could place themselves, or contract their intended circle and give the hand to one another, Hereward attacked them separately, and beat them one by one.

Nor did the Normans fare much better when they gave up their plan of circle and united their forces in one head. The Lord of Brunn, who had counted upon being driven from Spalding into the wilderness, found not only that he could maintain himself there, but that he could also hold his own good house at Brunn; for, when the Norman host marched upon that manor, they fell into an ambuscade he had laid for them, and suffered both loss and shame, and then fled from an enemy they had hardly seen; for the fenners had willow-trees for their shields, or they had bent their bows in the midst of the tall growing rushes.

Thus passed the summer months; and Duke William was still on the northern borders, fighting against Malcolm Caenmore; and as that Scots war became more and more obstinate, the Duke was compelled to call to his aid nearly the whole of his splendid chivalry, and almost every Norman foot-soldier that he could prudently withdraw from England.

With such mighty forces Duke William marched from the left bank of the Tweed to end of the Frith of Forth, and all through the Lothians; and thereupon the Scots king, albeit he would not deliver up the Saxon nobles who had taken refuge at his court, came and agreed with Duke William, and delivered hostages, and promised to be his man. But by this time another year was spent, and the fens were again impracticable; and, moreover, the Norman conqueror was compelled to tarry long at Durham, in order to settle the North country. Before the quinzaine of this Nativity the goodly stock of Lord Hereward was increased by the birth of a daughter, and Elfric was a father.

The two children were baptized on the same day; and at the feast, which was given in the same hall at Spalding wherein Ivo Taille-Bois and the Ladie Lucia had given their great feast for the christening of their first-born, the merry sword-bearer said, "Well, we be still here! And it is now my opinion that I shall be a grandfather before the Normans shall drive us out of the fens!"

The carefully guarded Norman prisoners of rank and note were very sad; but Ivo Taille-Bois was the saddest of them all on this festal day, for his wife and child were far away from him, living under the protection of the primate Lanfranc at Canterbury, and, much as he had tried, he could get no news of them; nor could he see any prospect of regaining his liberty, inasmuch as the Lord of Brunn declared that he wanted not money, and was determined to keep him and his men as hostages.

With another year there came fresh preparation for invading the fen country, and giving the deathblow to Saxon liberty by destroying Hereward. But again the saints befriended the last of the Saxons, for great commotions burst out in Normandie, and in the county of Maine the people rose to a man against the tyrannies and oppressions of Duke William; and thus the Conqueror was constrained to pass over into France with all the troops he could collect. Before he went he sent once more to offer a free pardon to the Lord of Brunn and a few of his adherents; but Hereward said that, in fighting for the liberties and old laws of his country, he had not done that which called for pardon: and as the terms proposed were otherwise inadmissible, the Lord of Brunn had rejected them all, and had told the proud Duke that he would yet trust to his sword, and to the brave fenners, and to the inexpugnable country he had so long occupied.

Aided by many thousands of native English soldiers whom he carried over with him into Normandie and Maine, and who there fought most valorously for him, Duke William conquered the men of Maine and reduced them to his obedience. But this occupied him many months; and when he returned into England, it was to put down another insurrection and a wide-spread conspiracy, which were headed not by the Saxon nobles, but by Roger Fitz-Osborne, Raoul de Gael, and other nobles of Norman or French birth, who were not satisfied with the vast estates and high titles they had obtained in England, but wanted more, and had long been saying that William the Bastard was a tyrant in odium with all men, and that his death would gladden their hearts.

Battles were fought and sieges were made before the Duke had triumphed over this confederacy; and while he was thus fighting and laying sieges, the Lord of Brunn reigned as a king in the fen country, and kept all the countries thereunto adjacent in a state of constant alarm.

The herds and flocks of Hereward and his associates increased and multiplied the while; the drained and enclosed grounds gave their bountiful crops; the rivers and meres seemed more than ever to abound with fish and wild-fowl; and whatsoever else was wanted was supplied by successful forays to the upland countries and to the sea-coasts: so great was the plenty, that even the poor bondmen often ate wheaten bread—white loaves which might have been put upon the table of my Lord Abbat of Ely.

The Ladie Alftrude and the wife of the sword-bearer were again mothers (so gracious were the saints unto them!); and Elfric's first-born son was grown big enough to show a marvelous similitude to his father, specialiter about the laughing mouth and merry eyes.

CONQUEST OF THE ISLE OF ELY

Having nothing else upon hand for that present, William sent another great army to try their fortunes in the fen country; and (grieves me to say!) many of these soldiers were native English, and some few of them men from the Isle of Ely, who had experience in fen-warfare. Now was the manor-house of Brunn retaken, and now was Lord Hereward compelled to abandon Spalding, and to get him gone into the heart of Lincolnshire with his family and his people, and all his friends, and his Norman prisoners; but he drove off his cattle with him, and he found other herds where he went; and he found, moreover, subjugated townships and Norman town-governors unprepared to resist him.

Some men do say that he had with him scant three hundred fighting men; but he flitted so rapidly from place to place, and so multiplied his attacks, that the Normans ever thought he had many thousands. And when the great Norman army marched against him in Lindsey in the north, Hereward doubled them, and marched back to the south into Kesteven; and when they came to look for him in Kesteven, either he was back in Lindsey, or continuing his course to the south, he got him into Holland and that flooded country near the Wash, where the Normans never could penetrate, and where every man that lived and went upon tall stilts was his liege man. Here, in Holland, and in perfect safety, chiefly abided the Ladie Alftrude, and the women and children, and the Norman prisoners. The name of the Lord of Brunn was more than ever sounded throughout broad England, and from the Wash to the Humber it was a name of dread to all Normans and friends of Normans. Every feat of arms or skillful stratagem inspired some new song or tale; and the gleemen were never idle, and were never unhonored.

CHAPTER XXVIII.

THE HAPPY END

There chanced to be one very hard winter, and the rivers and streams were frozen over, as well as the bogs and swamps. It was such a winter as one of those in which King Canute went to visit the monks of Ely. Then the nobles of Canute's court said, "We cannot pass; the king must not pass on the slippery, unsafe ice, which may break and cause us all to be drowned in the fen-waters." But Canute, like the pious and stout king that he was, up and said, "Hold ice or break ice, I will keep the feast of the Purification with the good monks of Ely! An there be but one bold fenner that will go before over the ice by Soham mere and show the way, I will be the next to follow!"

Now there chanced to be standing amidst the crowd one Brithmer, a fenner of the Isle of Ely that was called, from his exceeding fatness, Budde, or Pudding; and this heavy man stood forward and said that he would go before the king and show him a way on the ice across Soham mere. Quoth Canute, who, albeit so great a king, was but a small, light man: "If the ice can bear thy weight, it can well bear mine! So go on, and I follow!" So Brithmer went his way across the bending and cracking ice, and the king followed him at a convenient distance; and one by one the courtiers followed the king, and after a few falls on the ice they all got safe to Ely.

And, for the good deed which he had done, King Canute made fat Brithmer, who was but a serf before, a free man, and gave unto him some free lands, which Brithmer's posterity hold and enjoy unto this day by virtue of the grant made by King Canute. But there was not a fenner of Lord Hereward's party, fat or lean, that would show the

Norman a way across the ice; and the Duke was in no case to undertake any such adventurous journey, and hardly one of his chiefs would have exposed himself and his people to such a march, and to the risks of a sudden thaw; and the Saxons passed the season of frosts without any alarm, albeit every part of the fens was passable for divers weeks.

Duke William was now waxing old and growing exceedingly fat, in sort that he could not bestir himself as he had been used to do. At the same time his sons, who had grown into man's estate, had become very undutiful, and even rebellious. Robert, his first-born, who was short in his legs, but very lofty in spirit, claimed as his own the duchy of Normandie and the county of Maine, alleging that the dominion of those countries had been promised to him by his father, and that his father ought to rest satisfied with the great kingdom of England.

And although William had told Robert that he would not throw off his clothes until he went to bed—meaning thereby to say that he would give up none of his principalities and powers until he went to his grave—that impatient, furious young man showed that he would not wait and be patient.

The family of the Conqueror was a brotherhood of Cains. Robert, less favored by nature than they, thought that his father always gave preference to his younger brothers William and Henry: and being in France, in the little town of Aigle, William and Henry, after playing at dice, as was the fashion with milites, made a great noise and uproar, to the great disturbance of their elder brother; and when Robert remonstrated with them from a courtyard beneath, they called him Shorthose, and emptied a pitcher of water upon his head. Thereupon Robert drew his sword and would have slain both his brothers; but being prevented in that, he raised the standard of revolt against his own father, and endeavored to surprise the city and strong castle at Rouen. Here, too, Robert failed of success, but he fled into Brittanie; and he was now visibly supported not only by many Breton chiefs and by the great Count of Anjou, but also by Philip the French king, who never could stomach the power and greatness to which the son of the harlot of Falaise had attained. Now, while all this mischief was brewing, Duke William felt that there were many of the barons in Normandie in whom he could put no manner of trust, and he well knew that too many of the great Normans settled in England were unsteady in their allegiance to him.

In this state of things it behooved him more than ever to insure tranquility in England before he should again cross the seas, and to endeavour to secure the goodwill of the Saxon people, who were gradually becoming accustomed to his rule, and who had but so recently shown how valorously they could fight for him when he put his trust in them. And therefore had he somewhat relaxed the rigor of his government towards the English people, and had made promise to many native nobles that he would govern the country according to the good laws of Edward the Confessor.

Now some of these English nobles were closely allied by blood with the Ladie Lucia, and consequently with the Ladie Alftrude; and was not the Ladie Lucia the wife of Duke William's own nephew, Ivo Taille-Bois? And was not the Ladie Alftrude wife unto Hereward the Lord of Brunn, who held that nephew in duress, and who had for so many years prevented Ivo from enjoying the wide domains of his spouse? Perhaps Ivo had not been an altogether unkind husband, or it may be that the two children which she had borne unto him carried a great weight in his favor in the mind and heart of Lucia, who, certes, had long been very anxious for the liberation and return of her French husband. Some good Saxons at the time thought that this was un-Saxonlike and mean and wicked in the fair heiress of Spalding; but there were many young dames, and not a few Saxon dames that could hardly be called young, who felt much as the Ladie Lucia felt about their Norman husbands. But go and read the story of old Rome and the Sabine women! Nay, go read the Evangil, which tells us how the wife will give up everything for her husband. And, *crede mihi*, these womanly affections and instincts helped more than anything else to make disappear the distinction between the conquering and the conquered race.

Now after that many of her kindred and friends had supplicated Duke William to offer to the Lord of Brunn such terms as might procure the release of her husband and the pacification of the fen country, the Ladie Lucia herself found her way to the court, and at the most opportune moment she knelt before the Conqueror with her two fair children. The hard heart of the Norman ruler was touched; but politic princes are governed by the head and not by the heart, and it was only upon calculation that William determined to set at nought the opinions and the opposition of many of his advisers, and grant unto Hereward the most liberal terms of composition.

In the presence of Lanfranc and other learned priests he caused to be written upon parchment, that he would give and grant friendship and the protection of the good old laws not only unto Hereward, but also unto all his friends, partisans, and followers whatsoever, of whatsoever degree; that the life, eyes, limbs, and goods of the poorest fenner should be as sacred as those of Lord Hereward himself; that Lord Hereward should have and hold all the titles of honor and all the lands which he had inherited from his ancestors or obtained by his marriage with the

Ladie Alftrude; that he should be allowed to administer the Saxon laws among his people, as well at Ey as at Brunn; and that, in return for all these and sundry other advantages, nothing would be required from him further than that he should liberate, together with all other his Norman prisoners, Ivo Taille-Bois, viscomte of Spalding, and give the hand of friendship to Ivo, and restore to him the house and all the lands at Spalding, which were his by right of his marriage with the Ladie Lucia, and live in good cousinship with Ivo as became men so nearly connected through their wives, living at the same time in peace and friendship with all Normans, and pledging himself by his honor as a knight and by his vow pronounced with his right hand laid upon the relics of the Saxon saints he most esteemed, to be henceforward and always true liegeman to King William and to his lawful successors.

When a Saxon monk, known for his good English heart, and for the pious life he had led in Waltham Abbey, got into the fen country, and into the presence of the Lord of Brunn with this scroll, the gentle Ladie Alftrude, who had borne many toils and troubles without a murmur, was lying sick of a marsh fever, which she had caught in Holland. This afflicting event was calculated to have some influence over her lord's decision; but many other events and circumstances, too numerous to name, all led to the same conclusion.

No hope of the return of King Harold could be maintained any longer; the good old Saxon monk from Waltham vowed that his body was really buried in Waltham Abbey, that the river Lea, flowing fast by that Abbey gate, ever murmured his requiem, by night as by day, and that he himself, for years past, had said a daily mass for the peace of his soul. All the great Saxon chiefs had submitted long ago; Earl Waltheof, the last that had made a stir in arms, had been captured and beheaded outside Winchester town, and was now lying (though not without a strong odor of sanctity) in a deep grave at Crowland Abbey; Edgar Etheling, the last representative of the line of King Alfred, was living contentedly, and growing fat in a Norman palace at Rouen, with a pound of silver a day for his maintenance; for he had long since given himself up, and sworn himself liege-man to William.

Every rising had been put down in England, and all conditions of men seemed determined to rise no more, but to live in peace and good fellowship with the Normans; there was nothing but marrying and giving in marriage between the two races, and Saxon lords and other men of note were taking unto themselves Norman or French wives; and the great father of the whole Christian church, the Pope at Rome, Gregory, the seventh of that name, had given plenary powers to Archbishop Lanfranc to reorganize the Saxon church, and to excommunicate all such Saxons as submitted not to his primacy and to the government established. William, on the other hand, promised to take vengeance on none of Lord Hereward's followers, and to injure no fen-man for that which was past.

"Elfric," said the Lord of Brunn, "I think we must accept these terms, and cease this roving life among woods and meres. We have done what brave men can do: we have shown the Normans that England was not conquered in one fatal battle. We might yet hold out here, but for the rest of England we can do nothing; and our being here costs some Englishmen in the vicinage very dearly! What sayest thou, my ever-trusty sword-bearer? Wilt follow thy old master to London city, and make peace with Duke William and his Normans, who have never been able to overcome us?"

Quoth Elfric, "Where my lord goes there go I, be it to London city or to London tower. I think we have shown the Normans that England was not won by the battle of Hastings. And the Duke keep but his faith, we may live freely and happily in the good old house at Brunn, and among our honest fen folk."

Of the monks who had fled from Ely with Elfric some were dead, but the gentle and good Father Elsin and the fiery and old Father Kenulph, and several of the lay-brothers were yet alive; and therefore Hereward told the Duke's emissary, the good monk from Waltham, that there must be an especial agreement to relieve these monks of Ely from the rules of their order, and allow them to abide at Brunn or at Ey. The emissary was further told that, before Lord Hereward would submit, Duke William must swear upon the relics of his saints to observe the paction, to be true to every article of the agreement: and to give an earnest of his own sincerity and truth, the Lord of Brunn swore in the solemnest manner that he was ready to accept the conditions offered to him; and that, having once accepted them, nothing but treachery and violence on the other side would ever make him swerve from them so much as the breadth of a hair.

The monk of Waltham went his way unto London; and in as short a time as might be he came back again as far as the succursal cell at Spalding, attended by a goodly company of Norman and Saxon nobles, who came to bear witness that Lanfranc and the chancellor of the kingdom had put their signatures to the scroll as well as the king, and that William had sworn in their presence to be faithful to the deed. Now the Lord of Brunn went to Spalding with a goodly retinue of armed men, but not more numerous than the party which had come thither with the monk of Waltham; and having heard all that the monk and the lords had to tell him, and having carefully perused the deed (for Hereward had tasted books, and could read well in Latin), he wrote his name to the deed, and some of the principal men with him wrote their names; and then he swore upon the relics to be liege-man to King William. And now William the Norman might in truth be called a king, and king of all England. It was in the Kalends of October, in the year of grace one thousand and seventy-six, and ten years after the great assize of God's judgment at Hastings, that this thing was done and an end put to the resistance of the Saxons.

He had sworn upon the relics of saints before now, and had broken his oath; but this time King William was true to the vow he made, for great and manifold were the advantages he reaped from the submission of the Lord of Brunn. It needs not to say that the great Saxon warrior who had ever been true to his saints and a scrupulous observer of his word, was more than faithful to every part of his engagement. After he had been to London city to pay homage to the king which it was the will of Heaven to place over the country, he returned to his good house at Brunn, and hung his sword and battle-axe upon the wall, never to take them down again unless England should be invaded by the Scots or Danes.

King William, who went over into France to force his undutiful son Robert to forego his plots and rebellions, and to take vengeance on the French king (in both of which things he in the end succeeded), would with a glad heart have carried Hereward, the cunning captain, the great soldier, with him; and to tempt him into that service he made offer of lofty titles and commands, and of many hides of land in the upland country; but Hereward loved not to fight except for his own country and countrymen, and against those who had wronged him and oppressed them; and instead of clutching greedily at the king's offers, as many English lords had done, he preferred keeping his own in his own native parts, and ever remained plain Lord of Brunn.

Ivo Taille-Bois returned to the manor-house at Spalding with his wife and children; and albeit his brow was sometimes darkened by the recollections of the wedding at Ey, and the defeat and surrender in the marsh, and the hard life he had led as a prisoner in the fens, he lived on the whole, in very good fellowship with his neighbor and cousin of Brunn. Ivo never more harrowed the good Saxon monks of Spalding, who were left for a long time to their own peaceful and happy government. As for the traitorous monks of Crowland Abbey, who had brought back the Normans, they fared after the same manner as the false monks at Ely and the ungrateful monks at Peterborough; they were condemned by the Saxons, harassed and plundered by the Normans they had served, and fustigated by a sharp iracund abbat from France; and thus they did penance for many years, and until most of them were dead, when their cells were occupied by truer men, and the abbey of Crowland began again to be the revered place it had been in former times.

As Lord Hereward had ever been averse to cruelty, and constant in his endeavors to prevent his people being cruel to the prisoners they took in battle, the Normans had no scores of vengeance against him; and when they found that they were not to be gratified by dividing his broad lands among them, as they had long expected to do, they lived in a neighborly manner with him, and even sought his friendship.

Not one of them but allowed that he had been a great warrior; and when the monks of their nation, who had seen much of the war in England with their own eyes, began to chronicle the war and to relate the high emprises of William the Conqueror, maugre their Norman prejudices they paid a tribute of praise and admiration to the military skill, and the indomitable courage, and perseverance of Hereward, the son of Leofric, Lord of Brunn.

There were troubles in the land after the year of grace one thousand and seventy-six, but they came not near to Brunn. Twenty-four years after the submission of Hereward, when the Conqueror was in his grave, and his son Rufus had been slain by the arrow of a Norman knight, his other son, Henry the Clerk, ascended the throne, and in so doing he passed the good Charter called the Charter of Liberties, whereby he restored the laws of King Edward the Confessor, and engaged to redress all the grievances of the two preceding reigns. And shortly after his accession to the throne, King Henry still further conciliated his Anglo-Saxon subjects by espousing a Saxon wife, the fair Maud, daughter of Malcolm, King of Scots, and of Margaret the good queen, the relation of King Edward the Confessor, and of the right kingly kin of England.

Maud had been sent from Scotland at a very early age and committed to the care of her English aunt Christina, the pious Abbess of Wilton. Many great Norman lords, as Alain the Lord of Richmond, and William de Garenne, Earl of Surrey, had asked her in marriage, but she had refused them all; and even when Henry Beauclerc, a crowned and anointed king, made suit for her hand, and offered to place her by his side on the throne which her ancestors had sat upon for ages, she testified a preference for the quiet religious life she was leading; and it required the representations and entreaties of many noble Saxon friends to make her forego her purpose of entering into religion.

"Oh most noble and fair among women," said these Saxons, "if thou wilt, thou canst restore the ancient honor of England, and be a pledge of reconciliation and friendship; but if thou art obstinate in thy refusal, the enmity between the two races will endure, and the shedding of human blood know no end!"

To these representations she yielded; and those Saxons who had advised her lived to see much good to England proceed from the marriage, which was a great step towards that intermixture of the Saxon and Norman races which had been begun many years before, and which we have since seen proceed so rapidly. The elevation of the fair Maud to the throne filled the hearts of the English with joy, for not only was she their countrywoman and a descendant from the royal stock of Alfred the Great, but she was also at the time of her marriage beautiful in person, charitable unto the poor, and distinguished above all the ladies of her time by a love for learning and learned men. Elfric the sword-bearer, who was yet in the prime vigor of life, brought to mind the dying prediction of Frithric the Abbat of St. Albans, and said joyously to his lord, that "England would be England still, and that the Saxon tongue and laws were things that could not be rooted out!"

"Elfric," said Lord Hereward, "the great stream of our old Saxon blood is fast absorbing the less stream of Norman blood, and so will it continue to do. The children of Normans, being born in England and suckled by Saxon nurses, will cease to be Normans. All men love to keep that which they have gotten; and as our old Saxon laws are far more free than those of France, and give more security for life and goods, and oppose a stronger barrier to the tyranny of princes, the Normans that now live among us, or their sons that shall succeed them, will, for their own sakes, cling to our old laws, and help the chiefs and the great body of the English people to make the spirit of them to be enduring in the land."

CONQUEST OF THE ISLE OF ELY

Thus talked the Lord of Brunn and his faithful sword-bearer; and thus they lived to teach their children's children.

Hereward continued to live comfortably and peaceably with his neighbors and with all men, and he died in peace after he had lived many more years. Both he and the Ladie Alftrude reached a patriarchal age, and they left a patriarchal stock behind them. They were buried with all honors in Crowland Abbey, which, by this time, had become a holier and a better governed house than ever it had been before. A learned monk of Crowland wrote good verses in Latin upon the tombstone of the Lord of Brunn; but we find in our own home tongue lines which might have been a still better epitaph:—

> Him loved young, him loved old,
> Earl and baron, dreng and kayn,
> Knight, bondeman, and swain,
> Widows, maidens, priests, and clerks,
> And all for his good werkes.
> He loved God with all his might,
> And holy kirk and soothe and right.

And that there might be a lasting record of his prowess in battle and skill in war, his good and learned mass-priest Alefricus Diaconus, had written before he died, and in the same old English tongue, a goodly book of the deeds of Hereward, the great soldier; and albeit this goodly book, by some evil chance, hath disappeared, Hugo Candidus and Robert of Swaffham, two right learned monks of the abbey of Peterborough, have put the substance of it, and such portions as could be found, into their treatise intituled, *De Gestis Herewardi Inclyti Militis*.

THANKS ...

I am very grateful to my wonderful wife and muse Siegi, for the idea and support, without which this book series never would have been started, nor ever will be completed!

She always finds words of encouragement, sparks my own curiosity how everything evolves and is my first and best fan!

Many thanks to Horst from Switzerland, Walt, Jamie, John, Wolfgang and Paul from Vero Beach in Florida, Ralph from Switzerland, Marcio and Daniel from Brazil/ France, for giving me the assurance that there are still people in this world who are very much interested in true stories and real history.

Klaus Schwanitz
Vero Beach, Florida

About the scribe Klaus

He lives on the East coast of Florida and operates as an independent entrepreneur in the computer industry.
Nevertheless, he still has enough time to let his imagination run free as he pursues his passion of writing. Starting with some novels he changed his focus to more serious matters.
As a history buff he brings the almost lost past to life again by reviving very old historical books or documentations that have all been but forgotten.
We can learn from the past to make our future better; if not - from what else?

> *"There are three methods to gaining wisdom.*
> *The first is reflection, which is the highest.*
> *The second is limitation, which is the easiest.*
> *The third is experience, which is the bitterest."*
> *Confucius*

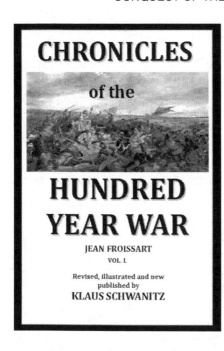

Available from Klaus Schwanitz

ISBN 13: 978-1514846056

Chronicles of the Hundred Year War

In 12 volumes

This is a very comprehensive narrative from the distant past. Over a period of more than 30 years, Jean Froissart collected and noted many historical accounts of life in Europe in the 14th century.

FROISSART, priest, canon, and treasurer of the collegiate church of Chimay, historian and poet, was born in Valenciennes, a town in Hainault, about the year 1337. He was a friend, confident and trustworthy acquaintance of many royalties, noble men, and knights. Jean traveled eagerly through Europe, became secretary to the Queen of England and known as an interested listener to all kinds of stories. Here you learn about true history from a person that was a contemporary of many stories in this time line. You will read of good and bad fights, noble behavior and intrigue; slaughter and murder, with hundreds of real names of Kings, nobles and knights and their destinies.

The CHRONICLES were original published in four huge volumes and several translations were undertaken during the past 600 years. This book series uses the best French to English version known that was done by Thomas Johnes, Esq, in 1803-1810. In this translation, the original four volumes were divided into twelve volumes with almost 5,000 pages.

These volumes were now edited, richly illustrated, and published so that this important part of our history will not be forgotten.

Incredible true history!

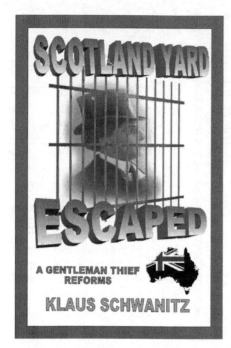

Available from Klaus Schwanitz

ISBN 13: 978-1507833759

Scotland Yard Escaped

A.J. RAFFLES and his friend Bunny are ... gentlemen thieves!

Yes, of course, they are criminals but lovely fellas, not hooligans, vandals, or worse. His creator, Hornung, had great success and published in the 19th century much of his work. In time he wanted to switch from this underworld theme and take on serious topics. Therefore, he heroically killed off Raffles in South Africa.

A lot of his followers and fans did not want to see this happen. Sir Conan Doyle let Sherlock Holmes die in the great Reichenberger waterfalls to protect the world from the evil Dr. Moriarty.

Now the same fate was to befall the gentleman thief, Raffles. His fans were upset when Hornung did not resurrect Raffles. I was also saddened about my hero's sudden demise, after devotedly so following him and his friend Bunny on so many adventures. Inspector MacKenzie and Sergeant Holly came very close to nabbing them, but eventually lost the battle.

But, - I know a lot more than all of Hornung's disappointed fans. Raffles escaped with his old flame to Australia and there ...

The best book I have read in a long time!
Read it – it is fun.

     Diane R.   A. Devine

Available from Klaus Schwanitz

ISBN 13: 978-1501047633

THE BANISHED
ANNO DOMINI 1519

Ulrich, Duke of Württemberg was the son of Heinrich of Württemberg, and declared of age in 1503. Ulrich was badly reared, became independent too soon, was unhappily married to Sabine of Bavaria, compensated himself by living in splendor, fell into debt that required increased taxes, against which 'Poor Conrad' in the Remstal revolted, and was compelled to accept the terms of the treaty of Tübingen.

The murder of the knight Hans von Hutten (the husband of his mistress) in the forest in 1515, the flight of his wife, the violence with which he attached the imperial city of Reutlingen to Württemberg, stirred up the nobility, and the dukes of Bavaria against him. In 1519 he was driven from his domain by the Swabian League. After several attempts to regain his lands, completely impoverished, Ulrich fled to Phillip of Hesse, who in the victory of Lauffen, restored to him his hereditary lands.

But Ulrich had to acknowledge Austria's sovereignty. In gratitude to God Ulrich introduced the Reformation, so following his defeat in the Smalkaldic War, Ulrich was compelled to humiliate himself before the emperor, pay a severe indemnity and to submit to the Interim, while Ferdinand threatened him with a court action on a charge of disloyalty as a subject, his death circumvented this misfortune. His difficulties and his return to Protestantism moderated the character of the prince and made him popular.

You have not heard the real story – here it is!

Available from Klaus Schwanitz

ISBN 13: 978-1500919290

SIR JOHN MANDEVILLE

Incredible Travels
ANNO DOMINI 1322-1356

Sir John Mandeville traveled between 1322 and 1356 from London through the known and unknown world of his century.

He described fantastic countries, strange people and brilliantly organized the eclectic travel material into an artistic first-person narrative. He begins with a guide to the Holy Land, relating many anecdotes of his experiences and observations. Then he describes the fabulous wealth and wonder of the court of the Great Khan and details of Prester John's kingdom in India.

Among the marvels he describes are various types of monsters such as dog-headed cannibals, flat faced people without noses or mouths, a race of herma-phrodites, people with ears hanging to their knees, and men whose heads grow beneath their shoulders.

You have not heard the real tale – here it is!

You have to read it – it's our unbelievable history.
B. Travers

Made in the USA
Charleston, SC
08 November 2016